9.00

Slavery in th

Herbert S. Klein is Professor of Latin American History at Columbia University. He is also the author of *The Middle Passage: Comparative Studies in the Atlantic Slave Trade* and *African Slavery in Latin America and the Caribbean.*

SLAVERY
in the
AMERICAS

A Comparative Study of
VIRGINIA
and
CUBA

By

Herbert S. Klein

Elephant Paperbacks
Ivan R. Dee, Inc., Publisher, Chicago

First ELEPHANT PAPERBACK edition published
1989 by Ivan R. Dee, Inc., 1169 South Plymouth Court,
Chicago 60605. Manufactured in the United States
of America.

ISBN 0-929587-04-9

To Harriet

Preface

For many years social scientists have recognized that the place of the Negro in contemporary North American society was molded by the historical experience of chattel slavery. Only recently, however, has it been understood that this historically determined role and status of the North American Negro is not a generalized American experience but is unique to the United States. This uniqueness has its roots in a system of slavery that was fundamentally different from other such institutions in the New World. Although even as far back as the seventeenth century contemporaries noted a sharp difference in the slave regimes of the English, French, Spanish, and Portuguese possessions, until recently few historians have attempted to analyze the causes and consequences of these distinctions.

The first contemporary comparative research was begun in the late 1940's by Frank Tannenbaum in his brilliant study on the legal structure of slavery in the New World.[1] This original work was greatly expanded and placed in a larger theoretical framework by Stanley Elkins.[2] Both scholars, however, concentrated on the vast structure of the law and on a comparative legal analysis upon which to draw their inferences. Because of this, critics have challenged their generalizations on the grounds that there exists a great difference between the ideal of the law and the reality of practice, and that the distinction between the Latin and Anglo-Saxon world is not as clear as has been conceived. In support of this, critics note that racial prejudice and accompanying pejorative terminology can still be found in all New World societies where the Negro exists, along with a strong correlation between race classification and social stratification.

[1] Frank Tannenbaum, *Slave and Citizen, the Negro in the Americas* (New York: Alfred A. Knopf, 1947).

[2] Stanley M. Elkins, *Slavery. A Problem in American Institutional and Intellectual Life* (Chicago: University of Chicago Press, 1959).

vii

Recent studies on the Negro in contemporary Latin American society, however, clearly demonstrate the primacy of socioeconomic classifications in contemporary Latin American race relations, in contrast to the United States.[3] But as yet, sociologists and anthropologists have not synthesized their findings with the new comparative historical models in their rapid surveys of the slave heritage. As for the historians, neither the critics nor defenders of the new comparative historical school have attempted to go beyond the legal materials to the social and economic dynamics of the New World slave systems to test the assumptions and conclusions that have been proposed.

This is the aim of my study. By subjecting to detailed analysis the operation of external institutions and internal conditions of the slave regimes of the two highly representative areas of Cuba and of Virginia, it is hoped that a start can be made in testing and modifying these models.

My reasons for selecting Cuba and Virginia for such a detailed comparative analysis are many. To begin with, each state was of prime importance in its geographic and cultural region because of the size and predominance of its slave population. Virginia was the largest and most influential state in molding the slave institutions of the North American continent, and Cuba in its turn was unquestionably the major slave colony of the Spanish empire. Equally important, both states were essentially similar in the size of their populations and their economic employment of slave labor. In both regions slave labor played a predominant role from the first century of

[3] The best research on race in Latin America has been the intensive work done in Brazil. Probably the most sophisticated of such studies in terms of theory and methodology is the work of Charles Wagley *et al., Race and Class in Rural Brazil* (Paris: UNESCO, 1952). This should be supplemented with the earlier study of Donald Pierson, *Negroes in Brazil: A Study of Race Contact in Bahia* (Chicago: University of Chicago Press, 1942), whose findings are supported by the results of Wagley and his associates; and by the study on colored mobility in Bahia by Thales de Azevedo, *Les élites de couleur dans une ville brésilienne* (Paris: UNESCO, 1953). Somewhat more controversial have been the numerous studies of the São Paulo school of Bastide, Fernandes, Cardoso, and Ianni on southern Brazil. This work is summarized in Florestan Fernandes, *A integração do negro na sociedade de classes* (São Paulo: Faculdade de Filosofia, Ciências e Letras da Universidade de São Paulo, 1964).

colonization, and a commercial crop plantation system based on this colored labor force was fully developed. Furthermore into each area a comparable colored population was imported by the middle of the nineteenth century, and within each state the colored-to-white ratios were closely parallel for almost the entire history of the slave regimes.[4] Although Cuba and Virginia obviously did not represent all varieties of New World slavery, their essential comparability and representativeness make them ideal models for testing the comparative thesis in the most basic of its assumptions and generalizations.

In undertaking the research for this book, which was carried out in Spain and in the United States during 1964–65, I had the aid of the Joint Committee on Latin American Studies of the Social Sciences Research Council. Mr. Bryce Wood of the council was extremely helpful to me in working out the committee's grant, which was supplemented by additional funds for secretarial assistance from the Research Committees of the College and the Division of the Social Sciences of the University of Chicago.

From the beginning of my work on this subject, I have had the individual support and criticism of my colleague Daniel J. Boorstin, of Stanley Elkins of Smith College and of Eric L. McKitrick of Columbia University. Others who assisted me in some part were Marcello Carmagnani of the University of Chile, James Fred Rippy, my original professor in the field, and the staff of the Archivo General de Indias of Seville. I would also like to thank the editors of *Comparative Studies in Society and History* and of *Caribbean Studies* for permission to use articles of mine that appeared in their 1966 issues. Finally I wish to acknowledge the help of my wife who has been an ever resourceful researcher, fellow translator, and critic.

HERBERT S. KLEIN

[4] Thus I have tried to control for extreme variations in demographic relations between the races, a factor upon which some recent anthropologists and historians have laid great stress as a primary cause in determining differences in race relations. See e.g., Marvin Harris, *Patterns of Race in the Americas* (New York: Walker and Company, 1963), chap. 7. Although this is an important element in explaining the divergences between race patterns of the British West Indies and the United States, it does not seem to have played anywhere near the central role across cultural frontiers these writers have implied.

Contents

Slavery in the Americas

PART I. Conquest, Colonization, and the Establishment of Imperial Control

Introduction. Although England and Spain may have had different motives for undertaking imperial expansion, may have been operating in different historical epochs and dealing with unique national characters, they nevertheless faced the identical problem of establishing their contol over frontier colonies thousands of miles from the metropolitan authority. In this attempt at impressing their wills upon these newly established communities, they faced their greatest difficulties, not primarily from physical distance, but from the opposition of their own colonial subjects, who sought as much independence from imperial direction as they could achieve. These colonists, indeed, wanted freedom from the metropolitan power in all but name.

This was a struggle inherent in both England's and Spain's colonizing efforts, a contest to determine where the true power was to be located—in the New World or in the Old, in the imperial monarchy and its institutions, or in colonial leadership and its own organs of power. For in both Cuba and Virginia the colonials were bent on achieving an initiative that they had never possessed in Europe and that they had come to America to achieve. Thus, the outcome of the struggle, given an equal drive of both Virginian and Cuban colonials for autonomy, would be determined by policies undertaken, whether active or passive, by the metropolitan authority in the early years of conquest and colonization.

For the institution of Negro slavery, the importance of this conflict was paramount, since it would determine whether the local or metropolitan institutions would create and administer the legal codes concerning the Negro in the New World. This in turn would largely determine what forces would exercise a significant influence in the development of the colonial slave regimes, for each of these authorities would be affected differently by various external factors.

With the leadership of the colony in the hands of the settlers, local economic needs would tend to be the dominant force in defining the legal structure of Negro slavery and social attitudes toward the slave. Understandably, a colonial legislature would reflect to a far greater degree the economic and social needs of the colonial community than would the imperial government.

Although these local economic and social factors may not be without their influence upon a central authority, other factors not in harmony with local desires may supersede them in importance. Not only is the central authority forced to think in terms of imperial requirements, but in the development of such a system as Negro slavery, the prior claims of traditional custom, religion, and concepts of royal government would be sure to make themselves felt, and these considerations would certainly influence to a marked degree the slave institutions that would finally emerge.

1. The Cuban Experience. The most striking feature in the Castilian conquest[1] of a New World empire, especially when compared with English colonization almost a century later, is the tremendous energy expended by the crown in

[1] The terms Castilian conquest and crown of Castile are used throughout this work because it was to that kingdom and its crown, rather than to the Spanish nation as a whole, that the right of conquest and colonization fell. In fact, it was not until the Bourbon monarchy of the eighteenth century that

giving meaning and direction to that conquest. The crown of Castile was fully cognizant of the immense task it was undertaking in its effort to bring under one imperial government an area of such magnitude as only Rome before it had been able to control. From the beginning it had constructed a coherent imperial organization sensitive to centralized direction. Although most of the instruments for creating and maintaining this centralized imperial structure were based on historic Castilian institutions, under Isabella and the early Hapsburgs the crown made major contributions in expanding these institutions to meet new imperial needs. Nor was the crown's effort limited to creating an efficient administrative machine, for this was merely the instrument to effect the basic goals of the monarchy. In an attempt to clarify these goals, the Castilian crown sought constantly to reevaluate its fundamental principles, and although its pecuniary interests in the New World were important, it will be seen that even these could be sacrificed at crucial points to fulfill its aims of creating an Hispanic and Christianized American Empire.

This drive of the Castilian crown to control and direct the conquest of the New World under its own will led to the imposition of that will on practically every matter of importance in the colonial world. This led to constant strife with its vigorous colonials, especially on the questions of the treatment of the conquered Indian, and of the place of the colonists in the government of the colonies. Although it was forced by sheer physical distance and the immensity of area to be controlled to accord some measure of local autonomy, the crown of Castile was remarkably successful in controlling the anarchistic forces unleashed in the conquest and colonization of a new world.

a united Spanish nation was created and the exclusive control of Castile over the Indies was finally absorbed by the rest of the nation. On this problem of the separate kingdoms and their overseas interests, see: Rafael Altamira y Crevea, *Historia de España y de la civilización española* (5 vols.; Barcelona: Juan Gilie, 1900–30), II, 441–43; Roger Bigelow Merriman, *The Rise of the Spanish Empire in the Old World and the New* (4 vols.; New York: Macmillan Co., 1918–34), II, 55–56, 220–22.

The Castilian monarchy was to achieve this success largely because of the experience gained within its own realms, an experience that gave that kingdom a unique preparation for the task of imperial organization and colonization. Unlike Aragon and most of the other nation-states of Europe, Castile had early and successfully addressed the fundamental problem of the rising monarchies of Europe—the destruction of the medieval power of the nobility. Joining forces with the powerful towns, Isabella succeeded in reducing the barons to military and political impotency, although still not completely destroying many of their old economic and social privileges. Then, under her rule and later under that of her· grandson Charles I, the towns and their parliamentary body the *Cortes* were denied many of their *fueros*, or ancient privileges, and were in turn so reduced in authority that the monarchy was left as the most powerful institution of the realm.[2]

Of prime importance to the crown in its suppression of contending political groups were two major institutions, a strong and devoted royal bureaucracy and the Roman Catholic church. Especially under the rule of Isabella, a unified system of government had been created and placed in the hands of the *letrados*. These letrados, or men of learning, were university-trained lawyers, thoroughly steeped in Roman jurisprudence, of middle class or untitled background, and extremely antagonistic to the ancient privileged classes.[3] They were organized by Isabella and her predecessors into a powerful and independent judicial and administrative bureaucracy, and were provided with a comprehensive code of laws by which to govern and unify the kingdom.[4] The Castilian bureaucracy proved so successful in the suppression of local

[2] J. H. Elliott, *Imperial Spain, 1469-1716* (New York: St. Martin's Press, 1963), chap. 3.
[3] Altamira, *Historia de España*, II, 14-15.
[4] The Consejo Real, which was the chief administrative and judicial council of the realm, as late as 1476 was still dominated by the nobles; however, by 1480 Isabella had succeeded in placing the *letrados* in full control, thus marking their complete domination over Castilian public administration. *Ibid.*, II, 452.

power at home that it became the model for the imperial structure created by the monarchy to administer its vast overseas possessions.[5]

The Spanish branch of the Roman Catholic church, under the rule of Ferdinand and Isabella, was turned into a church as nationalized and independent of papal authority as the Anglican Church of England. The crown was the head of the church with full and exclusive patronage over all its branches—including the powerful military orders. No papal bull could be published within the realm without royal sanction, and the Spanish church itself, through a tremendous reform program, was of such moral and intellectual stature that it actually exercised great influence over the papacy. Even the seemingly untouchable Holy Office was completely under the direction of the crown and its appointees, and many a noble, customarily protected from the crown by ancient privilege and law, was easily destroyed by the Inquisition.[6]

Thus, as Castile prepared to assume her role as an imperial power, her institutions had been subordinated to a centralized monarchy, and for that reason she was now equipped to undertake the most ambitious ventures. Castile's first advances beyond her continental borders were directed toward the

[5] Merriman, *Rise of the Spanish Empire*, pp. 221–22. For a general outline of the insular and imperial bureaucracies, see Juan Beneyto Pérez, *Historia de la administración española e hispanoamericana* (Madrid: Aguilar, 1958).

[6] *Ibid.*, pp. 409–10; Elliott, *Imperial Spain*, pp. 87–99. The crown won even greater control over the colonial church than it possessed over the Iberian church. Under the papal bulls of 1501 and 1508 and through other concessions, the crown was granted complete control over all ecclesiastical benefices and tithes, full rights of patronage, direction and maintenance of the work of conversion, and the authority to establish, maintain, and define the jurisdiction of all churches and monasteries. The crown also exercised full control over the emigration of clerical personnel to the New World and required a special royal license before emigration was allowed. The American church was totally dependent on the crown for its personnel, sphere of action, extent of power, and full financial support. Rather than debilitating the church, however, these practices gave it much strength and also guaranteed it as the most potent agency for the maintenance of royal power in the empire. Altamira, *Historia de España*, II, 485–86; Clarence Henry Haring, *The Spanish Empire in America* (New York: Oxford University Press, 1947), pp. 179–82. For a comparison of the power of the crown in the two churches, see Antonio Ybot León, *La iglesia y los eclesiásticos españoles en la empresa de indias* (2 vols.; Barcelona: Salvat Editores, 1954–63), I, 293 ff.

west in rivalry with her neighbor Portugal. Well before the advent of Columbus, Castilian adventurers were heading into the Atlantic to acquire new possessions. It was Castile who first contested Portugal's expansion into West Africa and after much dispute was finally able in 1479 to secure from Portugal complete sovereignty over the Canary Islands in return for recognition of Portuguese claims along the African coast. Not only did the conquest of the several islands of the Canary archipelago provide valuable experience in conquest and colonization for the Castilian crown and its subjects, it also provided Castile with an essential way station to what would become its New World empire.[7]

In the actual conquest of the New World, the Castilian monarchy worked out an extraordinarily effective system of private enterprise. Realizing that the tremendous energy required to carry out the subjugation of continents was beyond its resources, the crown exploited the pent-up drives within its own peoples and initially allowed the greatest freedom of action for its ambitious captains. Like the English crown in later centuries, the crown of Castile found it expedient and profitable to allow private individuals to carry out at their own expense the conquest of the New World in the name of the crown.

Although such a system was extremely effective in unleashing national energies and guaranteeing a rapid conquest, so that almost all of the New World had been subjected to Spanish control within a fifty-year period, it also had the obvious potential of destroying royal authority and creating an autonomous empire of conquistador princeling states. It was the genius of the sixteenth-century Castilian monarchy to understand this inherent danger from the beginning, and rapidly and effectively to prevent its development while still encouraging private initiative.

Although the crown was forced to contribute to the first major expeditions under Columbus and to the establishment of a secure outpost at Hispaniola, all further conquests were

---

[7] Merriman, *Rise of the Spanish Empire*, II, 172–73, 189–90.

carried out almost entirely by private initiative. Allowing any person with either resources or excellent connections at the court to organize an expedition, the crown signed with such an entrepreneur a *capitulación,* or contract, that was a kind of primitive charter conferring certain rights upon the adventurer, defining his area of conquest and the obligations he had to assume in terms of colonization and permanent settlement if his titles were to be recognized. This capitulación, given the fact that the entrepreneur was paying for the entire cost of the operation, was usually rich in seeming rewards for the conquistador. First of all, he was granted the very impressive title of *adelantado,* which had previously signified a border lord in the centuries of the *reconquista;* he received some sort of guaranteed financial return from any profits made; and finally, he obtained the crucial privilege of apportioning land and Indians among his followers. In turn, the capitulación granted to the crown the traditional royal taxes from the new territory, and the right to establish royal institutions. It also provided that a royal treasury official was to accompany the expedition to insure enforcement of royal revenue regulations.[8]

Most of the conquistadores obtained such documents beforehand, or bought out the original signature, but some bold and successful rebels actually usurped authority and led a conquest on their own initiative. But since this was usually done in the face of strong local challenges from other private entrepreneurs, these rebels were forced to get royal sanction to secure their rights. Not adverse to success, the crown was quite willing to sign such a post facto agreement, since it could usually extract more concessions from the individual entrepreneur. Such usurpation of authority, for example, was made by Cortés who, once the conquest was undertaken, made a direct appeal to the crown, accompanied by monetary tokens of success, to secure the royal assent.[9] Nor was the

[8] Haring, *The Spanish Empire,* p. 22; José Maria Ots y Capdequí, *Instituciones* (Barcelona: Salvat Editores, 1959), pp. 3–14.

[9] Robert S. Chamberlain, "Spanish Methods of Conquest and Colonization in Yucatan, 1527–1550," *The Scientific Monthly,* XLIX (1939), 239–40.

crown adverse to granting spectacular titles to the very first and most successful of the conquistadores such as Columbus and Cortés, especially when these titles could be used to pay for debts incurred without losing crucial governmental rights. By this capitulación system, the enterprise of the conquest proceeded at an unusually rapid speed. The reason for this success was, of course, the existence of a vast untapped wealth that could be had for the taking. In fact, the conquest actually paid for itself. Velázquez outfitted his private army of conquest for Cuba from the wealth he acquired in Hispaniola; Cortés and Velázquez invaded Mexico upon the resources that they had acquired in Cuba; and de Soto's Florida expeditions were financed from the treasures of Peru. Some of these expeditions represented the pooled capital of many individuals, as in the Peruvian conquest; but no matter how they were organized, the source for most of the funds came from the Indians. It was, in fact, the Indians, through their labor, gifts, and forced tribute, who ultimately paid for their own conquest.[10]

With their own private armies, loyal followers, conquered peoples, and even independent financial resources, the conquistadores had the power to gain almost unlimited freedom for themselves. But the crown did all in its power to prevent this from occurring. On every expedition, royal officials were present to guarantee the rights of the crown. These included not only exchequer officials, but, even more crucially, priests and missionaries, who were completely subservient to royal authority. Secondly, there always existed a large pool of entrepreneurs ever ready to attack the rights and riches of the successful conquistador, and thus the latter was forced to secure royal sanction as a vital support to his own authority, although even this was often not enough to prevent usurpation. That this was a prime concern of conquistadores is evidenced by the bloody, internal feuding that occurred after the success of practically every single conquest. No adelantado was immune from threats to his very survival.

---

[10] Silvio A. Zavala, *Las instituciones jurídicas en la conquista de América* (Madrid: Centro de Estudios Históricos, 1935), pp. 150–52.

In this the crown was a patient observer, which often maintained itself aloof from these bitter internal struggles until a victor emerged, and then it simply deprived the victor of the rich concessions his predecessor had legally acquired from the crown. Given this bitter strife, it was relatively easy for the crown to assure its authority, especially as it too was receiving a rich return in taxes, and was therefore able to pay the costs of an independent and powerful royal imperial bureaucracy. Thus, although the adelantado was granted extensive powers, and could, like the colonial proprietors of the English colonies, combine administrative, judicial, and military prerogatives under his control, and although he was often granted these privileges for more than one generation, few conquistadores ever actually enjoyed these grants of power. For even those original grantees who survived the initial struggles for power with their own followers saw their contracts violated by the crown of Castile and its astute lawyers, once colonization had been completed. Thus by the end of a decade or two, the original conquistadores were either reduced to the status of ordinary royal governors, carefully hedged in by opposing royal judicial, treasury, and ecclesiastical authorities, or were replaced altogether by royal officials on charges of misconduct. If these measures were not successful, the crown was even willing to buy off the conquistador with a title and residence in Spain, thus completely removing him from the New World. Thus by the latter part of the sixteenth century, all the New World territories were changed from proprietary domains to royal provinces.[11]

As the crown quickly undermined the vast concessions it had granted to its conquistadores in the political realm, it also fought for control over the conquered labor force in the economic sphere. While accepting the necessity of securing the free labor and tribute of the Indian peasant masses as a just compensation for the conquistadores, it carefully controlled the amount of this tribute and the form in which it was to be paid. Although it permitted the development of the *encomi-*

[11] Haring, *The Spanish Empire*, pp. 24–25.

enda, which was the right of a local colonist to collect tribute from a specified group of Indians in return for providing them protection and Christianization, it never allowed these encomiendas to become hereditary. In fact, despite fantastic colonial pressure, the crown refused to permit this right to pass more than two generations for fear of creating a colonial aristocracy, and because of its own desire to reap the tribute directly. Within a century of the conquest, therefore, the vast majority of the encomiendas would be taken over in forfeiture by the crown itself, and the system would have effectively eroded away.[12]

But in the debate over Indian labor, the crown was not only concerned over the fear of the development of a colonial aristocracy and of losing royal revenues to the colonists; it was also powerfully motivated by moral and juridical considerations. Since it claimed its right to conquest on the justification of conversion of the Indians, and since it faced the powerful moral force of the Counter-Reformation Spanish church and evangelical New World church, it was constrained to modify colonials' demands on the grounds of prior claims not only of the state, but more especially of the church itself. Thus it proceeded, under heavy pressure from the evangelical and humanitarian forces of the church at home and from its own Catholic conscience, to erode away the colonials' control over their Indian vassals. With royal encouragement there occurred in Spanish lay and ecclesiastical circles a great debate concerning the status of the Indian within the empire. This eventually raised the question of the very validity of the Castilian conquest and its destruction of the pre-Columbian Indian nations.

The humanitarian forces led by such men as the Dominican Fr. Bartolomé de Las Casas, a former Cuban *encomendero,* bitterly challenged the right of Castile to conquer the New World states, and held that, although the Indians were non-Christians, the crown had no right to destroy their sovereignty and make vassals of them. It was also claimed that such institutions as the encomienda and Indian slavery were morally

---

[12] For a full discussion of this struggle, see pp. 138–39.

wrong and should be abolished immediately. While the crown at first did not concur in this position and acted upon the assumption that the papal bulls had granted it the right of conquest, it also did not go quite so far as the humanist Sepúlveda who, in his famous debate with Las Casas before the Council of the Indies and a junta of eminent theologians in 1550, held that the crown as representative of the Pope could hold the infidel world in subjugation. No nation, he declared, had validity without Christ, and thus the crown was perfectly justified in conquering by military force non-Christian nations. But Francisco de Vitoria, among others, argued that acceptance of the faith was one thing and vassalage to the crown another, and that these Indian states should be considered fully independent and their conversion undertaken in the same way as between Portugal and the free Negro nations of Africa. Relying on such authorities as St. Thomas Aquinas, they held that belief was conditioned by free will, and that the Indian was thus free to accept or reject the faith.[13]

In the end, the crown accepted this missionary viewpoint and not only was Sepúlveda censured, but the famous *Recopilación de Leyes de las Indias* in 1680 would contain the statement "that war cannot and shall not be made on the Indians of any province to the end that they may receive the Holy Catholic faith or yield obedience to us, or for any other reason."[14] Not only did the crown thus reject its right to conquest, but under the influence of the reformers—and its desire, it should be added, to destroy local power as much as possible—the crown consciously began the long battle for suppression of the encomienda and Indian slavery. In this it was largely successful.[15]

The whole debate had thus committed the crown to a fun-

---

[13] Silvio A. Zavala, *New Viewpoint on the Spanish Colonization of America* (Philadelphia: University of Pennsylvania Press, 1943), pp. 30, 34–35.

[14] Quoted in *ibid.*, p. 46.

[15] For studies of these historic debates see Lewis Hanke, *The Spanish Struggle for Justice in the Conquest of America* (Philadelphia: University of Pennsylvania Press, 1949); Edward J. Brennan, "Spanish Debates Regarding the Conquest of America and the Treatment of the Indians, 1511–1559" Ph.D. dissertation (University of Chicago, Committee on International Relations, 1959); and Ybot León, *La iglesia y los eclesiásticos españoles*, I, 153 ff.

damental approach to Indian equality within the empire, and was testimony to the effect that the tremendously vital humanitarian forces of Spain's golden century (*siglo de oro*) had upon imperial policy. Nor did the fervor of reform stop with the Indian. Many even carried it to the question of Negro slavery as well, and it was in sixteenth-century Spain that the first abolitionists of modern history gave voice to the question of Negro rights and Negro freedom.[16] This movement never succeeded in carrying out abolition of Negro slavery, however, for the Negro slaves were not subjects for whom the Castilian crown felt a prime responsibility—coming into the Indies as they did by legal sale from the Portuguese, and already enslaved by their own peoples—and by the end of the century the movement had withered under the utilitarian current in favor of the slave trade.[17]

As in the original conquest and the early development of the labor system, the crown also permitted ample colonial initiative in the settlement of the new colonies. In Cuba, as

[16] Las Casas, who had at first favored the introduction of Negro slaves, later held that the Negroes were unjustly enslaved, "for the same reasoning," he claimed, "applies to them as to the Indians." Alonso de Montúfar, archbishop of Mexico, in 1560 questioned the enslavement of the Negroes, while Fray Tomás de Mercado in his work *Tratos y contratos de mercaderes* (1569) attacked the right of procuring and enslaving Negroes in Africa itself. Bartolomé de Albornoz in his *Arte de contratos* (1573) approved of the slave trade in Moors from North Africa, but rejected entirely the trade in Negroes from Ethiopia and the Portuguese traffic in it. Perhaps the most outstanding figures in the evangelical mission to the African Negro slave in the New World were two seventeenth century friars; Pedro Claver who worked among the Negro slaves arriving at Cartagena, for which he was later canonized, and the American Jesuit, Alonso de Sandoval, who wrote the famous evangelical tract, *De instaurada aethiopum salute* (1627). See Zavala, *New Viewpoints*, p. 65, and "Relaciones históricas entre indios y negros en Iberoamerica," *Revista de las Indias*, XXVIII, No. 88 (1946), 55-65; Altamira, *Historia de España*, III, 242; José Antonio Saco, *Historia de la esclavitud de la raza africana en el Nuevo Mundo y en especial en los paises américo-hispanos* (Barcelona: Jaime Jepús, 1879), pp. 252-55.

[17] Zavala, *New Viewpoints*, p. 65. As Zavala has noted elsewhere, the active criticism and liberal sentiment involved in this movement did not produce the positive results that were achieved for the Indian, but this humanist tradition again came to the fore in the eighteenth century in the philosophic thought of such liberal thinkers as the Mexican Francisco Xavier Alegre and was also to have a continuing influence on the attitude of the church toward the Negro throughout the colonial period. Zavala, "Relaciones históricas entre indios y negros," pp. 61-63.

elsewhere, the organizing instrument of colonization was the municipality. The establishment of permanent towns along carefully prescribed lines was considered essential to the maintenance of Hispanic civilization, and both by custom and design, the towns absorbed all the economic, political, and social life of the colonial regime. This tendency of the Castilians to view civilization in essentially urban terms was strongly encouraged by the crown, which permitted the colonists an unusual degree of initial self-government at a time this very municipal independence was being undermined at home. As with the conquest, this temporary grant of local control was to prove immensely helpful, for the towns were crucial instruments in the rapid settlement of the New World. This centralization of colonial affairs in urban centers would also prove extremely valuable to a centralizing imperial administration intent on concentrating power as much as possible under its own authority.[18]

When Velázquez landed in Cuba with his army of conquest in 1511, his first action was to create the municipality of Baracoa as a center for further expansion. With the creation of six more municipalities by 1515, the conquest of the island was considered complete.[19] The overwhelming majority of whites were established within these seven towns, and the latter consequently became the political and social centers of the island's civilization. The territory controlled by the municipality was considered to extend to the borders of the next town, and thus all the island was divided between these seven governments. At the heart of the municipal government stood the *cabildo* (municipal council), which not only carried out all the normal administrative duties of an urban executive council, but was also a court of law, a grantor of land titles, and a regulator of consumer prices, monopolies, and import-export require-

[18] For an excellent survey of these developments, see the two articles by Richard M. Morse, "Latin American Cities: Aspects of Function and Structure," *Comparative Studies in Society and History*, IV, No. 4 (July, 1962), 473–93; and "Some Characteristics of Latin American Urban History," *American Historical Review*, LXVII, No. 2 (January, 1962), 317–38.

[19] Ramiro Guerra y Sánchez *et al.*, *Historia de la nación cubana* (10 vols.; Havana: Editorial Historia de la Nación Cubana, 1952), I, 62, 70.

ments.[20] These municipalities and their environs, because of the island's impenetrable forests and mountains, became largely isolated from each other, and, at times, acted as independent units even to the extent of organizing their economic activities for entirely different outside markets.[21]

While these municipalities formed an essential part of the directed-colonization policy of the crown, they also became vehicles of political expression for the colonials. The cabildos and their representative assembly served as a major source of leverage for the colonists in their efforts to wrest control from the crown over their own institutions. But the crown, while at first supporting this show of vigorous initiative on the part of the colonials, soon managed by various means to bring their "democratic" organizations to near political impotency, and ended by gathering the major powers of the state into its own hands.[22]

Under Velázquez, the first cabildos were freely elected by the settlers, who chose not only the *regidores* (councilmen), but the *alcaldes* (chief magistrates) as well. Soon autocratic governors were appointing all alcaldes, but in 1529 the colonials were strong enough to upset this practice temporarily, and the *vecinos* (land-holding residents, and therefore citizens) were once again choosing these important officers. A compromise, however, was soon forced on the vecinos in the form of indirect elections for the alcaldes, and this office soon lost all pretense at directly representing the interests of the vecino class.[23] More direct intervention by the crown seriously diluted the representative quality of all the officers of the cabildo and their sensitivity to popular will. This was done by assigning perpetual regidores (at first to favored individuals, but by the end of the century, to anyone with the necessary money), and by having certain royal officials either enter

[20] Irene Aloha Wright, *The Early History of Cuba, 1492-1586* (New York: Macmillan Co., 1916), pp. 41, 62; also see Haring, *The Spanish Empire*, p. 168.
[21] For examples of this see H. E. Friedlaender, *Historia económica de Cuba* (Havana: Biblioteca de Historia Filosofía y Sociología, XIV, 1944), p. 37; and Julio J. Le Riverend Brusone, *Los orígenes de la economía cubana (1510-1600)* (Mexico: El Colegio de Mexico, 1945), pp. 47-50.
[22] Haring, *The Spanish Empire*, pp. 158, 164-68.
[23] Guerra y Sánchez, *La nación cubana*, I, 115.

into the deliberations of the cabildos, or seeing that their respective authorities overlapped.[24]

Under the vigorous leadership of the earliest Cuban settlers, the first cabildos had succeeded in organizing a representative assembly for the island along the lines of the Castilian Cortés. It developed out of the group of officials known as *procuradores;* these were the men who were elected by the municipal councils to present their problems and desires before the royal authority. The first Cuban procuradores sent to Spain in 1515 met with success and were able to secure for the cabildos valuable economic and political concessions.[25] Soon the procuradores from the seven towns were meeting periodically on the island, and they began to create an organization with its own attributes—as was the case in Castile—still connected with the cabildos but not subordinate to them. Although these procurador assemblies were to develop in many parts of the Indies, the Cuban assembly for a time was one of the most virile.

The Cuban procurador assembly in the early period met once a year at one of the island's towns (usually Santiago de Cuba, the capital), and each cabildo chose its own procuradores to represent it. The assemblies discussed every topic of any importance to the colonial welfare, and then chose representatives from among themselves to present the results of their deliberations before the crown. The crown at this juncture reviewed these proposals and either rejected or approved them, after which they were put into effect. The assemblies desired to have their proposals become legislative acts immediately put into law by the colonial governor, and only afterwards be subject to royal veto. This would have turned them into a legislative assembly similar to the Virginia General Assembly.

This attempt at strengthening the power of the procurador assembly was but one of many such proposals for making Cuba as autonomous as possible. Perhaps the most complete

[24] "Almost all the officers of the municipal councils ended by being either privileged individuals [i.e., holding life tenure] or employees of the king." *Ibid.,* I, 121.
[25] Wright, *Early History of Cuba,* pp. 68–69, 72, 79–81.

and vigorous expression of the white colonists' political aspirations was presented at the meeting held in 1528. At that time the assembly made a number of requests of the crown: to designate the governor from among the vecinos of the island, to limit the governor's term to three years, to abolish the *regidores perpetuos*, and finally, to permit the direct election of the procuradores by the vecinos rather than their appointment by the cabildos, as was the current practice. These proposals, had they been completely accepted by the crown, would have meant the crown's forfeiture of authority to the white colonials. They would have created representative cabildos, a sympathetic chief executive, and a powerful insular general assembly, and thus given virtual local autonomy for Cuba within the empire. It is also interesting to note that at the same meeting in which these "democratizing" proposals were made, the procuradores also petitioned the crown for an increased introduction of Negro slaves, the continuation of Indian slavery and slave hunting, and the granting of titles of encomienda in perpetuity.

Here was the greatest bid made by the settlers to wrest control over the colony from the crown. The crown's reaction was to grant only the most limited of concessions, and at the same time to resist most vigorously this threat to its own authority. Aided by the economic decline of the island and the draining off of a portion of the island's active leadership into further conquest, the crown was able to bring about the demise of the procurador assembly, and by 1540 the annual meeting of the procuradores was able to call forth representatives from only three of the seven towns.[26]

Thus although the crown of Castile often seemed to be making concessions, these were actually due either to mere expediency or to a temporary inattentiveness to colonial affairs caused by emergencies in other parts of the empire. Over a long period, the crown always emerged triumphant in maintaining the principle that the Indies were to be considered as its own exclusive possession, not only in opposition to the pen-

[26] Guerra y Sánchez, *La nación cubana*, I, 116–19.

insular legislatures, but to colonial ones as well. Under Isabella and the Hapsburg monarchs who followed her, the Indies were considered as several coequal states tied to the mother country only through the crown of Castile, with the crown's prerogatives far more extensive in these new "overseas kingdoms" than they ever were in the old.

The logical outgrowth of this principle was the establishment of a powerful imperial bureaucracy. Thus, following the initial period of freedom for the overseas conquest and colonization, the crown proceeded to suppress all opposition to its prerogatives and to inhibit the attempted decentralization of its authority by creating a powerful imperial structure. The first requirement for such a structure was to divide the Indies into manageable administrative units. In 1511 the first such unit was created at Santo Domingo, Hispaniola, where an *audiencia* (or high court) was established, and all of the West Indies and the northeastern coastline of South America soon fell under its judicial-administrative jurisdiction. As the conquest progressed, however, and more of these audiencias— seven by 1542—were established, the rest of the New World outside of the territory controlled from Santo Domingo was brought under two major administrative divisions, the viceroyalties of New Spain (1535) and Peru (1544). With the creation of the latter viceroyalty, the general form of imperial organization can be considered as having been fully elaborated by the monarchy.[27]

The establishment of the audiencia at Santo Domingo represented not only the crown's realization of the vast potentialities opened up by Columbus, but also the crown's desire to revoke the numerous and embarrassing concessions granted to this first conquistador. The audiencia was set up both to challenge Columbus' claims over the rest of the Indies, and to suppress his independence in Hispaniola as well. Cuba was made a test case by the monarchy, for while the island was legally under the control of Diego Columbus—

---

[27] See Haring, *The Spanish Empire*, pp. 19, 25, for the dates of organization; and Merriman, *Rise of the Spanish Empire*, III, 643–44, for the geographic breakdown.

heir to the concessions of his father and current governor of Hispaniola—the crown supported every move of insubordination and independence by Diego Velázquez, Cuba's conquistador and first governor. Thus by the end of the third decade Cuba and all the other islands and territory outside of Hispaniola were firmly in the hands of the monarchy. At the same time, under constant pressure from the crown, the House of Columbus finally sold out its rights to the Castilian crown for a pension.[28]

With all the islands under royally appointed governors following the demise or dismissal of the first adelantados, the audiencia of Santo Domingo became the highest authority and central administrator for all the Caribbean islands, including Cuba. The audiencia was first of all a court of appeals for all cases taken from the Cuban magistrates. It also provided the crown with a group of able judges who could undertake the frequent scrutiny of insular affairs that the crown deemed necessary. They did everything from investigating illicit trade in eastern Cuba to holding the famous *residencia* of audiencia judge Alonso de Cáceres in 1573, in which the first comprehensive code of laws specifically designed for Cuba was carefully worked out.[29]

The governor of Cuba was subordinate to the audiencia, and the latter would review his actions and remove him in special cases if it so desired. The audiencia also supervised the actions of the numerous royal officials on the island and usually was arbiter in the first instance of all disputes of authority on the island.[30] Unlike the other New World audiencias, the one at Santo Domingo was also the sole administrative head of the area under its control, and matters of defense and relations between the islands were decided by the court.[31] And finally, the court was charged with responsibility

---

[28] J. Vicens Vives (ed.), *Historia social y económica de España y América* (5 vols.; Barcelona: Editorial Teide, 1953–59), III, 444; Haring, *The Spanish Empire*, pp. 22, 84; Wright, *Early History of Cuba*, p. 24.

[29] *Ibid.*, pp. 161, 266–67; Guerra y Sánchez, *La nación cubana*, I, 120–21.

[30] Wright, *Early History of Cuba*, pp. 229–32, gives an example in which the audiencia decided the site of the capital after a bitter dispute between the governor and the cabildo of Santiago de Cuba.

[31] *Ibid.*, p. 271.

for protecting the freedom and rights of the Indians, and later of the Negroes, under its jurisdiction.[32]

The governor of Cuba was a royal appointee, and within a short time the office came to be filled by peninsular Spaniards who had no connections whatsoever on the island. In Cuban history, the governor stood forth far more resolutely in opposition to local power than did his counterpart in Virginia. There were constant disputes of authority between the governor together with his officials, and the cabildos and their procuradores. In these conflicts it was the former authority—possessing as it did not only the military power, but also the authority over the distribution of Indian labor through the encomiendas—that proved to be the crown's most effective instrument for the suppression of local autonomy.[33]

The governor was himself under close royal supervision. He was subject to the audiencia at Santo Domingo, and although as governor he could at times successfully appeal their decisions to the crown, the audiencia still represented a potent check on any autocratic tendencies. Another important factor was the type of individual appointed to the governorship: the appointee was usually a peninsular Spaniard with legal or military training and experience who had served the crown in many other positions and was in a sense a career bureaucrat whose performance at this post might lead to higher positions within the imperial hierarchy.[34] The average term of the governors was extremely short, and at the end of his term, he and his administration would be subject to a residencia. This was literally a trial, at which all complaints against the outgoing administration were heard—usually before the incoming governor or a judge of the audiencia—and

---

[32] For a discussion of the general organization and powers of the New World audiencia see Haring, *The Spanish Empire*, pp. 129–33; and J. H. Parry, *The Audiencia of New Galicia in the Sixteenth Century, A Study in Spanish Colonial Government* (Cambridge: Cambridge University Press, 1948), pp. 5–8.

[33] Guerra y Sánchez, *La nación cubana*, I, 121.

[34] In the eighteenth century, for instance, there were five viceroys who had previously served as captains general or governors of Cuba. Lillian Estelle Fisher, *Viceregal Administration in the Spanish-American Colonies* (Berkeley: University of California Press, 1926), p. 7.

many a governor was returned home in chains to face long years of litigation in his efforts to clear himself against charges often irresponsibly made.[35]

Another group that contended with the colonials for authority over insular affairs were the various royal officials appointed directly by the crown, and who were independent even of the governor's authority. These consisted of the royal treasurer, accountant, and factor, and the various military officers and customs inspectors who either frequented or were resident on the island. The military establishment, especially after the latter half of the sixteenth century, was to throw its shadow across Cuban government with the creation of permanent garrisons on the island and the constant visitations of the Royal Navy and Indies fleets.[36]

What really made the imperial bureaucracy most effective in suppressing the colonials' decentralizing efforts, and at the same time rendered the bureaucracy impervious to colonial influence, however, was the almost total exclusion of colonials from its membership. Thus the Mexican historian Lucas Alamán noted that of all the viceroys who ruled in the Spanish Indies up to 1813, only four were American born, and these four were sons of Spanish officials serving in the Indies. Of the 602 captains-general, governors, and presidents of audiencias who held office during the colonial period, only 14 were creoles, or native born, and of the bishops and archbishops ruling in the Americas, 601 had come from Spain.[37]

Not only was this distinction between American-born and European-born, between creole and peninsular Spaniard, a matter of imperial administrative policy, but in addition it represented distinct social and prestige cleavages as well. So far did these divisions reach that a lower-class European white

---

[35] Haring, The Spanish Empire, pp. 148–53.

[36] Guerra y Sánchez, La nación cubana, I, 78–79, 99–100. For a brilliant discussion of how such a divided and constantly challenged bureaucracy could still perform with initiative and efficiency, see the pioneer study by John Phelan, "Authority and Flexibility in the Spanish Imperial Bureaucracy," Administrative Science Quarterly, V (June, 1960), 47–65.

[37] Quoted in Haring, The Spanish Empire, pp. 209–10. The larger percentage for the church is explained by the fact that the church in the sixteenth and seventeenth centuries was more open to colonials than was the civil government.

in the Indies could consider himself the equal, if not the superior, of the colonial creole who had the noblest of European blood in his veins.[38] Although the creoles were left in undisputed control over the local colonial economy, they were totally excluded from political and social power. On the face of it, this seems an unusual arrangement of leadership in a modern Western society, where, since the end of the eighteenth century, economic power has been essential to political and even social dominance. In Virginia, the more modern pattern of economic leadership being equated with social and political power was to reach virtually a pure form for a pre-Industrial, pre-French Revolution society. To the Virginian, economic success meant complete admission into roles of both political and social leadership.

At the head of this European-dominated and -controlled imperial structure stood two powerful imperial royal organs, the Council of the Indies at Madrid, which was the supreme administrative and judicial head of the entire New World empire, and the *Casa de Contratación* at Seville, a combination admiralty court, navigation school, and ministry of trade that controlled the extensive commercial relations between the Peninsula and the Indies. It was these two supervisory organizations that saw to the smooth operation of the vast imperial bureaucracy. Its concerns embraced the maintenance of communications, the replacement and promotion of personnel, the compilation and execution of ordinances, and the careful preservation in priceless archives of all the records now available pertaining to Castile's New World empire. So well was this imperial structure created that it functioned even without the crown in almost all matters save final decisions of policy.[39]

[38] Thomas Gage, *A New Survey of the West Indies: or the English American his Travel by Sea and Land* (3d ed.; London: A. Clark, 1677), pp. 21–22.

[39] For the organization, history, and powers of the Council of the Indies, see Ernesto Schafer, *El consejo real y supremo de las indias* (2 vols.; Seville: Escuela de Estudios Hispano-Americanos de Sevilla, 1935–47). For the *Casa de Contratación* see Clarence Henry Haring, *Trade and Navigation between Spain and the Indies in the Time of the Hapsburgs* (Cambridge: Harvard University Press, 1918), chaps. 3–4. Both of these royal institutions were completely independent of home affairs and, together with their subordinate organizations, formed a bureaucracy completely distinct from the administrative organizations that controlled Castile and the Peninsula.

Finally, to bolster this entire edifice stood the separate, yet equally powerful, bulwark of the crown: the Catholic church. The church, being an integral part of the imperial organization, was not long in establishing its authority on the island. Priests went with the first expedition, and as early as 1516 the Pope had designated the first capital, Baracoa, as a bishopric. In 1522, Juan de Witte, the incumbent bishop, removed the cathedral from Baracoa to the new capital of Santiago, and in 1523 he established the cabildo, or chapter, of the cathedral that served as the base for the organization of the clergy in the colony. Yet even before the church had begun its full-scale secular operations on the island, Cuba was overrun with the lay orders—primarily the Dominican in this early period— who from the beginning were in contact with the Indians, undertaking their conversion.[40]

The Cuban white settlers had thus failed in any real way to wrest substantial direction over their affairs from the potent crown of Castile. Almost from the beginning the crown had imposed its authority and institutions on every aspect of colonial life. From taxes to the treatment of Indians, from land distribution and ownership to control over immigration and commerce, the crown had its own positive intentions and did everything within its power to have them carried into effect. Far different was to be the experience of the white Virginia colonists who, with the same determination as their Cuban counterparts, sought in their own way to establish their independence from imperial authority.

2. *The Virginia Experience.* In the development of the English colonization of Virginia, the lack of royal direction and control stands out in sharpest contrast to the Cuban experience. It was largely with indifference that the newly enthroned House of Stuart saw the first successful plantation established in America. It was an indifference that allowed

[40] Guerra y Sánchez, *La nación cubana,* I, 58–59, 148–49; Wright, *Early History of Cuba,* pp. 120–23; Ramiro Guerra y Sánchez, *Historia de Cuba (1492–1607)* (2 vols.; Havana: "El Siglo XX," 1921–25), I, 331 ff.

the early Stuarts to surrender royal authority over the New World colony at almost every point at which it was challenged. Nor would the crown allow any other political authority to exercise a unified control in its place, and for almost half a century was successful in denying Parliament any jurisdiction over colonial affairs. The establishment of Parliamentary authority would later bring an attempt to subordinate the empire to central direction, but by then the colonials had so thoroughly established their claim to self-government that even when certain of their rights were successfully whittled away by the metropolis, their control over essential domestic institutions was left entirely alone, as traditionally belonging to the colonial regimes themselves. Thus, for the most formative period of growth, the Virginia colonials would find themselves unchallenged in their drive to create their own institutions and entrench their authority.

Any analysis of the Cuban conquest and colonization had of necessity to focus on the crown and its actions. In the case of Virginia, however, the starting place must be with the commercial classes of Great Britain. For it was the mercantile interests and not the monarchs who would undertake the financing and organization of the expansion of England into the New World.

It was the late sixteenth century that not only saw the rise of the famed British naval power, but also the great expansion of English commerce, which was soon to rule the world's markets, even penetrating behind the very barriers of the Spanish Empire. By the beginning of the sixteenth century, the English commercial classes had achieved control over their own commerce with the outside world, first from the Venetians and then from the Hanse Towns. With this overthrow of the foreign merchants had come the rise of London as a commercial center and the organization of the first overseas trading adventurers into regulated companies. Such companies, especially the Merchant Adventurers, were soon challenging the Hanse towns for leadership on the continent. The first of the great joint-stock corporations, arising out of these more primitive, individualistic, "regulated companies," was the Muscovy Company chartered in 1555. This first corporate company was soon followed by a host of other such commercial ventures in all the major areas of the world. The joint-stock companies early provided the vehicles for England's leadership in world trade, for they were able to organize large amounts of capital savings for purposes of foreign trade and colonization, and with their free issuance of stock, limited liability, concentrated management, and many other unique features, enabled England to outdistance its rivals in the Western world's carrying trade.[1]

Through the activities of these companies, England soon found itself in possession of a large merchant fleet, a strong navy, and surplus capital. So vigorous were these developments that with the fall of Portugal to Spain in 1580, England was able to undertake successfully the establishment of British intervention in the fabled Far East; in 1588 to challenge successfully the mightiest naval power of the time; and by the end of that century to challenge Spain in her New World empire.

The economic theories that rose with the mercantile classes of England held that colonization and expansion were necessary for commercial survival. This theory of mercantilism and the obvious benefits being conferred upon Spain by her wealthy empire convinced English leaders that their nation's prosperity lay in establishing permanent colonies overseas, and especially in disputing Spain's exclusive control over the entire Western Hemisphere. The late sixteenth century was a most propitious time for England to lay down this challenge, for Castilian energy had finally dissipated itself in the conquest, and the crown of Castile, after successfully rebuffing French interference in the early part of the century, contented itself with merely holding the strategically vital Florida peninsula while relinquishing all physical control over the territory to the north.[2] Stressing these considerations, and espe-

---

[1] Charles M. Andrews, *The Colonial Period of American History* (4 vols.; New Haven: Yale University Press, 1934–38), I, 27–28, 30–31, 41.

[2] Attempts had been made by various lay orders to establish a "mission frontier" along the Atlantic Coast possibly as far north as Virginia, but

cially emphasizing England's position as a rising commercial state needing new outlets for capital as well as new markets and sources of raw materials, such vigorous publicists as the Hakluyts were able to convince England's commercial leaders that expansion had become a necessity.[3]

The first attempts at New World colonization were carried out by individual adventurers, much in the style of the conquistadores. In the last quarter of the sixteenth century, Gilbert had tried and Raleigh had temporarily succeeded in planting a colony along the Carolina coast, but both eventually failed. For unlike the Spanish Indies whose wealth quickly supplied the means for support and further colonization, the North American coasts proved barren of precious metals, or of such established Indian agricultural communities as encountered by Spain. Such a colonial area to be economically successful had to create goods and/or services needed in European markets. The failure of Roanoke Island proved that individuals alone could not supply the capital necessary to sustain such overseas colonies until this kind of commercial crop or product could be found to take the place of Indian labor or precious metals.

This inability of individual enterprise constantly to supply a colony with the necessary resources until it could find the means to sustain itself, and the long period before it would even begin to show a profit, early led to the question of royal support. But English colonization encountered an extremely parsimonious crown, to an extent unmatched even by the often debt-ridden and hard pressed Castilian monarchs. The English crown, as early as Elizabeth, offered moral support and sanction to colonization, but refused entirely to supply the needed capital. Not only did this limit the size of the colo-

---

failure had attended all such efforts. See Wesley Frank Craven, *The Southern Colonies in the Seventeenth Century, 1607–1689* (Baton Rouge: Louisiana State University Press, 1949), pp. 16–17.

[3] And it was not until these London merchants were convinced and their support substantially obtained (in the years after 1606) that the movement for American settlement was a success. *Ibid.*, p. 38. For details of the program and propaganda activities of the Hakluyts as well as their influence on English colonization see *ibid.*, pp. 27 ff.

nizing effort to the amount of private capital that could be drawn into such a highly speculative investment as overseas settlement, but it would ultimately mean that the crown would capitulate its authority over the entire colonization movement to the English mercantile classes.[4]

At the beginning of the seventeenth century, a group of London merchants who had longstanding interests in colonization and were also involved in the great joint-stock companies of their time, decided to pool their resources in a joint-stock adventure and make another try at colonization. In the first charter (1606) granted to this group of merchants and financeers known as the London Company, the crown attempted to retain direct control over the colony, however it refused to commit itself financially to its development or support. Under this charter a royal council was established in England that was granted full administrative authority over the entire New World region from Cape Fear to Ste. Croix. The company was to appoint all members of a resident colonial council, which was allowed to control local affairs. But all political and administrative authority was vested in the so-called Royal or Superior Council, all of whose members were crown appointees; whereas to the company was left only direction over the actual business of settlement, maintenance, and trade. In effect, this Royal Council was the English crown's first step to the creation of something akin to the Council of the Indies and was the forerunner of later attempts at centralized imperial control.[5]

The crown also maintained that the newly discovered territory was to be considered as its own possession, much in the manner of the Castilian throne's relation to its empire. But although it was initially successful in maintaining its rights as opposed to Parliament in this area, it was forced to abandon its direct administrative and political control over the Virginia colony to the London merchants. For such assertions of exten-

[4] *Ibid.*, pp. 36 ff.
[5] Andrews, *The Colonial Period*, I, 84, 103; George Louis Beer, *The Origins of the British Colonial System, 1578–1660* (New York: Macmillan Co., 1908), p. 298.

sive royal control deterred private capital from investment, and in the charter of 1609 the Royal Council was eliminated entirely, and the crown relinquished all active control over Virginia to the London Company.

The charter of 1609 was to establish a pattern that the crown would follow, not only in the Virginia charter of 1612, but in all the subsequent individual and company colonial grants. Bitterly involved in a desperate struggle for power at home and on the continent, unwilling to supply any capital for overseas settlement whatsoever, the crown gave up any cohesive control over its burgeoning empire. Every colonizing enterprise was given complete freedom over its undertaking, with little or no interference from the crown and its administrative organization. In the grants and charters following that of 1609, all immediate control over the colony was given to the proprietor, whether an individual or corporation, and he became virtually the sole connecting link between the colonists and the metropolis, his only challenge to undivided authority being the provincial legislature that might develop.[6]

Like the crown who had been forced to concede authority because of its financial position, the London Company itself did not prove immune to the problems involved in financing a long colonization and was early forced to provide liberal grants to stimulate investment and immigration. In the joint-stock issue of 1609, the principle of equality between planter in Virginia and adventurer in London was established when the majority of emigrating colonists were given coequal shares in the enterprise (shares that were to be retired in 1616). In the years that followed, the company was reduced to offering patents or charters to groups of adventurers for the setting up of private plantations or colonies, usually known as hundreds, within the territory covered by the company charter. In these grants the subsocieties usually received extensive control over their plantations, to the detriment of the over-all power of the company itself.[7]

---

[6] *Ibid.*, pp. 299–302.
[7] Craven, *The Southern Colonies*, pp. 85–88; Andrews, *The Colonial Period*, I, 128–30.

In the charter of 1612, there occurred within the company a shift in power from a select council to a general assembly of the stockholders. For the colonists—coequal shareholders— this democratization of the company organization would ulti- mately mean the shift of power over Virginia from London to Jamestown. With the maturation of the stock issue of 1609, the emigration of many London stockholders, and the coming of peace and prosperity to the colony, this step was taken by the leaders of the company; and in 1618 they proposed setting up a governmental organization in the colony along the lines of the general assembly of the London Company. In the Great Charter of 1618, the London Company provided for the crea- tion of a colonial general assembly with representation in the lower house for all the boroughs, hundreds, and private plan- tations.[8] The culmination in this extraordinary reorganization came in 1621 in the Ordinances and Constitutions issued by the London Company, which provided that "no orders shall bind the colony unless they be ratified in the Virginia general assembly."[9]

Even the form of Virginia colonization, like the control over government, was determined by the will of the colonials. For while the township organization had been envisioned by the company as the soundest and most secure means of organi- zation, it was abandoned by the colonials once the company control had been relaxed. Under the authoritarian rule of the first company governors, the settlement had been confined to fortified areas with communal arrangements for planting, harvesting, and selling the various crops produced. In their long-range plans the company leaders had hopefully divided the colony into boroughs. Once the first communal organiza- tions had been dissolved, however, and the power of the Indians finally broken, the colonists dispersed over a vast area, their plantations racing along the rivers (James, York, Rappa- honic, and Potomac) toward the falls. As each of these rivers

---

[8] *Ibid.*, 103 n, 182–83. Although the acts of 1618 were grants from the company to the colonials and had nothing to do with the crown, they are of such importance that they are usually referred to as the Great Charter of 1618.

[9] Quoted *ibid.*, p. 187.

was navigable as far as the falls and much of the area was heavily forested, the majority of plantations were connected to the outside world directly through their own docks. In such a situation, urban development proved impossible, especially as the economy became almost totally absorbed in one commercial crop and therefore provided few possibilities for intracolonial trade. It was not until after the close of the seventeenth century, when the line of settlement had passed the falls, that urban communities began to develop, and even then only on a very modest scale.[10]

The Virginia General Assembly, taking cognizance of this dispersal of settlement, abandoned the borough system and in 1634 organized the colony into eight counties. By so doing, the Assembly provided a form amenable to the economic realities of the dispersed community, and by 1644 the colony had added nine more counties.[11] The administrative center of this county organization was the powerful county court, which was both an executive and judicial organ.

The county court was in many ways similar to the Cuban cabildo both in the extent of its powers, and in its representation of the power of the propertied classes. Organized and put into operation as early as 1619, the powers of the county court were steadily augmented over the years. Besides having legal jurisdiction over innumerable civil and criminal problems, it was charged with the execution of all government ordinances, and for these purposes it was provided with an assortment of minor officials. Its authority extended to all local economic matters, including the regulation and control of tobacco, maintenance of standard weights and measures, regulation of

[10] Craven, *The Southern Colonies*, pp. 87–88, 107–8, 129–30; Philip Alexander Bruce, *Economic History of Virginia in the Seventeenth Century* (2 vols.; New York: Macmillan Co., 1896), II, 524–25; Thomas J. Wertenbaker, *Patrician and Plebeian in Virginia, or the Origins and Development of the Social Classes in the Old Dominion* (Virginia: By the author, 1910), pp. 39–42. In 1697 it was reported that "the major Part of the House of Burgesses . . . [consists] of *Virginians* that never saw a Town, nor have no Notion of the Conveniency of any other but a Country Life. . . ." Henry Hartwell, James Blair, and Edward Chilton, *The Present State of Virginia, and the College*, ed. Hunter D. Farish (Williamsburg: Colonial Williamsburg, 1940), p. 14.
[11] Craven, *The Southern Colonies*, pp. 166, 169, 269–70.

the price of local commodities, and the upkeep of lines of communication such as ferry services and highways. The county court was also a court of records, and with its clerk were filed licenses, deeds, certificates, contracts, wills, and most important of all, land titles. In short, it was the prime keeper of the vital statistics of the county. Nor was its jurisdiction in legal affairs confined, for by separate acts of the Assembly it was granted the powers of a probate and equity court in 1645, and in 1658 those of admiralty court.[12]

As the court came to symbolize local power, it tended to merge all local authority in its hands.[13] Although the militia system had been created as a separate organization in all counties, in actual fact its personnel became members of the court, and to the court itself fell all the responsibility for the maintenance of the troops and for the selection of the men.[14] The same held true for the vestry, which was composed of the same men and in reality proved a complementary institution in the realms of ecclesiastical and welfare matters on the county level.[15]

Membership in the county court was based on appointment by the governor, and candidates were chosen from among the most powerful and respected planters of the community. Although the eight to ten magistrates appointed were placed in office supposedly for short terms, the very nature of the select group from which they were chosen created a strong tendency for prolonged membership on the court.[16] It was this same select class of wealthy and dominant planters who formed the membership of both the Council and the House of Burgesses, and the same individual often held a position

---

[12] Philip Alexander Bruce, *Institutional History of Virginia in the Seventeenth Century* (2 vols.; New York: G. P. Putnam's Sons, 1910), I, 484, 541 ff.; Craven, *The Southern Colonies*, pp. 272–78.

[13] So important was the county court considered as a source of power by the Virginians that: "On each frontier the earliest expression of the will to self government was a demand for the creation of a local court. . . ." *Ibid.*, p. 172.

[14] *Ibid.*, p. 277.

[15] George Maclaren Brydon, *Virginia's Mother Church, and the Political Conditions under which it Grew* (2 vols.; Richmond: Virginia Historical Society, 1947), I, 94–96. Bruce, *Institutional History*, I, 62.

[16] *Ibid.*, pp. 488–89, 504.

in one of these two houses of the General Assembly and on his local county court as well.[17] Thus colonial leadership fell to the most prominent planters of the community, who entrenched themselves, especially after 1624, in all of the major political and administrative offices of the colony, bringing surprising political concentration for such an economically and geographically decentralized colony.

The fall of the London Company in no way threatened this entrenched power; rather it insured the final triumph of the colonial leadership over imperial England. It was largely because of political differences in England between the leaders of the company and the Royal Councillors that the crown pressed for, and succeeded in gaining, repudiation of the London Company's charter in 1624. Yet despite this reworking of Virginia into a royal province, the crown was as unwilling as ever to contribute its funds to colonial development, and for a time thought to revert back to the scheme of 1606 with a royal council and a subordinate company of adventurers. When this fell through there was even serious consideration given to rechartering the old company.[18]

Nor did the end of the London Company in any significant way alter over-all colonial policy, for the old types of proprietary patents were still being issued to the numerous companies that followed, including that extraordinary grant to the Massachusetts Bay Company in 1629. From year to year the crown vacillated about the type of centralized administration it should create to control the affairs of Virginia, and in the meantime it created nothing of permanence. To replace the company's centralized directorship, various subcommittees of the Privy Council and special commissions were set up. None of these, however, lasted more than a short time, and no separate administrative machinery such as Castile's Council of the Indies and Casa de Contratación—which existed apart from the administrative agencies already in existence for home affairs—was even contemplated at this time. Anything of

---

[17] Craven, *The Southern Colonies*, p. 170.
[18] *Ibid.*, pp. 148, 150–53. It was largely the opposition of the Virginia colonials that prevented recharter.

importance that was accomplished by the first two Stuarts in the direction of imperial centralization was wiped out by the chaotic years of civil war. Imperial control would eventually come to England's New World empire, but this would not begin until after the Restoration, and then it would not fall under the influence of the crown so much as under that of the potent merchants of London who had a vital interest in Virginia's economic development.[19]

The only issues that truly shocked the English crown out of its acquiescence to planter leadership in Virginia were issues in which its revenue was threatened. As early as 1636, the royal customs on one shipload of tobacco from Virginia yielded an impressive £3,334, and although the early Stuarts voiced pious wishes to see diversified agriculture come to Virginia and discoursed on·the evils of tobacco, they did nothing seriously to suppress its production. In that same year of 1636 it was estimated that the total royal revenue from tobacco should have been £20,000, if it had been properly collected. Thus the crown—even before the first Parliamentary Navigation Acts of 1651—decided to do all in its power to discourage the foreign trade of the colony because of the loss it entailed for the royal revenues.[20]

The constant years of overproduction in Virginia brought depression prices in the decades of the 1650's and 1660's, and in 1662 the colonials petitioned the crown for one year's total cessation of production—only to be bitterly rebuked by the Privy Council for even petitioning for such a thing. A similar petition in 1664 was again vetoed by the crown despite the economic privations of the colony. As the crown was averaging £100,000 annually by the '80's a third such petition for crop restriction, presented in 1681, was heartily disapproved, for no matter how extreme the fluctuation in price for Virginia leaf, the crown received a fixed return and the greater the production, the greater its own revenues.[21]

This reasoning held true in regard to the crown's interests

---

[19] Andrews, *The Colonial Period*, I, 200; Beer, *Origins of the British Colonial System*, p. 340; Perry Scott Flippin, *The Royal Government in Virginia, 1624–1775* (New York: Columbia University Press, 1919), pp. 44–59.
[20] Bruce, *Economic History*, I, 320, 326, 347–48.
[21] *Ibid.*, pp. 389, 392, 402–3.

in the African slave trade, from which it derived extensive revenue. Among the few acts of the Virginia General Assembly ever repealed by the English crown were those of 1723 and 1727, which attempted to place tariffs on imported African slaves—tariffs which in spite of colonial statements to the contrary, seemed to the crown to be prohibitive in intent.[22]

Yet on truly essential matters that had no direct relationship to the royal customs monopolies, the crown was either indifferent or indecisive. Given this royal attitude, the colonials were not slow to assert their "rights" and demand the fullest measure of support for their self-governing institutions. Thus from 1624 until 1639, the General Assembly continued meeting despite nonrecognition until, in the end, the crown gave it its sanction. Eventually, for want of a more positive conception of imperial government, the crown decided to accept what had been established in the colony by custom and usage.[23] The crown gave powerful sanction to the county court system—despite its extensive powers unknown to the local English judiciary—and in 1642 it declared that permanent sites be established in every county for the local court, thus insuring its continued maintenance.[24]

With no centralized agency appearing in the British Isles before the Protectorate to take control over colonial affairs the situation in Virginia showed itself equally unsubordinated to royal direction. Although, with the dissolution of the London Company, the task of appointing the governor and the council now fell to the crown, this did not insure acquiescence to royal authority, nor destroy the independence of colonial leadership. The council, even though it consisted of royal appointees, was in fact chosen almost exclusively from the pool of planter leadership. For the crown habitually confirmed without question the nominations of the governor, and the latter was forced to accept the colonial leaders in his council if anything like an effective administration was to be main-

[22] William Waller Hening (ed.), *The Statutes at Large: being a collection of All the Laws of Virginia from the first session of the Legislature in the year 1619* (13 vols.; Richmond: Samuel Pleasants, Jr., 1819–23), IV, 118, 182.
[23] Andrews, *The Colonial Period*, I, 198–205; Craven, *The Southern Colonies*, p. 153.
[24] Bruce, *Institutional History*, I, 486.

tained.[25] At the same time, the crown, ever desirous to spend as little as possible, fostered the use of colonial planters in other public offices of importance so that their salaries might be of the most minimal nature, for the honorific reward would be considered sufficient inducement. Thus of the seven royal officials created in the colony prior to 1700—aside from the governor and his council—almost all were filled by native Virginians.[26] In an attempt to insure the native quality of the colonial leadership, the General Assembly in 1676, with the approval of the crown, provided that at least three years residence in the colony was required for office-holding.[27] There is no doubt that the English crown in Virginia was saved the vast sums that were required to keep the Cuban administrative machinery going, but at the price of its own authority.

The crown did have one representative sensitive to its interests, however, in the person of the governor, whose term of office and actions were directly dependent upon royal sanction. In the majority of cases the holder of this office was chosen from the ruling classes of the home government rather than from the Virginian leadership, and he was personally provided with a salary that removed him from the threats of an opposition General Assembly. Although the positions of governor in Cuba and Virginia proved uniquely advantageous for royal suppression of local autonomy, the Virginia executive was faced by an opposition far more powerfully armed than the Cuban colonials with their cabildos ever were. For key rights of the governor, such as the appointive, military, and other executive functions, were shared by the very powerful and often hostile council, whereas control over initiation of legislation was in the hands of a strong General Assembly.[28]

Because of the crown's crucial refusal to provide adequate funds for colonial administration, it was forced to concede to the General Assembly not only the rights of petition and legislation, but those of taxation and control of finance as well.[29]

[25] Thomas J. Wertenbaker, *Virginia Under the Stuarts, 1607–1688* (Princeton: Princeton University Press, 1914), p. 41.
[26] Flippin, *Royal Government in Virginia*, pp. 358–59.
[27] *Ibid.*, p. 355.
[28] *Ibid.*, pp. 85–87.
[29] Craven, *The Southern Colonies*, p. 159.

It was the House of Burgesses' almost absolute control over colonial finances that enabled it to withstand repeated assaults by autocratic governors and also to participate in the executive functions. The first royal treasurer did not arrive in the colony until 1639, and even then the crown was unable to collect the quitrents that had belonged to the London Company, and finally in 1691 the office itself came under the direction of the House of Burgesses, which chose its own treasurer.[30]

Another area in which the royal authority was equally ineffective was in the creation of an imperial judiciary. Whereas Cuba had been subordinated to a tight judicial hierarchy, its history encumbered by countless litigation battles fought at all levels and especially at the Council of the Indies in Spain, an imperial judiciary in England was a long time in the making, not coming until the end of the century and then by the devious route of admiralty courts. During the seventeenth century few cases were carried from the colony to England, and Massachusetts even challenged the appellate jurisdiction of the Privy Council for disputes concerning colonial affairs.[31]

As far as defense was concerned, Virginia largely provided for the maintenance of its own harbor and frontier fortifications, as it had under the company, and as Virginia was isolated both from the main areas of imperial conflict and from the regions of major piratical raidings, no permanent military organization was established in the colony by England. For all invasions, Indian wars, and insurrections, the colony relied upon its own militia, and this militia formed an important branch of colonial self-government, giving essential police powers to the planter leadership.[32]

Although the Anglican church, or Church of England, was made the established church of the colony from the beginning

---

[30] Flippin, *Royal Government in Virginia*, pp. 208–12. Prior to 1680 the House of Burgesses had very extensive judicial powers as well, *ibid.*, 202. Also see Beer, *Origins of the British Colonial System*, pp. 321–22.

[31] *Ibid.*, pp. 334–35.

[32] Bruce, *Institutional History*, II, 3–4. The accepted planter leadership was as fully in control here as in the county courts system, the officer corps of the militia consisting almost entirely of men of wealth and great social and political influence. *Ibid.*, pp. 23–27.

of company rule, no resident bishop would ever be sent to the colony, nor to any of the other continental colonies in which the church was established. It was not even decided to which metropolitan bishopric these colonies pertained until after the Restoration. Only then was the Bishop of London selected, but his representative did not arrive in the colony until 1689.[33] During this period of complete neglect, both on the part of the Anglican hierarchy in England and the crown —the official protector and head of the church—the Virginians were able to reconstruct the high church structure of Anglicanism into a vestry-dominated congregational type of organization completely unknown to the mother church in England. So profound were the changes in structure and control, that the Viriginia church became anathema to the majority of English-trained clergy. And although the Church of England did construct a missionary society after the close of the seventeenth century, the S.P.G., as it was called, never sent missionaries to Virginia.[34]

For the most crucial period of its development, Virginia was thus unencumbered by a numerous non-native bureaucracy and was largely ignored by such institutions as a national church and an imperial monarchy. Because of the financial difficulties involved in its colonization, as well as strong royal indifference, the colony had early been granted the most liberal concessions of self-government, and its institutions, once created, were successfully strengthened and fortified against all opposition by the rising planter leadership. Virginia was thus allowed to grow in the light of its own immediate needs, and was able to ignore to a large extent such external forces and institutions with which Cuba had to contend from the beginning of its settlement.

[33] Brydon, *Virginia's Mother Church*, I, 232.
[34] See below, chapter 6.

PART II. The Legal Structure

Introduction. The degree of administrative, judicial, and religious autonomy or centralization that these two colonies possessed had its most profound impact on the creation of the legal system of slavery for the imported African Negro. For while slavery has existed in almost every pre-industrial society known to man, it has differed as fundamentally as the societies themselves, and especially so in its legal aspects. For slavery can include or exclude a whole range of rights, duties, and obligations, and no two slave codes have ever been identical in this respect.

In traditional legal theory, the absolute individual rights of a human are considered to be the rights of personal liberty, personal security, and property. In addition to these absolute rights, the individual, as a legal personality, possesses the relative rights of parent, spouse, master, and so forth.[1] Although by the very nature of slavery the slave forfeits the right of personal liberty, he need not lose his other absolute and relative rights. In this retention or loss of portions of the slaves' individual rights lies the basis for the differences of legal bondage

---

[1] John Codman Hurd, *The Law of Freedom and Bondage in the United States* (2 vols.; New York: D. Van Nostrand, 1858–62), I, 37.

among nations.[2] In Virginia and in Cuba, there existed a very fundamental difference in their slave codes, based on this primary distinction of what rights, if any, the slave was to possess under the law.

Legally, a slave may be considered anything from an inanimate possession to a human being with extensive rights. He can either be chattel, that is a *thing*, only the object of rights and never the subject of them, or a *legal person* held to bondage for life, who has various obligations on his part as opposed to the condition of privilege on the part of others.[3] This in essence was the underlying distinction between the Virginian and Cuban slave codes. The Cuban codes never forgot the legal personality of the Negro; the Virginian codes ultimately reduced the Negro to chattel slavery. This may seem but an academic distinction, having no influence over the daily life of the slave, but it in fact forms a crucial part of his whole existence within these colonial societies.

Under chattel slavery there may be restrictions placed on the power of the master over his slave, but this in no way vests legal rights in the latter. Without legal personality the slave has no right to such things as personal security, property, marriage, or even parenthood. He may be granted these by a benevolent master, but he has no right to them, and this is crucial. For if a slave is given a legal personality, which implies his capacity for choice and action, then it recognizes as well a legal capacity for absolute and relative rights. As a legal person the slave retains rights over which his master has absolutely no power.[4] As chattel however, he in no way challenges the master's full property rights. So thoroughgoing was the right of possession of the slave's person and the consequent loss to the latter of even the right to personal security, that under Virginia law, killing of a slave by his master was not considered a felony for, as the code logically reasoned, "it cannot be presumed that prepensed malice (which alone makes murder ffelony) should induce a man to destroy his own

[2] James Curtis Ballagh, *History of Slavery in Virginia* (Baltimore: Johns Hopkins Press, 1902), p. 28.
[3] Hurd, *Law of Freedom and Bondage*, I, 40–42.
[4] *Ibid.*, pp. 40–43.

estate." Such reasoning is obviously foreign to traditional Western thought, whether classical or Judeo-Christian in origin, yet it well represented the ultimate direction in which the Virginia codes would run. As one Virginia jurist put it, chattel slavery reduced the slave "below the rank of human beings, not only politically, but physically and morally."[5]

Not only were these two slave codes of an entirely different structure, but as has been implied in the first part, they sprang from entirely different sources of authority, a fact that had much to do with their subsequent development. In Virginia, chattel slavery was created entirely by the customary, judicial, and statutory decision of colonial origin, whereas in Cuba, the source of its slave code was fundamentally royal enactments and prior metropolitan law. As one famous defender of North American slavery has pointed out:

> The severity of the slave laws in the commonwealths of English origin, . . . was largely due to the historic possession by their citizens of the power of self-government. A distant autocrat might calmly decree such regulations as his ministers deemed proper, undisturbed by the wishes and apprehensions of the colonial whites; but assemblymen locally elected and responsive to the fears as well as the hopes of their constituents necessarily reflected more fully the desire of social control. . . . If this should involve severity of legislative repression for the blacks, that might be thought regrettable and yet be done without a moments qualm.[6]
> It may fairly be said that these laws for the securing of slave property and the police of the colored population were as thorough and as stringent as their framers could make them, and that they left an almost irreducible minimum of rights and privileges to those whose function and place were declared to be service and subordination.[7]

---

[5] St. George Tucker, *Blackstone's Commentaries . . . with an appendix to each volume* (4 vols.; Philadelphia: W. Y. Birch and A. Small, 1803), Book I, Part 2, in an appendix on Slavery (H), p. 55.

[6] Urlich Bonnell Phillips, *American Negro Slavery, A Survey of the Supply, Employment and Control of Negro Labor as Determined by the Plantation Regime* (New York: Appleton-Century Co., 1936), p. 495.

[7] *Ibid.*, p. 501. The above analysis and the argument presented in the next two chapters is in fundamental disagreement with the recent and rather inaccurate legal study undertaken by Arnold A. Sio, "Interpretations of Slavery: The Slave Status in the Americas," *Comparative Studies in Society and History*, VII, No. 3 (April, 1965), 289–308.

3. Virginia and the Establishment
of Chattel Slavery.
Under English imperial law the guarantee of common law rights, or the rights of Englishmen, was usually conferred by the original charter. These natural rights, however, did not apply in determining the relations and rights of aliens such as Africans and Indians, which meant that the power to effect such relations and statuses was divided between the imperial and the colonial governments. The colonial government had the authority to establish the rights and obligations of these individuals in internal affairs, and those rights that were incident to the relations of commerce and international intercourse were left in the hands of the imperial sovereignty. This power of the colonial governments was in fact granted by default, for throughout the colonial period there was no imperial legislation enacted to determine the condition or status of either Indians or Negroes.

Nor did any judicial decision of the English courts of common law determining the condition or status of the Negro in England have any effect whatsoever on the colonial courts, or vice versa. In fact, colonial judicial decisions of any nature were exempt from review by any English court, save possibly by the King in Council, and even this was disputed.

As there existed no precedent for Negro slavery in English common law, the Virginians, through their customary, judicial, and statutory practices and decisions, thus created their own slave regime. Although the English crown did have undisputed right of review on all colonial statutory codes, it never exercised this right in regard to the creation of the Virginia slave codes.[1]

Because of this lack of precedence of a slave code and the already established pattern of indentured labor, the first Negroes introduced into Virginia in 1619 appear to have been

---

[1] Hurd, *Law of Freedom and Bondage*, pp. 208–12.

treated as indentured servants.[2] Coming from the Spanish West Indies and therefore being Christians,[3] the majority of these first Negroes were treated in the matter of labor and rights much as their fellow white servants, some receiving an education, and most being granted their freedom dues after their period of labor.[4]

But with the beginning of direct heavy African importations after 1640, the colored population of Virginia began to be increasingly divided between servants and slaves, with the majority who came after the fourth decade being immediately reduced by the planters who bought them to servitude "for life." It also became increasingly difficult for the Negro servant to prove his right to freedom, and the class dwindled rapidly.[5] For the colonial leaders early recognized that they could possess the labor of the Negro for his lifetime with little opposition from any outside power. Doing this, they were able to provide themselves with a form of labor that was the cheapest that they had yet been able to obtain. Compared to the short terms of the white indentured servant, an enslaved Negro might be held for life and his progeny forever, all for only one initial outlay. Negroes could more easily be controlled and policed, throve on cheaper fare, and lived in poorer dwellings. Finally, there would be no payment of freedom

---

[2] On the Spanish origin of these first slaves, see Helen Tunnicliff Catterall, *Judicial Cases Concerning American Slavery and the Negro* (5 vols.; Washington: Carnegie Institute of Washington, 1926–37), I, 55–56.

[3] John H. Russell, *The Free Negro in Virginia, 1619–1865* (Baltimore: Johns Hopkins Press, 1913), p. 23.

[4] Philip Alexander Bruce, *Economic History of Virginia in the Seventeenth Century* (2 vols.; New York: Macmillan & Co., 1896), II, 126. Convincing proof of the servant status of these Negroes is found in a legal document dated December, 1652: "Whereas Emanuel Driggs and Bashasar Farnando Negroes now servants unto Capt. Franc Pott have certain cattle, Hoggs & poultry now in their possession ye wch they have honestly gotten and purchased in their service formerly under ye sd Capt. Pott & since augmented and increased under the service of Capt. Steph. Charlton now we, sd Pott & Charlton, doe hereby declare yt ye said cattle, hoggs, & poultry (with their increase) are ye proper goods of the above sd Negroes; and yt they may freely dispose of them either in their life tyme or att their death." Quoted in Russell, *The Free Negro in Virginia,* p. 27. Thus these Negroes possessed property rights in the fullest extent, a right never held by the slave.

[5] *Ibid.,* pp. 29, 31.

42 The Legal Structure

dues, which were a heavy and periodic financial burden upon the planter.[6]

That racial prejudice was one of the factors, aside from economic considerations, that may have influenced the enslavement of the Negro and the development of the legal institution of slavery is seen in the curious documents on the early reaction to miscegenation between the races. In September of 1630, it was ordered by the governor and council that "Hugh Davis be soundly whipped, before an assembly of Negroes and others for abusing himself to the dishonor of God and shame of Christians, by defiling his body in lying with a negro."[7] In 1640 Robert Sweet was also convicted of dishonoring himself with a Negro, and this time the Negress was whipped.[8] And in 1662 those found "ffornicating with a negro" were to be fined double the amount usually meted out for such offense.[9] All this would seem to lead to the conclusion that as far back as the 1630's there existed an antipathy of some kind on the part of the white colonials against the black, an antipathy or prejudice that was entirely lacking in the racial relations of the Castilian Cuban and the Afro-Cuban. This antipathy was to have a damaging effect upon the life of the free Negro as well as that of the slave, and possibly forms as important a cause of certain later developments in the slave regime—particularly as regards moral attitudes toward the Negro—as did economic considerations.[10]

But whatever the specific cause for enslaving the Negro,

[6] Bruce, *Economic History*, II, 57–60.
[7] William Waller Hening (ed.), *The Statutes at Large: being a collection of All the Laws of Virginia from the first session of the Legislature in the year 1619* (13 vols.; Richmond: Samuel Pleasents, Jr., 1819–23), I, 146.
[8] *Ibid.*, I, 552.
[9] *Ibid.*, II, 170.
[10] On the subject of racial prejudice and the origins of the slave regime, see the provocative article by Carl N. Degler, "Slavery and the Genesis of American Race Prejudice," *Comparative Studies in Society and History*, II, No. 1 (October, 1959), 49–66. An attempt to balance the Degler argument of racial prejudice origins, is well presented in the article by Winthrop D. Jordan, "Modern Tensions and the Origins of American Slavery," *Journal of Southern History*, XXVIII, No. 1 (February, 1962), 18–30. Both Degler and Jordan severely attack the Handlin thesis on the origins of the slave regime, although Jordan attempts to come to some type of moderate compromise on this issue.

there is no doubt that the Virginia planter had little scruple about reducing anyone to an enslaved status. That he did not more systematically enslave the Indian was due to their nomadic nature and to the inability of these largely hunting and gathering Indians to adapt to intensive agricultural labor. But this failure of Indian slavery did not occur for want of experimentation.[11] Nor were the planters slow in adopting the slave system, even despite the first years of indecision about the status of the Negro. Although the legislative or statutory structure of Negro slavery was not begun until 1662, there already appeared as early as 1640 county court cases recognizing the institution as it was being created in practice by the planters. In that year John Punch, a Negro, was made to serve for life as a punishment for running away, whereas the two whites with him had but four additional years added to their time.[12] In 1644 the Assembly, acting as a court, heard the case of a mulatto boy named Manuel who was supposedly sold "as a slave for-Ever," but who petitioned the Assembly in that year to be considered no slave, but to serve as other Christian servants did.[13] That there were many who were considered slaves even prior to this can be seen in the evaluation of estates of deceased planters that listed the worth of Negroes and white servants. In the estate of William Burdett, recorded in 1643, a white boy with seven years to serve was rated at 700 pounds of tobacco, a Negro girl of eight was rated at 2,000 pounds, and Caine, a Negro boy, was rated at 3,000 pounds. The obvious reason for the differentiation in value was that the two Negroes were slaves and were held for life.[14]

As the increasing tide of Negroes from Africa swelled the ranks of the Virginians, especially under the growing trade with the Dutch in the fifth and sixth decades of the seventeenth century, the class of Negro slaves grew appreciably. With no indentures or contracts, with no knowledge of English, with no Christian training, and with no question of their

[11] Bruce, *Economic History,* II, 64–65.
[12] Russell, *The Free Negro in Virginia,* pp. 29–30.
[13] *Ibid.,* p. 31.
[14] *Ibid.,* p. 36.

subsequent treatment having an effect upon those who were to follow them, as it did with white indentured servants, it was extremely difficult for the African immigrant after the middle of the century to escape being reduced to slavery.[15] Perhaps the best case for illustrating how difficult it was for a Negro to secure the status of indentured servant was that of Anthony Johnson and his suit against John Casor, also a Negro. Johnson claimed that he held Casor for life, whereas the latter maintained that he had been indentured and was to serve only for seven or eight years. With the aid of white neighbors, Casor was able to secure his release from Johnson, but the latter eventually took the case to court, and in 1653 it was decided that Casor was to be returned to his "rt Mayster Anthony Johnson." If one Negro was able to reduce another one to slavery so easily, despite the fact that white members of the community supported the servant's contention that he had indeed signed indenture papers, then how difficult it must have been for those Negroes, whatever their background, who fell into the hands of white planters ever to attain their freedom.[16]

The Virginia planter, in his drive for a more economic system of labor, was the first to reduce the Negro to the status of a servant for life. But the judiciary and the legislature, which were uniquely representative of and in fact entirely composed of the members of the planter class,[17] were not far behind in

[15] The thesis of original coequal treatment of blacks and whites as indentured servants and the subsequent rise of slavery owing to the lack of ill treatment affecting colored importations is presented in the controversial study by Oscar and Mary F. Handlin, "Origins of the Southern Labor System," William and Mary Quarterly, 3d Series, VII (April, 1950), 199–222.

[16] Russell, The Free Negro in Virginia, pp. 32–33. It was, however, still legally possible for an entering Negro to become an indentured servant until the statutory laws of 1670 and 1682—the latter closed all possible loopholes by naming the immigrants to be enslaved by color rather than by religion. In fact, it appears that the last Negro to be treated as a servant was Andrew Moore, a "Servant Negro," who in 1673 was granted his freedom dues for five years of service. H. R. McIlwaine (ed.), Executive Journals of the Council of Colonial Virginia (3 vols.; Richmond: Virginia State Library, 1925), I, 354.

[17] The colonial judiciary consisted of but two types of courts, the county courts (see above, pp. 29–31) and the General Court—the latter was made up of the governor and the council and was the highest colonial court. It

taking cognizance of this growing customary law governing the Negro's condition, and they early gave recognition to this whole body of practice. The elaboration of the slave status in law, however, took more time than did its development in practice, for the legal structure of Negro slavery was not really begun until 1662, when the Virginia General Assembly, by statutory law, undertook to work out as sytematic a slave code as possible, and the process was not satisfactorily completed until the beginning of the eighteenth century. The reason for this nearly forty-year period of construction can be explained by the Virginia planters' lack of legal sophistication. Since these men made up the county courts and colonial legislature, the process of creating a slave code would undergo many revisions and corrections before it would be considered satisfactory for firmly establishing the place of the Negro slave in Virginia.

Although the conscious construction of the status of the Negro in the statutory codes was not to begin until 1662, there were references to the condition of slavery in prior acts of the Assembly. The first use of the word "slave" occurred in an act dated 1655, which declared that "if the Indians shall bring in any children as gages of their good and quiet intention to us and amnity with us . . . the countrey by us their representatives do engage that wee will not use them as slaves."[18] The first use of the phrase "Negro slave," however, did not occur until March 30, 1660. On that date appeared an act that was designed to encourage the importation of Negroes, especially

was written about the county courts in the 1690's that: "these County Courts having been held by Country Gentlemen, who had no education in the Law, it was no Wonder if both the Sense of the Law was mistaken, and the Form and Method of Proceeding was often very irregular. . . ." Henry Hartwell, James Blair, and Edward Chilton, *The Present State of Virginia, and the College*, ed. by H. D. Farish (Williamsburg: Colonial Williamsburg Inc., 1940), p. 45. As for the General Court, according to these same witnesses, "the Forms of Proceeding in this Court, are, almost in every Thing, disagreeable to the Laws of *England*, and very irregular." *Ibid.*, p. 47. They found that the justices of this high court "are unskilful in the Law, and it is thought an inconvenient thing in all Governments, that the Justices and Policy of the Government should be lodg'd in the same persons, who ought indeed to be a check upon one another. . . ." *Ibid.*, p. 46.

[18] Hening, *Statutes at Large*, I, 396.

by the Dutch. It provided "that if the said Dutch or other forreiners shall import any negro slaves, ..." they were to be granted reductions on the duty for the tobacco they received as payment for the said Negroes.[19] In the same month came another law that required "that in case any English servant shall run away in company with any negroes who are incapable of makeing satisfaction by addition of time, ..." they were to have double the penalty of years of added service for running away.[20] The reference here is obviously to the class of Negro slaves. One further mention of this status occurred in 1661, when it was declared that any "Englishmen, trader, or other [who] shall bring in any Indians as servants and shall assigne them over to any other, shall not sell them for slaves nor for any longer time than Englishmen of the like ages should serve by act of assembly."[21]

Once these first hints about the existence of a status of slavery within the colony had been made by the legislature, there seems to have developed at this point a conscious effort on the part of the Virginians to create a statutory framework on which to firmly base this condition. It was first deemed important to legalize the transference of slave status to the posterity of the Negro. This was accomplished in December of 1662:

Whereas some doubts have arrisen whether children got by any Englishman upon a negro woman shall be slave or ffree, *Be it therefore enacted and declared by this present grand Assembly,* that all children borne in this country shall be held, bond or ffree only according to the condition of the mother. . . .[22]

Although this follows the Roman precedent and was adopted by all the English colonies, it seems to have been adopted for very pragmatic reasons.[23] That is, that there already existed the usual problems of miscegenation in Virginia, and the most frequent occurrence by far was, as the act stated, between white males and Negro females. This act also implies that

[19] *Ibid.,* I, 540.
[20] *Ibid.,* II, 26.
[21] *Ibid.,* II, 143.
[22] *Ibid.,* II, 170.
[23] Ballagh, *Slavery in Virginia,* p. 44.

where both parents are Negro and slave it was usual in customary law to have the master possess their progeny as well.

As important as defining which parent shall carry the descent of bondage was the question of who shall be included in the class of slaves. It was first felt that the distinctions of importation and religion would be sufficient to classify the Negro as a slave. Thus on October 3, 1670, it was declared that "all servants not being christians imported into this country by shipping shalbe slaves for life."[24] The act was careful to exclude Indians from this definition, and they were not enslaved in the colony until 1676.[25]

But the definition of 1670 was to prove inadequate, not only because Indians were later brought into slavery through war and trade, but, more important still, because many imported Negroes were Christians and therefore could not be held as slaves. It was decided in 1682 to rectify this by specifically naming the groups to be classified as slaves:

. . . all servants except Turks and Moores . . . which shall be brought or imported into this country, either by sea or land, whether Negroes, . . . Mullattoes or Indians, who and whose parentage and native country are not christian at the time of their first purchase of such servant by some christian, although afterwards, and before such their importation . . . they shall be converted to the christian faith; . . . shall be judged, deemed and taken to be slaves. . . .[26]

In short, any imported Negro was presumed to be a slave, no matter what his religious or national background. So logical a connection would the status of slave and the color black or brown have in Virginia slave codes that, in later years, a Negro or mulatto was automatically presumed to be a slave, and it was incumbent upon him to prove otherwise.[27]

As great as the concern was for these codes to define the

---

[24] Hening, *Statutes at Large*, II, 283.
[25] *Ibid.*, II, 346.
[26] *Ibid.*, II, 490-91.
[27] See the famous case of Hudgins *v.* Wrights in William W. Hening and William Munford (eds.), *Reports of Cases Argued and Determined in the Supreme Courts of Appeals of Virginia* (3 vols.; Flatbush, N. Y.: I. Riley, 1809), I, especially 135, 139-41.

rights of the planters in case of disputes of ownership or control, the Virginia slave code, as it evolved, showed no interest in providing for the rights or personality of the slave. It consciously began to reduce him to the abject level of a thing or a chattel. This is clearly seen in the law of 1668, which deprived the Negro of the fundamental legal right to self-preservation and security. By this act, it was declared that "if any slave resist his master (or other by his masters order correcting him) and by the extremity of the correction should chance to die, that his death shall not be accompted ffelony," for as we have already noted, "it cannot be presumed that prepensed malice (which alone makes murder ffelony) should induce a man to destroy his own estate."[28] And in 1672, it was made lawful for any white to kill runaway slaves if they offered resistance.[29]

A sudden fear of Negro insurrection overwhelmed the General Assembly in 1680, and a new series of restrictions were passed. The Negro slave was denied the right to: (1) "carry or arme himselfe with any club, staffe . . . or any other weapon of defense or offense," (2) or "to goe or depart from of his masters ground without a certificate," (3) and "if any negroe or other slave shall presume to lift up his hand in opposition against any christian, shall be for every such offense . . . have and receive thirty lashes on his bare back well laid on. . . ."[30] This last part curiously illustrates the legal inconsistencies to which the Virginia legislatures were prone. For under chattel slavery, the state, by ignoring the personality of the slave, ignores his capacity for moral action as well, and thus commits the control of his conduct as a moral agent to the master. The Virginia legislators, insofar as they held the slave morally responsible to the state for his conduct, so far recognized his legal personality.[31] But the Virginians did not seem to be bothered with this inconsistency, for they tried the slave for various crimes on the one hand, and if he was found guilty

---

[28] Hening, *Statutes at Large*, II, 270.
[29] *Ibid.*, II, 299.
[30] *Ibid.*, II, 481.
[31] Hurd, *Law of Freedom and Bondage*, p. 208.

and was executed, paid the master from public moneys for his destroyed property on the other.[32]

One of the most fundamental English common law rights of personal security was of course denied to the Negro slave when in 1692, it was provided that Negro slaves involved in cases of capital offense were to be tried "without the sollemnities of jury."[33] In 1692, the slave was denied the third primary right, the right of possession of personal property. It was held that "any negro or other slaves" could not brand as his own horses, cattle, or hogs, and any animals so branded were to be considered property of the slave's master.[34] Free movement of slaves was again denied in 1682, with the addition that they could not remain on another plantation over four hours.[35] In 1687 they were denied the right "to hold or make any solemnity or funeralls for any deced Negroes,"[36] thus removing another cause for their possible congregation and intercourse.

Although these restrictions on the rights of the Negro slave cover a wide range of diverse topics, they present an even harsher picture when one considers the innumerable rights about which the law was glaringly silent. Thus the Negro male never possessed any of the rights associated with fatherhood, and slave marriages were totally unrecognized in customary law—a fact to which the church conveniently accustomed itself despite the harsh distortion of one of the sacraments. And so strong was the economic motivation upon Virginia slave legislation that the slave code refused to recognize the sacrament of marriage for the Negro. For recognition of marriage would have meant a serious infringement upon the property right of the master and it was this consideration, above all others, that heavily influenced the Virginia codes.

Another facet of the slave code, as important as the status

---

[32] See e.g., Hening, *Statutes at Large*, III, 269–70.
[33] *Ibid.*, III, 102–3.
[34] *Ibid.*, III, 103.
[35] *Ibid.*, II, 493.
[36] McIlwaine, *Executive Journals of the Council*, I, 86.

of the slave while he was a slave, was the question of what rights, if any, he may have had to claim his freedom. As one author has stated it, "the attitude toward manumission is the crucial element in slavery; [for] it implies the judgment of the moral status of the slave, and foreshadows his role in case of freedom."[37] In the Virginia code, quite opposite from the Castilian imperial law, manumission was made as difficult to execute as possible, and at the same time the position of the few freedmen that were left was made as precarious as possible.

This systematic denial of freedom to the Negro began at an early date in Virginian law. In 1667 came the denial of the right of baptism to "alter the condition of the person as to his bondage or ffreedom."[38] This had been a belief that had gained widespread acceptance and that was thought to be a fundamental justification for the Negro's enslavement, that is, the need to Christianize him. In 1691 it was declared that "no negro or mulatto" could be "set free by any persons whatsoever, unless such person or persons, their heirs executors, or administrators pay for the transportation of such negro or negroes out of the country within six months of setting him free. . . ."[39] And if this was not sufficient, in 1723 it was further declared, "that no negro, . . . shall be set free, upon any pretence whatsoever, except for some meritorious services, to be adjudged and allowed by the governor and council. . . ."[40] These acts were to remain very much in force until the temporary loosening up of the Virginia slave code in the revolutionary fervor of the 1770's and 1780's.

The area that most clearly demonstrated the Virginians' judgment of the moral status of the Negro and revealed that curious racial antipathy previously noted was the very sensitive area of intermarriage and miscegenation—and here the laws were careful not to differentiate between slave, servant, or free Negro. In 1691, it was declared by the Assembly that

[37] Frank Tannenbaum, *Slave and Citizen, the Negro in the Americas* (New York: Alfred A. Knopf, 1947), p. 69.
[38] Hening, *Statutes at Large*, II, 260.
[39] *Ibid.*, III, 87–88.
[40] *Ibid.*, IV, 132.

any free English woman having a child by a Negro or mulatto was to lose the child to the parish, which sold it into bondage for thirty years, and was herself to pay a heavy fine or serve for five years.[41]

And for a further prevention of that abominable mixture and spurious issue, which hereafter may increase in this her majesty's colony and dominion, as well by English, and other white men and women intermarrying with negros or mulattos as by their unlawful coition with them . . . ,

it was enacted in 1705, that any "white man or woman, being free shall intermarry with a negro or mulatto man or woman, being bond or free, shall be . . . committed to prison" and the minister marrying them severely punished.[42] This law interestingly enough talks of bond or free, Negroes and mulattoes. As in many of the laws of the codification of 1705, the freed Negro was brought under the same restrictions as the enslaved one.[43]

---

[41] *Ibid.,* III, 87.
[42] *Ibid.,* III, 453.
[43] In Virginia, also, there was no attempt made to catalogue carefully the various shades of racial intermixture, all being simply called mulattoes. And although the term mulatto was used, in reality there was little or no difference in his status before the law as distinguished from that of a Negro. Any Negro blood, no matter how "whitened" by intermixture, implied a colored and degraded status. Only in so far as a person could physically pass as white was miscegenation of any value. In short, before the law, Virginia very rapidly became a caste-like system, with all colored persons being grouped together regardless of their physical features or cultural attributes.
Just the reverse is true of the Spanish legal system, which, as we shall see, tried to create a carefully graded hierarchy of colored ranking based on physically distinguishable features. In the end this system simply recognized the practical effects of miscegenation, which tended to change dramatically the status of the person, and by the eighteenth century the crown would be forced to adopt a cultural criterion for defining status, largely ignoring physical features and color. In the sixteenth century, however, the range of color terms was enormous, each supposedly bringing to the individual different rights and duties, and even distinctive dress patterns. There was no simple class of mulattoes, but gradations such as *chinos* and *zambos,* which indicated whether the parents were Indian or white or of mixed blood already, and there were whole sets of terms to describe the particular person's color and features (e.g. *mulato pardo, mulato prieto,* etc.). With such fine gradations, passing upward from generation to generation was relatively easy, especially as the Spaniard himself was considered *bermejo,* or of ruddy complexion. G. Aguirre Beltran, "Races in 17th Century Mexico," *Phylon,* VI, No. 3 (1945), 212–18, and chart on p. 201. Also see Irene Diggs, "Color in Colonial Spanish America," *Journal of Negro History,* XXXVIII (Octo-

From the series of laws of 1705 came new additions to the definition of the status of slave. Indians were now excluded from the class of slaves by a law that read "that there be free and open trade for all persons, at all times, and at all places, with all Indians whatsoever."[44] "That a slave's being in England, shall not be sufficient to discharge him of his slavery,"[45] was Virginia's recognition that the status it was creating for the Negro had recognition only within its colonial territory and by force of positive legislation, and that under English common law court decisions, the air of England was becoming too pure for a slave to breath.[46]

In this 1705 series of laws concerning servants and slaves, much of the legislation previously enacted was compiled, along with new laws, into a comprehensive legal code for the Virginia slave regime. It restated the law of 1682 about who should be a slave. The law concerning the transference of slave status through the maternal line appeared here in its third reenactment. Manumission received consideration with the laws regarding baptism and the new one of residence in England, and the entire code on runaways in all its harshness was treated upon. All the disenfranchisements of rights to physical mobility, assembly, property, trial, and so forth,

ber, 1953) 403–27. On the widespread practice of falsification of birth records to change color status see Richard Konetzke, "Documentos para la historia y crítica de los registros parroquiales en las indias," *Revista de Indias*, VII, No. 25 (Julio-Septiembre, 1946), 581–86.

It should be noted that the North American treatment of the mulatto is even in sharp contrast to the practice of English planters in the British West Indies. This whole comparative subject is brilliantly explored in the essay by Winthrop D. Jordan, "American Chiaroscuro: The Status and the Definition of Mulattoes in the British Colonies," *William and Mary Quarterly*, 3d Series, XIX, No. 2 (April, 1962), 183–200.

[44] Hening, *Statutes at Large*, III, 468. This law, in its effect upon ending Indian slavery, does not seem to have become operative for another twenty years or so. The first court decision on it, in fact, did not come until April, 1787, at which time there was discovered an even earlier law (of 1691) which stated the same thing. Tucker, *Blackstone's Commentaries*, Appendix, p. 47.

[45] Hening, *Statutes at Large*, III, 460.

[46] "In the Eleventh of Elizabeth, one Cartwright brought a Slave from Russia, and would scourge him, for which he was questioned; and it was resolved, That England was too pure an Air for Slaves to breath in." Catterall, *Judicial Cases*, I, 1.

were again restated, with freed Negroes and mulattoes now included in many of their provisions.[47]

The compilation of 1705, although not an all-inclusive code, can be regarded as the completion by the Virginians of the legal foundations of their slave institutions. And throughout the rest of the colonial period the codification of 1705 would be considered, with but few modifications, sufficient to define Negro slavery.

Nevertheless, many ramifications of the institution still had to be dealt with, and in 1723 came a new series of laws defining the outer limits of the system. In that year it was decided that not only were slaves not to possess property of their own, but that as a logical consequence they were not allowed to sell or receive any commodity whatsoever without their masters' consent.[48] Also, in 1723, the laws concerning the right to correction and slave deaths caused by this denied even the little right to personal security that may have been left to the slave by the codes of 1705. For to the provisions that if "any slave shall happen to die . . . during his or her correction" was added "or for any reason of an accidental blow whatsoever . . . no person concerned in such . . . correction, or accidental homicide shall undergo any prosecution or punishment for the same."[49] And for the fugitive slave, under the old English laws of "hue and cry," when all gave chase, there was absolutely no right to personal security afforded at all.[50]

[47] Hening, *Statutes at Large*, III, 447–48, 453–54. One ambiguous and difficult question that was treated in these laws of 1705 was whether the slave was to be held as personal property or real estate. By that time it was felt "necessary to advance the property notion of the slave from personality to realty for the sake of justice to owners and heirs in settling and preserving estates." Although potentially this could have turned the status of the slave into something akin to the land-tied serf, it was found to be a highly uneconomic and difficult system to carry through even on a modified scale and was dropped altogether in 1748, with the slave again being considered as personal chattel, liable to seizure for debt, and being completely mobile property. Ballagh, *Slavery in Virginia*, pp. 63–67. The issue was not completely settled until 1792–93. *Ibid.*, p. 70.

[48] Hening, *Statutes at Large*, III, 451.

[49] *Ibid.*, IV, 132–33.

[50] *Ibid.*, IV, 168–73. The extent to which the fugitive slave lost this security is well revealed in a law of 1769 on castration. In its preamble, the act declared that: "Whereas by an act of the General Assembly made in the

In fact, the only time the law considered the slave a human being was in cases of conspiracy and revolt. Fear of insurrection led the masters to make the only exception in ascribing chattel status to the Negro, for to have the state punish a Negro for conspiracy it had briefly to consider him to have volition to act. But this temporary expedient only confirmed the essential quality of chattel status. For the slave was denied even the most rudimentary of legal rights before the law in this one time that his human personality was recognized. Thus, the conspiracy act of this same year declared:

> That if any number of negroes, or other slaves, exceeding five, shall at any time hereafter consult, advise or conspire, to rebel or make insurrection, or shall plot or conspire the murder of any person or persons whatsoever, every such consulting, plotting, or conspiring, shall be adjudged and deemed felony, and the slave or slaves convicted thereof . . . shall suffer death, and be utterly excluded the benefit of clergy. . . .[51]

Thus the Negro was tried for merely plotting a crime in the same manner as if that crime had been committed—which was indeed a concept alien to traditional English law. Nor did the trial proceed along traditional concepts of English justice, for only two judges were appointed as a special trial court just to try the Negroes, and all that was needed to convict was evidence from two witnesses or "one with pregnant circumstances," and execution prior to 1748 was immediate and without appeal.[52]

Although the Revolutionary period would bring relaxation of the laws regarding Negro slavery all along the line, this

twenty-second year of his late majesty George the second, intituled An Act directing the trial of slaves committing capital crimes, and for the more effectual punishing conspiracies and insurrections of them, and for the better government of negroes, mulattoes, and Indians, bond or free, the county courts within this dominion are impowered to punish outlying slaves who cannot be reclaimed, by dismembering such slaves, which punishment is often disproportioned to the offence, and contrary to the principles of humanity," and it therefore ordered, "that it shall not be lawful for any county court to order and direct castration of any slave, except such slave shall be convicted of an attempt to ravish a white woman, in which case they may inflict such punishment," *Ibid.*, VIII, 358.

[51] *Ibid.*, IV, 134.
[52] Ballagh, *Slavery in Virginia*, pp. 82–83.

was only temporary, for the resurgence of the economic importance of slavery in the late eighteenth century and the dissipation of the revolutionary ferment would lead to the return to a harsh slave regime, in this instance even more degrading than the colonial slave codes. By the time of the discovery of the supposed Gabriel "plot" of 1800, the slow hardening of white racial attitudes had already replaced the mild reformist sentiment, and the comparative relaxation and reform of the Revolutionary period came to a bitter end for the Negro in Virginia. Although the issue of emancipation had been reopened in 1782, and an outpouring of philanthropic and religious interest had started movements toward the mass Christianization and education of Negroes, slave and free, during the Revolutionary period and immediately afterward, by 1800 these movements had come to an end. Church after church began to accede to white communicant demands that they stop agitating for emancipation and education of the Negroes, and in the famous prelude to the Civil War in the early decades of the century, they began to split into northern and southern branches on the slavery issue. Finally came a deep-seated reaction from the vast majority of planters to even the mild reformist aims of the revolutionary leadership, and this reaction became even stronger when northern radicals began taking up the emancipation issue where Virginia leadership left it.[53]

Given this background, the legislation of the nineteenth century would prove in many ways even more detrimental to slave rights than all the preceding enactments of the slave code. For these codes assumed that the Negro was an inferior being, and to maintain him in his docility and obedience, denied him every possible access to independence and avenue of self-expression. First came prohibitions to all forms of literacy: schools were denied slaves; planters were prohibited from teaching them; and especially church groups were denied the

[53] On the rather mild "reformist" and emancipationist attitude that the planters expressed even at the height of "revolutionary ferment," and their very rapid return to a hard line on slavery see Robert McColley, *Slavery and Jeffersonian Virginia* (Urbana: University of Illinois Press, 1964), pp. 114 ff.

right to teach literacy with Christianity.[54] Then came a frontal assault even on church gatherings, for in 1804 and in later acts of the 1830's, all religious meetings at night were prohibited; all Negroes, free and slave, were denied the right to hear colored preachers or ministers; and finally, slaves were required to accompany their white master or a member of his family if they wished to go to church. Even then they could only listen to white preachers, and only during the daytime.[55]

In the economic sphere, slaves—again along with free Negroes—were prohibited from peddling any goods whatsoever, and colored slaves were totally denied the right to hire themselves out.[56] They were also denied the right to gather socially without white supervision, and they were elaborately hemmed into the plantation by a complex procedure of warrants and patrol systems, whereby all the Negroes of the state were carefully and constantly accounted for.[57] There also appeared a host of antisedition laws, hue and cry legislation, and other acts to prevent slave insurrections and sabotage following the Gabriel and Turner insurrections of 1800 and 1831, respectively.[58] Finally, as we shall see, came a progressive attack on the rights and independence of the free colored class to reduce its status to as close to the level of the slave as was possible.

Here then, briefly sketched, is the slave code of Virginia. No one can deny that it was a harsh and brutal code, leaving the master with full protection over his chattel, and the Negro with a legal position as degraded as any possibly ever held in Western civilization. That the law presents the extremes of the actual institution of slavery, and that self-interest and humanity on the part of the master mitigated its harshness can

[54] See below, p. 246.

[55] On the 1804 act and its 1805 revision see Samuel Shepherd, *The Statutes at Large of Virginia (1792–1806)* (3 vols.; Richmond: Samuel Shepherd and Co., 1835), III, 124. For the later revisions, see General Assembly, *Supplement to the Revised Code of the Laws of Virginia [1819–32]* (Richmond: Samuel Shepherd and Co., 1833), p. 246.

[56] See Shepherd, *Statutes at Large*, II, 94, 300.

[57] For the laws of the patrol system, see James M. Matthews, *Digest of the Laws of Virginia* (2 vols.; Richmond: C. H. Wynne, 1856–57), II, 550–51.

[58] See e.g., severe punishments for arson of crops and barns, the latter being a capital crime, in Shepherd, *Statutes at Large*, III, 125.

still be accepted without denying that the legal codes present a horribly true picture of the attitude of the white Virginians toward "their" Negroes.

The Negro was chattel, and there stood no opposing institutions in colonial Virginia to claim that in this the master class was wrong. The whole outlook of Virginia slave law was to the perpetual enslavement of Negroes, with a basic feeling that the free Negro class was an anomaly to be obliterated as far as possible from a society that fundamentally refused to accept such a community or concept as feasible. The Negro was branded by these laws and attitudes with an inferiority upon which even that principle of the Enlightenment of "life, liberty, and the pursuit of happiness" had no effect. If anything stands out in sharpest contrast in these two New World colonies, it is Virginia's "Legislation of Iron"[59]—created as it was by "pure" capitalism[60]—and Cuba's slave regime, a product of historic institutions and ancient philosophies alien to the modern capitalistic temperament.

4. Cuba and the Transplantation of a Historic Institution. Whereas the development of the Virginia slave code can be seen as a comparatively compact unit formed between the years 1619 to 1705, the development of the slave codes of Cuba, by the very nature of the sources from which they came, forms a continuum in legal history from Justinian to the nineteenth century. Because of the presence and intervention of the state in the Castilian colonization of the Indies, and because of the careful and successful assertion by the Castilian crown of its authority as the source of all law, the legal institutions of the

[59] "A legislation of iron, is what the North American colonists had given to themselves, independently of the Brittanic Metropoli" Fernando Ortiz, *Hampa Afro-Cubana: Los negros esclavos* (Havana: Revista Bimestre Cubana, 1916), p. 362.

[60] For an incisive statement on the "Dynamics of Unopposed Capitalism" and its effect upon the Virginia slave regime see Stanley M. Elkins, *Slavery. A Problem in American Institutional and Intellectual Life* (Chicago: University of Chicago Press, 1959), pp. 37 ff.

metropolis were the essential sources of the colonial codes. Although the crown, as has been noted, allowed others to finance the exploration and conquest of the New World, nothing of validity occurred without its consent, and its consent was obtained only on the grounds that the government of the colonies was to devolve upon royal officials. So successful was this policy and its enforcement that within a few years of the original conquest, all the conquistadores and companies of conquest had been completely eliminated from the government of the Indies.[1]

The several viceroyalties and their subdivisions, as has already been noted, were considered kingdoms just as much as León and Castile on the peninsula. In these "overseas kingdoms," however, the authority of the crown was even more absolute than in Iberia. The peninsula kingdoms had been able to establish forces in opposition to the absolutist tendencies of the Castilian monarchy, and these parliamentary institutions, nobilities, and other ancient privileges circumscribed royal authority as no colonial institutions were able to do. For the crown saw to it that none of these institutions was ever allowed to develop in their New World dominion, and thus never had to compromise or divide its sovereignty. Under Spanish imperial law, the crown was the source of all legal, political, and even economic rights (since it alone owned all the land as well as all the subsoil under the land) in the New World kingdoms.

It was decided by the crown, that "because the Kingdoms of Castile and the Indies are under one Crown, the laws and ordinances of government of the one and the other ought to be as similar and consistent as possible," and it therefore declared that the laws and customs of these overseas kingdoms should be the same as "the customs and ordinances with which the Kingdoms of Castile and León are ruled and governed with regard of course for making room and allowing for the

---

[1] Richard Konetzke (ed.), *Colección de documentos para la historia de la formación social de hispanoamérica, 1493-1810* (4 vols. to date; Madrid: Consejo Superior de Investigaciones Cientificas, 1953-62), I, Introduction, vii.

diversity and dissimilarity of these lands and nations."[2] Although the allowance for the uniqueness of the New World would eventually necessitate the famous *Recopilación* in 1680, which was a comprehensive codification of all the laws that applied specifically to the Indies,[3] a great deal of the ancient Castilian legislation would remain the basic core for colonial institutions. This was nowhere better illustrated than in the Negro slave codes.

The fact that the laws of Castile were to be fully applicable to the Indies was of extreme importance for Cuban slavery, because the colonials were presented ab initio with a complete and historic slave legislation, which had already been applied to the African Negro for at least a century before 1511. Fundamentally the slave code of Castile rested upon the Justinian Code of ancient Rome, and more specifically on the famous codification of Castilian law that occurred in the thirteenth century A.D. under the rule of Alfonso X. Between the years 1263 and 1265 the comprehensive *Las Siete Partidas del Rey Don Alfonso el Sabio* was compiled under royal direction, and within these seven divisions can be found an elaborate slave law, a code that was transplanted almost intact into the New World.[4]

Las Siete Partidas provided a slave code that was indeed unusual, for influenced as it was both by later Roman law and by Christian philosophy,[5] it held as a fundamental principle that slavery was *contra razon de natura*.[6] Slavery was against natural reason, as an introductory declaration stated, because "slavery is the most evil and the most despicable thing which can be found among men. Because man, who is the most noble,

---

[2] *Recopilación de leyes de los reynos de las indias* (3 vols.; Madrid: D. Joaquin Abarra, 1791), I, 234–36, Libro II, Título II, Ley XIII.

[3] Konetzke, *Colección de documentos*, I, vi.

[4] Fernando Ortiz, *Hampa afro-cubana: los negros esclavos, estudio socio-lógico y de derecho publico* (Havana: Revista Bimestre Cubana, 1916), pp. 335, 342–43; Frank Tannenbaum, *Slave and Citizen, the Negro in the Americas* (New York: Alfred A. Knopf, 1947), p. 45.

[5] *Ibid.*, pp. 45–48.

[6] *Las Siete Partidas del rey Alfonso el sabio, cotejadas con varios codices antiguos, por la Real Academia de la Historia* (3 vols.; Madrid: La Imprenta Real, 1807), III, 117, Partida IV, Título XXI, Ley I.

and free creature, among all creatures, that God made, is placed by it in the power of another. . . ."[7] Thus while slavery was accepted as a historic institution and one of long standing and custom,[8] which was of necessity to be continued, it was conceived of as an evil necessity rather than a positive good, and thus the law would do all in its power to insure the slave his God-given humanity. In direct contrast to the tortured Virginia codes, the slave, under Las Siete Partidas, was considered a human being, a legal personality possessing, as will be seen, innumerable rights as well as obligations.

The slave's legal personality was recognized by the state through his right to personal security and property. Moreover, through the slave's right to admittance into the faith, he secured a whole series of relative rights such as sanctity of marriage, parenthood, fraternization, and so on. These relative rights especially, would become of major concern to the church in the Indies, and would occupy much of its legislative attention.

Of the right to personal security, it was declared that:

> The father may punish his son moderately, and the master his slave . . . and the teacher his student. But because there are some of them who are so cruel and so excessive in doing this, that they do evil with stone, or with wood, or with other hard thing, . . . and someone dies because of these wounds, although it was not done with the intention of killing him, the killer should be banished to some island for five years. And if the one who punished with these wounds did it knowingly with the intention of killing him, he should have the punishment of homicide.[9]

It was also expressly declared that in the case of their murder, all differences between a freedman and a slave were erased, and the murderer was punished the same way whether he killed either one or the other with the intent to destroy.[10]

[7] *Ibid.*, III, 30, Partida IV, Título V, introducción.
[8] "Slavery is a position and institution which ancient peoples created. . . . And this [institution] was established by the emperors, because in ancient times as many as they captured they killed, but the emperors were sustained by good and ordered that the captives not be killed, but that they protect them and make slaves of them." *Ibid.*, III, 117, Partida IV, Título XXI, Ley I.
[9] *Ibid.*, III, 570, Partida VII, Título VIII, Ley IX.
[10] *Ibid.*, III, 566, Partida VII, Título VIII, Ley II.

Whereas castration of slaves was acknowledged to be an ancient custom practiced by the Romans as well as the Moors, it was deemed by Las Siete Partidas to be a crime of very serious circumstances, and if guilty the master was tried before the royal courts and the slave was freed.[11]

Not only was the slave in his own person protected by law against the violence and power of his master, but so was his family as well. Thus it was provided that the master could not perform adultery with the slave's wife, nor dishonor his daughter, and if this should occur the slave could appeal for justice in the courts, whereby if the charges were proven against the master, he was to lose all power over the slave.[12]

Under these thirteenth-century codes, the slave had far less right to personal property than he was to possess later in the New World. His right to property was heavily dependent upon the will of his master, for it was felt that if he did not possess his own person he could have very little claim to other property; he was, however, granted the right to transact business if he were self-employed or if he were employed by his master in a business establishment.[13] From other laws it can be seen that there was some type of legal recognition given to the slave who was allowed to possess property, aside from his master's volition. Thus a slave could inherit property as any other legal person, although by so becoming an heir, this status, as will be seen, did change.[14] The law also recognized as a legal transaction the action of a slave giving money for his price to a third party, so that the party might buy him from his master and then set him free. And it was provided that the slave could have recourse to the courts if this third party did not fully carry out the agreement.[15] From this it can be inferred that at least in customary law, the slave possessed some property outside of his master's will. But the actual right to possess property and with that property buy his freedom for

[11] *Ibid.*, III, 572, Partida VII, Título VIII, Ley XIII.
[12] *Ibid.*, III, 120, Partida IV, Título XXI, Ley VI.
[13] *Ibid.*, II, 734, Partida III, Título XXIX, Ley III.
[14] *Ibid.*, III, 381, Partida VI, Título III, Ley III.
[15] *Ibid.*, II, 357, Partida III, Título II, Ley VIII.

himself, a whole system that was to receive the name of *coartación*, did not devolve upon the slave until the institution of slavery had been transplanted to Cuba and the New World.

Although the right to property may have been extremely circumscribed, the slave possessed without any reservations, save that of being a Christian (and all could be admitted to the faith), the right to marriage. Slaves could marry against the will of their masters if they continued serving him as before. And if they belonged to two separate masters they had to be sold and placed under one master, and if neither master was willing to buy the slave, the church had to do so.[16] Also if a slave spouse was taken out of the country, the church had to see that the two were reunited, again by its buying one of them and keeping them under one master, for it was held as an absolute, that "husband and wife cannot live apart."[17] It was even provided that a slave could marry a free person without the consent of the master, so long as the free partner was fully aware of the slave condition.[18]

Although as in the Roman, and the later Virginian codes, the child was made to follow the condition, either free or slave of its mother, it was also expressly added that the child of a male slave and a free woman was free.[19] In fact, in its whole attitude toward manumission Las Siete Partidas was an extremely unique document, and the spirit that animated these provisions was to find expression in all subsequent slave codes and was to govern imperial and colonial thought and action on this vital topic until the end of slavery in the nineteenth century. Holding that slavery was essentially an evil thing, and that the slave was a human being, Las Siete Partidas justified its lenient and very complex and extensive legislation of manumission on the grounds that "all of the laws of the world should help toward freedom."[20]

A slave could be freed by two sources of power, either by

---

[16] *Ibid.*, III, 31, Partida IV, Título V, Ley I.
[17] *Ibid.*, III, 31–32, Partida IV, Título V, Ley II.
[18] *Ibid.*, III, 31, Partida IV, Título V, Ley I.
[19] *Ibid.*, III, 118, Partida IV, Título XXI, Ley II.
[20] *Ibid.*, II, 419–20, Partida III, Título V, Ley IV.

the state or by his master. Since the master was allowed the greatest amount of freedom in declaring his slave manumitted, the act could legally be carried out in a church, before a judge, in a testament, or with a letter signed by five witnesses. Since freedom was considered so precious and the manumitting of slaves such an extremely honorable act, the law specifically provided that the freed slave was to pay all kinds of homage to his former master and his family. He was never to speak ill of such a master, and in times of the latter's distress or discomfort he should do all in his power to aid him.[21]

Direct manumission was thus strongly encouraged by the law, but this was by no means the only way a slave could attain his freedom. By performing an act of service to the country, namely: by denouncing the rape or molestation of a virgin, by denouncing acts against the government—specifically identifying counterfeiters and guards and soldiers who had deserted their frontier posts, by accusing the killer of his master or by avenging him, or by discovering treason against the crown, he was to be freed without any regard to his master's wishes. In all cases save the last, the state reimbursed the master for his slave's freedom;[22] the last case can be considered in a legal sense to constitute a forced expropriation for public utility.

In other cases, a master who abused his slave would have that slave taken from him; and although all cases did not prescribe that the slave be freed—he was often given instead to a new master—in some cases this was done. Such crimes as castration, ill treatment of the slave's wife or daughter, excessive punishment, or poor care and food usually saw the slave removed from the guilty master to a new one. If a female slave was put to public prostitution by her master to make money out of her, then she was declared to be free.[23] As José Antonio Saco has pointed out, the Justinian Code was more liberal in instances of abuse in that it, more often than Las

[21] *Ibid.*, III, 121–22, 124, Partida IV, Título XXII, Leyes I, VIII.
[22] *Ibid.*, III, 123, Partida IV, Título XXII, Ley III.
[23] *Ibid.*, III, 123, Partida IV, Título XXII, Ley IV.

Siete Partidas, allowed the slave to go free rather than go to a new master.[24]

But no matter how "illiberal" these thirteenth-century codes were in this respect, they at least provided the slave with a wide range of protective legislation that directly interposed the state between the slave and the master, and greatly weakened the latter's property rights over his slave. In Virginia's chattel slave code, the master's property right never allowed for the admittance of the church or state into the master-slave relationship. The master's self-interest and humanitarianism was all the Virginia Negro could rely on, whereas the more worldly Castilians knew that power corrupts and were much less concerned with what to the Virginian was the prime consideration—that the property right of the master in the slave be in no way questioned by the state.

A fourth means of freedom for the slave involved his being the recipient of some right through his relations with others or through his assumption of rights that only a freedman could hold, and therefore necessitating that he be made a freedman commensurate with his newly won rights and duties. Thus if a slave became a member of the clergy with the consent of the church, despite his master's wishes he had to be freed, and if he became a bishop he seems to have been required to free two slaves in his own name.[25] If a father appointed a slave as the guardian of his children, the slave by that act was freed.[26] A slave who became the heir of his master, unless he was involved in adulterous relations with the testator's wife, could inherit the estate either wholly or in part and in so doing was emancipated.[27] As has been seen a slave could marry a free person without the master's consent, and the marriage was binding so long as the free party knew of the enslaved status; but if a master willingly agreed and consented to this type of

---

[24] José Antonio Saco, *Historia de la esclavitud desde los tiempos más remotos hasta nuestros días* (3 vols.; Barcelona: Jaime Jepús, 1875–77), III, 273.
[25] *Las Siete Partidas*, III, 124, Partida IV, Título XXII, Ley VI.
[26] *Ibid.*, III, 498, Partida VI, Título XVI, Ley VII.
[27] *Ibid.*, III, 381, Partida VI, Título III, Ley III.

marriage, then the slave was free. Also, if a master married his slave then the slave was automatically freed. If a slave was owned by more than one person, and at least one of the owners wished to free him, then all the others were required to do so too, despite their wishes.[28]

The slave was given the right to initiate legal suit before a court, primarily in cases where he was fraudulently prevented from gaining his freedom by any one of numerous ways.[29] The slave could also initiate suit in cases involving defense of his master's property, and if a slave was owned by the crown, he could appeal both for defense of his master's property and also for defense of his own person—the latter being a special right granted to a royal slave because of the eminence of his master.[30] Slaves could appear as witnesses against another person only in certain cases, for it was felt that "slaves are like other desperate men because of the slavery which they are in" and therefore their testimony may not be just in all cases. Nevertheless they could appear in all cases of treason, and although slaves usually could not appear as witnesses against their masters—being like other legally dependent persons such as wives and children—they could testify in cases in which the master or his wife were accused of treason, murder, or adultery.[31]

While these thirteenth-century codes obviously did not take into cognizance the still unorganized modern African slave trade, the sub-Saharan African Negro had been, along with Arabs, Berbers, Slavs, and even Spanish Christians, a part of the Castilian slave population upon which these laws operated. For especially after the Moorish invasion of the Iberian peninsula in the eighth century, sub-Saharan African Negroes had been brought into Spain in fairly large numbers. As slaves they played an important role in the armies of the Moorish regimes and were also extensively traded to the Christian

[28] *Ibid.*, III, 122–23, Partida IV, Título XXII, Leyes V, II.
[29] *Ibid.*, II, 357, Partida III, Título II, Ley VIII contains most of these possible fraudulent means of preventing a slave from gaining his freedom.
[30] *Ibid.*, II, 357–58, Partida III, Título II, Ley IX.
[31] *Ibid.*, II, 352, Partida III, Título XVI, Ley XIII.

kingdoms by Moorish traders from North Africa.[32] Even as late as the opening up of the water routes to West Africa by the Portuguese in the fifteenth century, Negro slaves were still being imported into Spain, where slavery, though reduced in importance, still flourished.[33] And as the modern West African trade developed, large numbers of Africans were brought directly to Spain, and there, especially in Seville and the province of Andalusia, achieved some prominence well before the discovery of America.[34]

Thus although no new codes were needed after 1492 to deal with the African Negro as such, the unique problems of the modern slave trade and of the control of heresy and purity in the Indian population forced the crown to expand the old Castilian slave legislation into new areas previously unconsidered. The crown's assertion of absolute control over all emigration to its Indies along with its desire to control and secure a profit out of the slave trade led the crown into its first additions to traditional law.[35] Although it first had scruples over the admittance of *bozales*, or raw blacks direct from Africa, into the Indies in the first decades and demanded that only *ladinos*, or Spanish-speaking Christianized Negroes from Spain could be imported, this policy was abandoned as early as 1510. Finding the ladinos difficult to control and expen-

---

[32] On the role of the African Negro in medieval Spain see E. Lévi-Provençal, *Histoire de l'espagne musulmane* (3 vols.; Paris: G.-P. Maisonneuve, 1950–53), III, 72, 74–75, 177–78, 208 ff; Charles Verlinden, *L'esclavage dans l'europe médiévale, peninsule iberique-France* (Bruges: "De Tempel," 1955), pp. 225–26, 358–62; Saco, *Historia de la esclavitud*, II, 140–41.

[33] *Ibid*, III, 36; Elizabeth Donnan, *Documents Illustrative of the History of the Slave Trade to America* (4 vols.; Washington: Carnegie Institution of Washington, 1930–35), I, 1.

[34] So important did the colored population of Seville become that the government appointed a special Negro "count," or judge, who ruled over the community. See Antonio Domínguez Ortiz, "La esclavitud en Castilla durante la edad moderna," *Estudios de Historia Social de España*, II (Madrid: C.S.I.C., 1952), 369–428. In 1565 the archdiocese had a population of 14,760 slaves (*ibid.*, pp. 376–77), whereas Lisbon, the center of the Portuguese slave trade, had a population of 9,950 slaves in 1551; see Frédéric Mauro, *Le Portugal et l'Atlantique au XVII* siècle (1570–1670) (Paris: S.E.V.P.E.N., 1960), p. 147.

[35] A full discussion of the licensing and other regulations for the slave trade is contained in the classic study by Georges Scelle, *Histoire politique de la traite négrière aux Indes de Castille* (2 vols.; Paris: L. Larose et L. Tenin, 1906).

sive, the crown reevaluated its attitude and concluded that the bozales were at the same primitive, pre-Christian, religious state as the New World Indians, and therefore were not in danger of religiously polluting the Indies.[36]

But while a compromise over the bozales was almost essential, considering the heavy demands from the New World colonials for Negroes and the limited and expensive supply that the ladinos represented, the crown would not compromise with Mohammedanism, whether it professed itself in white skin or in black. In 1531, it prohibited the carrying of Berber slaves to the Indies; and in 1543 it ordered the expulsion of all Berbers and Moors found in the Indies. In 1550 another *Real Cédula* prohibited the carrying of Negro slaves from Sardinia, Majorca, Minorca, and other regions of the Mediterranean because, it was claimed, they were of Moorish castes or married to Moors, even though being the caste of Guinea Negroes.[37]

Also uniquely involved with the modern slave trade were the *asientos*. Ever since the first asiento had been granted, the crown had been forced to back up this grant with much protective legislation: demanding licenses, designating ports of call, providing protection for the ships of the asiento fleet, providing for the price in the Indies and the registration of numbers transported, as well as seeing that the holder of the asiento carried out all its provisions.[38]

Although the complex legislation on importation and the slave trade was the first legislation added to the traditional codes, there soon began to develop a host of local and imperial laws dealing with the everyday operation of the slave system in the New World. Unlike the trade regulations, the laws dealing with the actual functioning of the internal slave regime, though issued in Spain, were heavily based on local custom, needs, and precedents. Although the crown would modify large amounts of this colonial legislation, either for

[36] José Antonio Saco, *Historia de la esclavitud de la raza africana en el nuevo mundo y en especial en los paises américo-hispanos* (Barcelona: Jaime Jepús, 1879), pp. 68–70.
[37] Ortiz, *Los negros esclavos*, p. 343 n.
[38] *Recopilación de leyes*, II, 539–42, Libro VIII, Título XVIII, Leyes I–XI.

its own economic, political, or military interests, it tended to accept planter and master needs so long as they conformed with the basic outline of the imperial slave codes, as defined in Las Siete Partidas. The laws dealing with the Negro and the American institution of slavery, like the vast majority of imperial legislation, came from a combination of New World sources and royal enactments. The crown, in fact, took great care in obtaining exact information on the unique problems of the Indies, as well as collecting the opinions of local officials, and if these opinions were in accord with its moral and judicial positions it would carry them through to law.[39] Thus the crown formed and modified its new slave law from the diverse New World institutions generating law: the municipal ordinances, diocesan and provincial synods, the proclamations of viceroys, governors, and captains-general, and finally from the proceedings, sentences, and resolutions of the audiencias.[40] The metropolis also permitted the colonial officials to suspend metropolitan ordinances if they felt it necessary, allowed them to question the legitimacy of these acts based on their experiences, and gave them the right to propose other solutions in their stead.[41] This suspension, however, was never indefinite, and if the crown still felt that the law had to be carried through, it sent new officials to the Indies who would replace the old ones and enforce its legislation.

Probably the earliest additions to the royal slave codes necessitated by new American conditions, aside from those about the ladino-bozales problem, concerned the control of the colored population. Although the slave population on the peninsula had been important, it had never been so essential or so dominant a part of the economic life and population of the community as was the Negro slave in the Caribbean. Not only were the Negro slaves greater in number than the whites in many places but the vast uninhabited areas of this tropical New World provided the Negro with ample opportunity to escape successfully his masters and at the same time survive

---

[39] Konetzke, *Colección de documentos*, I, viii.
[40] Ortiz, *Los negros esclavos*, p. 347.
[41] Konetzke, *Colección de documentos*, I, ix.

in a type of climate with which he was long familiar. As early as 1526, when the ladinos were excluded altogether, it was noted that Hispaniola and the other islands were already infested with these wild bands of rebellious *cimarrones* who were secluded in the innermost mountain fastness of the several islands.

All during the sixteenth and seventeenth centuries, these cimarrones existed throughout the Caribbean and constantly proved a serious threat to Spanish government in the area. For the cimarrones not only ruled on their own, but they gave constant and essential aid to all enemies of Spain, from the pirates and freebooters who roamed the Caribbean to the large military expeditions from Europe that were bent upon conquest.[42]

Nor did the problem of the cimarrones disappear in later centuries, although the Caribbean was eventually cleared of freebooters by the middle of the eighteenth century, and large tracts of previously unsettled interior land was colonized in the eighteenth and nineteenth centuries. Losing their free-booting qualities and becoming primarily sedentary farmers, the escaped slaves now formed regular palisaded or stockaded villages known as *palenques*. Although pushed further into outlying mountainous and infertile or swampy regions, these palenque villages had an active and fruitful existence until the very end of slavery in the late nineteenth century. Appar-

---

[42] For the role of the cimarrones in the operations of Drake, for example, see: Saco, *Historia de la esclavitud de la raza africana*, p. 221; Arthur Percival Newton, *The European Nations in the West Indies, 1493-1688* (London: A. & C. Black Ltd., 1933), pp. 86–93.
Probably the earliest description of Negro cimarrones working closely with corsairs in Cuba came in 1539 when the French attacked and burned Havana and also attempted to take Santiago de Cuba. See the Colección de Juan Bautista Muñoz in the Real Academia de Historia, Madrid, tomo 81, folio 275. There does not seem to have been quite as many Negro cimarrones raids in these early years as José Antonio Saco has listed in his studies. For early records, as inscribed in the Colección Muñoz, tended to use the term cimarrones indiscriminately for Indians and Negroes, and it seems that many of the earliest cimarrones rebellions of the 1510's to the 1550's were in fact fugitive Indian revolts and raids; see e.g., the letter of Hernando de Castro, dated Santiago de Cuba, August 31, 1543, which makes this clear, in Colección Muñoz, vol. 83 folio 99. Saco made the mistake of assuming all cimarrones were Negroes even in this early period. By the mid-sixteenth century, however, cimarrones were identified exclusively with Negroes.

ently known to the vast majority of plantation slaves, these hidden and self-sufficient villages became the chief escape route for the bozales and other unskilled rural Negro slaves.[43]

To deal with this endemic and often dangerous problem of runaway slaves, there appeared on the statute books of the Indies a large body of repressive legislation on the control and capture of cimarrones. Heavily basing the legislation on colonial experience, the crown as early as 1542 ordered that no Negroes could be out at night in the cities of the Indies, or in the villages or other places, and that they should remain under their master's roof.[44]

More specifically aimed at the cimarrones were a host of laws designed to strike down their communities and hunt them effectively, for as one royal decree noted, they were responsible for mutinies, seditions, rebellions, highway robberies, and other thieveries.[45] Prior to 1530 the Cubans themselves had resorted to a classical Spanish institution, the *hermandad*, or rural voluntary constabulary. These hermandad patrols were maintained by a tax upon all masters of slaves, and their sole purpose was to retrieve fugitive Negroes.[46] But these efforts were insufficient, and there soon grew up a class of professional slave hunters known as *rancheadores*, whose methods were none too pleasant, for as early as 1540 the crown had to require that in no instances were Negro cimarrones to be castrated. In another Real Cédula it was provided that these rancheadores should not molest free persons of color.[47]

In 1571 the crown demanded that "Viceroys, Presidents, and Governors should always endeavour to subdue the Negro *Cimarrones*, putting in this reduction the greatest possible diligence" and that captains of greatest experience should be placed in charge of these wars against the cimarrones. The penalties for fugitive slaves were made extremely severe: any

---

[43] For a full discussion of the problem of runaways and fugitive slaves, aside from the palenque and full cimarrones, see pp. 155–57.

[44] *Recopilación de leyes*, II, 363, Libro VII, Título V, Ley XIII.

[45] *Ibid.*, II, 369, Libro VII, Título V, Ley XXVI.

[46] Ortiz, *Los negros esclavos*, p. 398.

[47] *Recopilación de leyes*, II, 365, 368, Libro VII, Título V, Leyes XXIII, XIX.

Negro absenting himself without leave for more than four days would receive fifty lashes, more than eight days one hundred, and so on. If the escapee were found in company with cimarrones, the penalties applied were to be even more severe —an escapee away more than six months and found in company with cimarrones was to be hanged.[48]

In their wars against the cimarron bands, the government first provided time for peaceful surrender, and if the cimarron so surrendered and it was his first offense, then he was excused the penalties assigned for this act. If a band of cimarrones was captured during such a "war," then the leaders were summarily executed without benefit of judicial proceedings, and the rest of the Negroes reduced to slavery. Severe penalties were assigned to those who aided the cimarrones, from reenslavement for free Negroes to expulsion from the Indies for whites, and if anyone maintained active communication with them, then the penalty was death.[49]

Virginia's "hue and cry" laws were fully as severe in their treatment of fugitive slaves as the Cuban codes, but she never experienced the tremendous problems encountered by the Spaniards with their cimarrones. For the cimarrones were everywhere in the Indies and maintained permanent towns on all the islands, including British Jamaica, as well as along the Panama coast and even in Mexico. On the other hand, such settlements were almost impossible for the Virginia Negro, since he could not survive in the colder Virginia climate in such independent communities, especially as he faced a landlocked forest and often unfriendly Indians. Thus fugitive slaves in Virginia were really "outlying slaves" who never went far from plantations, surviving only by stealing food from the white community. The Cuban Negro on the other hand, could escape with relative ease to areas unknown and inaccessible to whites, come upon established fugitive slave communities, and not only grow his own food undisturbed and even raise a family, but in the earlier centuries he could

---

[48] *Ibid.*, II, 365–66, Libro VII, Título V, Leyes XX, XXI.
[49] *Ibid.*, II, 366–69, Libro VII, Título V, Leyes XXIV, XXVI, XXII.

even arm himself and gain all the necessities of life through contact with the innumerable freebooters who roamed the Caribbean, ever willing to aid the cimarrones. The cimarrones in turn not only supplied hides from the wild herds of cattle and acted as illicit handlers of contraband goods, but were also invaluable guides for raids on the Cuban communities.

Even when the cimarrones settled down into the defensive and isolated palenque pattern of primitive agricultural villages, they still proved a major problem to the Spaniard and creole masters, since they were a prime drawing source for dissatisfied and rebellious slaves. These slaves often used the palenques as bases for depredations against the plantations, and the palenque itself offered a safe refuge for the extremely large number of outlying slaves who stayed close to their home plantations and could use these villages in times of crises. It is little wonder then that the cimarron problem was of such persistence and magnitude in the history of Cuban slavery.[50]

[50] Although the government made constant raids and often used professional troops, as well as the civilian agencies, the independent fugitive village system continued to survive and prosper until the end of slavery. Even when discovered, these villagers tended to defend themselves or successfully elude capture, and the average dweller spent a good portion of his adult life in freedom. For example, in 1749, in the Cape Cruz peninsula near Bayamo, a special government force attacked such a village and succeeded in capturing only a small number of the inhabitants. Of the 11 adults captured, the average time that they had been fugitives from their masters was 9.6 years, and the two children taken had both been born in the village. One of the adults captured was not even a resident of the village but was merely visiting from his own stockaded fugitive community. Archivo General de Indias [hereafter cited as AGI], Sevilla, Audiencia de Santo Domingo, legajo 367, no. 37, April 23, 1749.

Nor did this one attack on the Cape Cruz area seem to have made much of a change, for two years later troops from Bayamo succeeded in capturing 43 more fugitive slaves, although after this major campaign the local officials admitted that "many more" fugitives eluded capture than were taken. AGI, Santo Domingo, leg. 368, no. 40, July 13, 1752.

Located principally in the Oriente and Pinar del Rios regions on the western tip of the island, there were nevertheless important pockets of these villages scattered throughout the island between these two areas. For a discussion of such villages and their activities in the Matanzas region in the 1840's, see [J. G. F. Wurdemann], *Notes on Cuba* (Boston: James Munroe & Co., 1844), p. 262. For a description of a *ranchería*, or fugitive slave hunt, and of the varieties and types of fugitive villages, from one or two huts

But the problem of fugitive slaves was only one of many new problems the crown encountered in establishing the legal framework for Negro slavery. It was not only required to enact laws on the control of the slave population and the suppression of runaways, but it also had to enforce the major humanitarian goals of its general slave code. These problems are well reflected in the first comprehensive legal code ever written for Cuba, which occurred in the sixteenth century.

In 1574, an *oidor* from the audiencia of Santo Domingo by the name of Alonso Cáceres made a *visita* to Cuba to bring uniformity to its chaotic laws and practices. The bulk of the famous ordinances of Cáceres that finally emerged concerned the crucial issues of municipal government and property rights. But an important part of these fundamental laws were concerned with the slave system. Of the 88 ordinances, some 15 dealt with the slave and colored population, and a large part of these slave ordinances were concerned with self-employed and hired-out Negro slaves who Cáceres felt were leading too independent an existence.[51] As he described it,

... many citizens have Negroes, and Negresses who are employed, and that these Negroes occupy themselves in diverse things, and go about like free workers, and do what they want, and at the end of the week, or month, give to their masters a fixed wage, and other masters have inns, providing food and lodging for passengers, and employ their women Negro slaves in these inns. . . .

To better control this almost free status of urban slaves, Cáceres provided that no Negro slave, even if self-employed, could have his own house and required that he live with his master (ord. 55). Not only could these slaves not live in their own houses, but they were also prohibited from boarding out in the homes of other persons (ord. 57), and were required to be in the home of their masters every evening unless they were given special permission by their masters (ord. 56).

(*ranchos*) to full-scale palenques, see the observations of another American visitor, Demoticus Philalethes (pseud.), *Yankee Travels through the Island of Cuba* (New York: D. Appleton & Co., 1856), pp. 38–39. Also see F. Ortiz, *Los negros esclavos*, chap. 22.

[51] The ordinances of Cáceres, dated May 13, 1574, can be found in AGI, Santo Domingo, leg. 331.

Although recognizing that self-employed Negro slaves, or day laborers, or those working with their masters could drink wine in taverns, he limited them to a daily ration. Cáceres was also outraged by what appeared to be slave control over the taverns of Havana and ordered that no Negro slave could sell wine for his master, or otherwise operate a tavern, without a license from the cabildo, and this license was to be given only on the good conduct of the licensee (ord. 50). This desire to make masters responsible for the acts of their self-employed slaves was urgently felt by Cáceres, and he pointed out in support of his plea the case of the washerwomen who deliberately disappeared with the clothes of their transient ship customers the day these persons sailed for home (ord. 54).

How effectively these ordinances controlled self-employed slaves is questionable, for throughout later centuries it appears that the slaves who hired themselves out lived virtually free lives in the cities, and that by not providing food and shelter, the master was saving himself large sums of money. In fact, it was because Cáceres found so many of these self-employed also poorly housed and clothed, as well as because of his desire to control their movements and account for their actions, that he legislated on their state.

He also sought to eliminate some of the more basic causes for slave unrest, these being primarily inadequate food and clothing, and harsh and excessive punishments. "Because many use their slaves, and do not give them meals, or clothes to cover their flesh," Cáceres noted, there was much stealing and running away, and he therefore ordered that:

all of those who have Negroes on *estancias, hatos,* or cattle ranches, or other places, must give them sufficient food for the work that they do, and that they likewise give them two pairs of pants, . . . at least once a year, and that they must not give them excessive and cruel punishments, and that in order to see that they comply with this, . . . the alcaldes of each village, the first in the month of March, and the other alcalde in the month of October are obliged to visit the *hatos* and *estancias;* and inform themselves of the treatment of the said negroes. . . .[52]

[52] Ordinance no. 60.

It does not appear that masters in Cuba were excessively motivated by humanitarianism or self-interest, for in the code that follows the previous one on inspection, there is listed an index of what Cáceres felt to be excessive and cruel punishments.

Because there are many who treat their slaves with great cruelty, who whip them with great cruelty and scourge them with different kinds of resin, and burn them, and do other cruelties from which they die, and they remain so punished and intimidated that they come to kill themselves, and throw themselves into the sea, or flee or rebel . . .

it was therefore ordered that in such cases the slave be taken from the master and the latter be brought to justice.[53]

Cáceres also concerned himself with the fugitive slave problem and the threat of rebellion. He ordered that no Negro slaves could be armed, except Negro cowboys and other rural workers. Free colored persons were specifically excluded from this act, however, because they were citizens of the town and were required to do night-watch duty in this major port city (ords. 52, 53). He also provided very severe penalties for ranchers, farmers, and other persons who deliberately gave shelter to runaway slaves or permitted them to work on their estates (ord. 58). It seems that these planters then went to the runaway's master and bought the supposedly lost slave for a nominal fee. He also declared that any free person had the right to apprehend and capture fugitive slaves (ord. 59), and he provided a sliding scale of rewards that the masters were required to pay slave captors, the amount depending on the distance the capture took place from the home of the master (ord. 61).

Aside from these laws on runaways, and the attempts to deal with the unique growth of urban slavery and with the native development of the coartación—the self-purchase system,[54] the major part of the imperial slave code was concerned with implementing the fundamental rights of the slaves in oppo-

[53] Ord. no. 61.
[54] See pp. 196–99.

sition to the property rights of the masters; and essentially it reenforced the classic pre-Columbian codes. Thus, as early as 1540, the crown demanded of "our Royal *Audiencias*, that if any Negro or Negress or any other held for slaves proclaim their freedom, they hear them, and do justice and provide that for this they are not maltreated by their masters."[55] And in 1570, it declared, reminiscent of Partida IV, Título V, Ley II of Las Siete Partidas, that Negro slaves who were married in the peninsula kingdoms could not be transported to the New World without their families—wives and children included—and provided strict registration to see that this was enforced.[56]

Another sign that the traditional moral attitude toward the slave prevailed in imperial thinking is to be found in the famous law of 1563, which claimed that "some Spaniards have slave children and wish to buy them in order to free them. We order those parents who wish to buy them for this reason to have a preference when they are sold."[57] Although in 1527 the crown declared that the marriage of Negroes, and by inference their conversion to Christianity, did not entail the automatic right to manumission, the law specifically recognized and encouraged marriage among them.[58]

Perhaps nowhere did the underlying philosophy of Las Siete Partidas manifest itself so obviously as in the Real Cédula of 1693. Written to the captain-general of Cuba, it expressed the desire of the king regarding Negro slaves in Cuba and the institution of slavery. It was ordered that if at any time the masters mistreated their slaves the captain-general:

will apply the necessary remedy. [For] it is not just to consent to, or permit any excess in this matter, for their slavery is a sufficient sorrow without at the same time suffering the distempered rigor of their masters.[59]

To complete the first centuries of royal concern with the Negro and with the growth of New World slave legislation there arose a whole body of canonical law, which specifically

[55] *Recopilación de leyes*, II, 362, Libro VII, Título V, Ley VIII.
[56] Konetzke, *Colección de documentos*, I, 451 (document no. 317).
[57] *Recopilación de leyes*, II, 361–62, Libro VII, Título V, Ley VI.
[58] *Ibid.*, II, 361, Libro VII, Título V, Ley V.
[59] F. Ortiz, *Los negros esclavos*, pp. 350–51.

dealt with the problem of the African as a pagan, a slave, and a Christian. These church enactments were given immediate royal sanction and thus legalized as both civil and canon law, and were supported by royal cedulas. Thus these canonical actions would have a profound impact on the life of the slave as they dealt with his moral, religious, and even economic rights and duties. Equally important, this whole canonical code dealing with the Negro was created by the various dioceses and provinces to which Cuba belonged and originated from laws that were the direct result of practical, clerical experience on the island.[60]

As the centuries passed, the crown more and more came to concentrate its energies on the problem of the Negro slave and his particular position in the New World society. Although excessively absorbed in the problems of the Indian in the first two centuries of colonization and faced by a relatively small number of Negro slaves within its dominions, the crown did not begin fully to comprehend slavery and the Negro as a vital problem requiring constant concern and legislation until the eighteenth century. Although the outlines and shadings of the slave legislation were long since fixed, the crown constantly had to prevent the erosion of traditional patterns under the impact of new economic conditions or local developments.

By the end of the seventeenth century and the beginning of the eighteenth, a number of developments converged to bring this problem into sharp focus. The first and most important of these developments was, of course, the regularization and vast expansion of the slave trade under French and then English asiento agreements. Along with this came the growth of sugar, coffee, and other plantation slave-labor crops that greatly promoted slave importations and reinvigorated the entire Caribbean economy, making the islands and continental shoreline a new area of wealth and importance for the new Bourbon governments. In its trade with Europe under the new and tremendously modified ideas of royal mercantilism, which were heavily tinged with free trade notions, the crown was seriously concerned with developing the commercial crop

---

[60] For a full elaboration of this extraordinary code, see below, chap. 5.

system and went to unusual lengths to guarantee the growth
and rational development of this new agriculture. It offered
such modern concepts as protection of colonial crops and
fomentation of agricultural societies, and it permitted unlimited and untaxed trade within the entire Spanish empire.
Finally, of course, added to the old Catholic humanism was
the tremendous impact of the thought of the Enlightenment,
which greatly deepened royal humanitarian thinking.[61]

All of this led in the eighteenth century to such institutions
as the *procurador síndico*, or royal defender of the slaves for
each local district, and to the recognition of coartación, or the
right of slaves in Cuba to purchase their freedom and to seek
court protection in all the formal proceedings. This latter
was a customary practice to which the crown gave important
legal sanction in the 1760's.[62] Finally came a whole new code
dedicated for the first time exclusively to the problem of
American Negro slavery—the famous code of 1789.

As the crown itself admitted in the preamble to the code,
it was deeply concerned with infractions of traditional legislation regarding slave rights and duties, and because it had
just created absolute free trade in slaves the year before fully
recognized that something substantial had to be done. For as
the crown rightly foresaw, and the statistics in Cuba bear out,

---

[61] For the impact of the Enlightenment and Bourbon rule on Spain, see
Jean Sarrailh, *L'Espagne éclairée de la seconde moitié du XVIIIe siècle* (Paris:
Imprimerie Nationale, 1954), and Richard Herr, *The Eighteenth Century
Revolution in Spain* (Princeton: Princeton University Press, 1958).

[62] An institution developed primarily by local custom, *coartación* was not
officially dealt with by the crown until the 1760's. At that time it asked for
a complete analysis of the operation of the system to see what taxes, if any,
should be charged in the transaction, and specifically if the *alcabala* or sales
tax should be applied. In the resulting investigation the crown decided that
the tax not be charged and also strongly supported the whole practice of
coartado and weighted it heavily toward the side of the slave. It decreed
that, despite whatever education or skills the slave had acquired, the master
could ask only the price which he paid for the slave originally because,
stated the crown, "all should be sacrificed for the benefit of freedom,"
which it claimed was always in the public interest and therefore superseded
private concerns. The crown also fully supported the right of a slave to
have himself coartado even against the will of his master. See AGI, Santo
Domingo, leg. 890, book 58, June 21, 1768; AGI, Santo Domingo, leg.
890, book 58, June 21, 1768; and AGI, Santo Domingo, leg. 1138, no. 3,
February 17, 1778.

the end of the exclusive asiento system and the opening up of free trade in Negro slavery brought a flood of Negro slaves into the New World domains of Spain, making the three previous centuries of importation seem totally insignificant by the next half-century of growth. As the crown concluded in its preamble, "taking into consideration, that with the freedom of the slave trade which I have conceded to my vassals . . . February 28th of the past year, the number of slaves in both Americas will be considerably augmented, this class of human beings deserve from me their just attention."[63]

Known as the "Royal Cédula of His Majesty, on the education, treatment and occupation of the slaves, in all his dominions of the Indies," the code concerned itself exclusively with the rights and obligations of the slaves as human beings and the special obligations that attached to those royal subjects who were masters. Representing the culmination of years of practical experience of Negro slavery in the New World, and particularly with the plantation system of the Caribbean, the code was one of the most sophisticated and adoptive pieces of royal legislation ever enacted. It did as much as could possibly be done by a legislator, in a practical sense, to guarantee the rights and privileges of slaves "as human beings" by carefully providing for local conditions and for a host of carefully tested checks and balances to guarantee the enactment of the codes. An over-all standard was declared, but wide latitude was allowed for local variations and modifications. This code, then, the most liberal of all the Iberian and New World legislation ever written on slavery, embodied the essence of Enlightenment thought, heavily tinged with the evangelical Catholicism of the Bourbon rulers of Spain.

As in the classic codes, the 1789 collection began with the essential requirement that the masters educate the slaves in the Catholic religion and guarantee their enjoyment of the

---

[63] The code, divided into 14 chapters, is found reprinted in "Real Cédula de Su Magestad sobre la educacíon, trato y ocupaciones de los esclavos, en todos sus dominios de Indias, e islas Filipinas," *Revista de Historia de América*, III (September, 1938), 50–59. The introduction to the code also specifically declared that the codes on slavery were based on *Las Siete Partidas*, which were still legally operative.

sacraments. As the first chapter declared, "All owners of slaves, of whatever class and condition that they are, must instruct them in the principles of the Catholic religion and in the true necessities in order that they be baptized within one year of their residence in my dominions. . . ." For this task, the master was to pay a priest to say mass and give instruction on every Sunday and holiday and also pay for all other masses that special occasions dictated or that the slaves requested. The master was also required to see that the slaves said their rosaries every evening after work, either in his presence, or in that of their overseers.

The code also repeated the traditional thirteenth-century enactments on marriage, providing that "masters of slaves must avoid illicit contact between the two sexes, foment marriages" and not impede their slaves from marrying off the hacienda. If slaves did so, and the plantations were far apart, then the woman slave's master had to sell her to the other master at an equitable price. If the two could not agree, then the local justices were to make a fair settlement (chapter vii).

But only two chapters of the code concerned themselves with these traditional matters, which seemed to be taken for granted for the most part and needed little retelling. What the code most concentrated on was the physical welfare of the slaves and the full legal protection by the state of their basic right to security and protection as human beings. This was a constant theme in a tremendous amount of individual cedulas and local legislation, but the crown now made it a permanent part of a fully detailed and coherent code. To begin with, the second chapter of the code concerned itself with the problem of food and clothing. Recognizing that the diversity of climates and conditions prevented a uniform code, the crown provided that the procurador síndico meet with the local town governments and local justices to determine local rules and regulations guaranteeing to slaves and their families the proper clothing and food. These rules were then to be posted in all the local churches, on the doors of the cabildo, and in the parade grounds or shrines of the local haciendas, giving full notice to all masters "in order that none can allege ignorance" of them.

By the same means, local working conditions were also established and published abroad in the local districts. Work was broken down into types of occupations by sex and age, and was carried out only "from sun up to sun down" with two full hours off each workday for the slaves to use for their own benefit. Men over 60 and under 17 and women of all ages were not obliged to give full field labor. Women slaves were not to work as day laborers nor be required to mix with men (chapter iii).

Detailing a whole chapter to "Diversions," the 1789 code provided that on festival days[64] the "masters cannot oblige, nor permit their slaves to work, after they have heard mass, and attended the teaching of the Christian Doctrine. . . ." Rather the slaves were to be allowed, until the sounding of evening prayers, to do as they pleased, providing that the masters prevented excessive drinking, the mixing of sexes, or the gathering together of slaves from other plantations (chapter iv).

In its concern for the living conditions of the slaves, the crown required that masters provide separate quarters for unmarried men and women and that this housing be well made to withstand inclement weather. When slaves lived more than two in a room, the master was also required to maintain a separate residence as an infirmary. If he sent his slaves to a hospital, the master was to pay for their daily maintenance in the hospital and was to pay all burial fees for his slaves when they died (chapter v). For the old and infirm, who often seemed to have been badly neglected or simply freed by the average plantation owners, the code provided that children and aged and infirm slaves, "must be fed by their masters, without allowing the masters to concede freedom to them in order to discharge himself of them" unless he provided for their maintenance (chapter vi).

Turning to the obligations of the slave, the crown declared

[64] One expert in the early nineteenth century estimated that the Cuban work-year consisted of only 290 days, leaving 85 days of rest and recreation, these being holidays and Sundays. Alexander von Humboldt, *The Island of Cuba*, trans. with an introduction and notes by J. S. Thrasher (New York: Derby and Jackson, 1856), p. 212 n.

that if the masters sustained, educated, and usefully employed the slaves according to their strength and conditions, then the slaves by the same reasoning had to obey and respect their masters and overseers, doing what work they asked, "and venerating them as Padres de familia." If they did not follow instructions or obey the commands of their masters, then they could and should be corrected in accordance with their delinquency. However, no slave was to receive more than twenty-five lashes with a whip, which lashes could not cause bleeding or severe contusion. Nor could the slave be corrected by anyone except the master or his overseer (chapter viii).

If a slave's crimes and disorders merited greater punishment, the state was to intervene, and in a trial before the local justices with the presence of the procurador síndico, the state would exact the punishment required. In all cases, the punishment was to be exactly the same as in the cases of free persons (chapter ix). This proviso was particularly important, for it made all crimes of the slaves equal in punishment to that of whites, an extremely unusual feature for slave societies and in distinctly sharp contrast to the Virginia codes, which held the slave and the Negro to entirely different sets of penal standards.

As for the master, for any infraction of the above rules and regulations on the education or welfare of his slaves, in the first instance, he was to pay a 50-peso fine; in the second instance, a 100-peso fine; and the third time, a 200-peso fine. The master was to pay these fines even if it was the exclusive fault of his overseer, if the latter could not pay. As in all such legislation, the traditional rule was applied whereby the person who denounced the action received one-third of the fine, the judge one-third, and the government one-third. If the above fines were not sufficient to stop the improper action of the master, then government officials were to see that more severe action was undertaken against the guilty master (chapter x).

Placing the problem of excessive punishment in a separate paragraph to indicate its unique importance, the crown dictated that masters or overseers who caused dismemberment, grave contusion, or bleeding during correction were not only to be fined the above amounts, but were to be tried in courts of law by the síndico. In their court cases they were to suffer "the punishment corresponding to the crime they committed, as if the injured party were a free person." Here again, the slave was given exactly the same rights and privileges before the law as the free white, in order that his basic right to personal security could be fully defended. Like the child in normal legislation, the slave could be punished for wrongdoing, but only to a point, the point being anything that seriously threatened his basic right to security of life and limb. Also, in such cases the maltreated slave was to be sold to another master, but if the slave had been incapacitated for work, then the master had to pay for his maintenance for the rest of the slave's life.

The code also made clear in a separate chapter (xi) that only the master or his overseer could correct a slave. No other party was permitted to punish, castigate, wound, injure, or kill a slave "without incurring in the punishments established by the laws for those who commit similar excesses, or crimes, against persons of a free status." Here as well the procurador síndico was to act in the first instance for the slave, even though the slave's master might be the injured party. In short, it was not left to the master to determine injury but, as in the case of the free citizen, to the state.

To guarantee that no master could cause the disappearance and death of his slaves, the crown provided that a list of all the planters' slaves be notorized and deposited with the municipal clerk. In the instance of the absence or natural death of a slave, the master had to notify the municipal government of the fact within three days, or otherwise he would be under suspicion of murder and would be proceeded against on these grounds by the síndico (chapter xii).

Aside from making provisions for the síndico to make triannual visits to all the haciendas in his district to guarantee conformity to the law, the crown specifically provided that the itinerant clerics who said mass at the haciendas on Sundays, holidays, and other special occasions should act as secret informants to the síndico if there were any breach of obligations and duties on the part of the master or any crime committed against the slaves. The code also provided that all informants who gave details and accusations of crimes were to be protected in their privacy, without having their names revealed at any time; and they were also to receive a third part of any fines imposed against the masters (chapter xiii).

To promote this complex government system of protection of the security, health, and welfare of the slaves, the crown provided that all monies that it procured from fines against masters were to be used by the síndico in all measures necessary to bring protection to the slaves and to bring all masters to justice. To guarantee that the monies were spent toward these ends, the síndico had to account for them annually, in detail, to the local intendant, the most powerful royal official under the revised Bourbon administration.[65]

There is some debate about how much of this famous code was actually implemented, but there is no question that it had a major impact on all nineteenth century legislation. From the 1806 free-marriage decree ending the last vestiges of caste ar-

---

[65] The masters were not slow in protesting the new code, and in January, 1790, some 69 Cuban planters, seven of them aristocrats, claimed that the code, though well meaning, was harmful to the economic and peaceful functioning of the sugar estates. In an attitude reminiscent of the Virginia planters, the Cubans protested that the very act itself was not needed because "it suits the masters to treat their slaves well, since in their hands rests their own subsistence and the progress of their estates. Not only are the masters thus inclined to humanity, but it is in their particular interest to do so. For this reason, in this area the best law is that each one think of his own interests." On the specific chapters of the code, they claimed that their slaves were well treated and certainly not starving, as the ability of many of them to save money and to buy their own freedom indicates. As to clothing, food, shelter, and other essentials for their slaves, they felt that they, the masters, rather than any local official, could best determine the needs on each plantation. What most irked the masters were the severe prohibitions on physical punishments. On the one hand, they pointed out that their slaves had plenty of opportunity for dancing, recreation, and religious services and that the harvest work was far from excessive. On the other hand, they claimed that their slaves were always mutinying, running away, or becoming cimarrones, and that if the masters could not determine their own punishments, the whole system would collapse. The planters concluded that the crown should not listen to false information about ill-treatment of slaves from local informers, but should base its new legislation on the advice of interested parties, and especially recommended the use of the cabildos rather than the royal officials. For this long memorial see AGI, Papeles de Estado, leg. 7, no. 4.

rangements to the 1842 Cuban *Reglamento de Esclavos* and the important 1863 code that provided effective new juridical rights to slaves, the 1789 act was the moving spirit upon which all this legislation was based. Although work rules might at times be less liberal than the 1789 charter, the provisions of marriage, religious instruction, coartación, health and living conditions were always the same.[66]

Throughout its centuries of development the Cuban slave law had shown a remarkable cohesion and a consistent extension of rights to the slaves. Although the law might be more or less enforced in given periods, we can nevertheless assume that by the nineteenth century the attitudes universally expressed in the vast body of canonical and civil law of Spain and Cuba had come to be accepted as legitimate and morally operative by the majority of Cuban whites.

These Cuban slave codes had created a powerfully modified form of slavery that carefully preserved for the slave his rights to property, to security, and to full religious equality. Not only did the royal government concern itself with these traditional rights to legal personality, but by the nineteenth century it was legislating such things as health standards, diets, working hours, clothing, and even minimum housing standards for the slave work force. In short, no aspect of the rights, duties, or living and working conditions of the slaves was neglected by the Cuban and imperial codes, and it was this emphasis on the slave and his world as opposed to Virginia's exclusive stress on the master and his rights that would so fundamentally distinguish the legal regimes of these two slave systems.

[66] Ortiz, *Los negros esclavos*, pp. 367 ff.

PART III. Anglicanism, Catholicism, and the Negro Slave

Introduction. In concluding this survey of the primary institutions that mediated between master and slave, we come to the unique role played by the church. Although royal official and judicial officers did set the general outlines of the world of the slave and from time to time even directly involved themselves in the everyday operation of the slave regime, it was the priests and clerics who concerned themselves most intimately with the daily life of each and every African slave. For whatever else an African Negro might be in the great age of missionary activity, he was still a human soul uneducated to the true faith.

Dealing with these non-Christian, imported, African Negro slaves was one of the most difficult tasks faced by the churches of the New World from the earliest days of the slave trade. Whether Roman Catholic or Protestant, each church suddenly found its colonial parishes flooded with human beings held in bondage and ignorant of the doctrines of the church. For each church the question of the validity of that bondage had to be dealt with, and for each the human and Christian nature of the African Negro had to be decided. The problem might be ignored in the first hours of establishing a functioning church among the white colonists and dealing with the problem of evangelization among the Amerindians, but these questions had to be resolved before a Christian kingdom could be established on the shores of the New World.

How the two metropolitan churches dealt with the African Negro slaves would be determined by a host of considerations, from the question of organizational differences to the problem of religious climate. But whatever the case, the patterns of dealing with these slaves, which they both evolved, would have a profound impact on the life of the bondsmen. For expecially in the pre-Enlightenment world, when religious thought and action completely pervaded the life of colonial America, the attitudes and actions of the church did much to create and define the moral, legal, social, and even economic position of the Negro, slave and free, within colonial society.

5. The Church and Its Negro Communicants in Colonial Cuba.

Within colonial Latin American society the Spanish Catholic church was the prime arbiter in the social and, to a considerable extent, intellectual life of all men. Not only did it define the moral basis of society and determine the limits of its intellectual world view, but it also sanctified and legalized the most basic human relationships. Although this was the traditional role of the church in Catholic Europe, and especially in Spain, the church in the New World also faced the unique task of dealing with non-European peoples and defining their place within traditional social patterns.

Acutely aware of this problem from the first days of the conquest, the church conceived of its primary function in the New World as an evangelical one. Putting aside its harsh and negative role as defender of the faith, which dominated its European attitudes against the other "peoples of the book," it adopted a positive role of sympathetic conversion of virgin peoples to the true faith.[1]

Although the thrust of this missionary activity was directed toward the American Indians,[2] the evangelical Catholic church of the New World also intimately concerned itself with the other great religiously primitive peoples, the African Negro slaves. From the beginning of slave importation, in fact, the church took up the position that the African Negroes were to be considered part of the New World church on much the same level as the untutored Amerindians. And while the church was often forced to concede the colonists' prior claims for the labor of these black and brown races, it never relinquished its position as the guardian of the moral, religious, and even social life of the untutored Indian and Negro races within its New World domain.

This dominant role of the church in the life of the Negro slaves is well illustrated in the history of the Cuban church. Because of the virtual extinction of the Indians who lived on the island before colonization and the subsequent dominance of the slave population, the Cuban church was forced

---

[1] The evangelical mission of the Catholic church in the New World was, in fact, a truly novel and powerful departure from previous experience. While the wars of reconquista against the Moors had brought the expansion of the faith, this had been by means of fire and the sword. Only in rare instances were attempts made to convert peacefully Mohammedans and Jews to Christianity, and thus despite the religious overtones of the centuries-long reconquista, the whole concept of evangelization was practically nonexistent.

Even when the opening up of virgin territories suddenly brought this great movement to life within Spanish Catholic circles, it was entirely directed overseas, with no parallel in Europe. While the New World church was pacifically preaching a gentle Christ to the Indians, the peninsular church, during these same three centuries of colonial rule, waged an unrelenting war against Jews, Moors, *mudejares, moriscos, conversos,* judaizers, Lutherans, and Calvinists. An intolerant defender of the faith at home, it proved to be unusually tolerant, patient, and intelligent assimilationist in its encounters with the New World pagans. As one scholar concluded: "Militant Spain guarded its religious purity in the metropolitan territory with the sword, and turned itself into a missionary at the service of the same faith in the New World." Antonio Ybot León, *La iglesia y los eclesiásticos españoles en la empresa de indias* (2 vols.; Barcelona: Salvat Editores, 1954–63), I, 347–50.

[2] See e.g., Robert Ricard, *La "conquête spirituelle" du Mexique* (Paris: Institut d'ethnologie, 1933).

to give its undivided attention to its Negro communicants almost from the first years of colonization. Eventually becoming the most heavily populated Negro colony in Spanish America, Cuba, more than any other area, tended to set the pattern of church-slave relations.

In defining its attitude toward the African slave, the Cuban clergy was, of course, governed by the ideas that had evolved on the institution of slavery and on African Negroes from the contemporary mores of Iberians and from the decrees of the metropolitan church. And in both sets of standards there had been built up in the Iberian peninsula a historic pattern that preceded the creation of the modern Spanish state. The sub-Saharan Negroes as well as the North African peoples had had intimate contact with the population of Spain from recorded times to the sixteenth century. The Negro had been especially important in the armies and slave populations of the Spanish Moslem states, and the Iberian peoples had long accepted his individuality, personality, and coequality. Since North African Berbers blended into mulatto and black sub-Saharan Negroes, there was no reason for the white Iberians to conceive of these Africans as anything but normal human beings, no stranger or more incomprehensible than the barbarous Slavs and the fierce Berber tribesmen. Thus, under the slave systems developed by the Christian kingdoms of northern Spain, the Negroes were treated as coequal to all other non-Christian peoples, and as slaves had the same obligations, duties, and rights.

Because of this familiarity both with the institution of slavery and the sub-Saharan African Negro, the church had long become accustomed to dealing with these two phenomena. The Moslemized African slave had been treated like all Moslems, and the institution of slavery, long used for Christians, Moslems, and Slavs in the Iberian penisula, was fully recognized by church law and practice. In the thirteenth-century Las Siete Partidas, for example, the church had been made responsible for guaranteeing that married slaves lived together in legal wedlock, and that the sanctity of the family should not be broken by sale of members to overseas owners or by separation of any kind. Under these codes, it had also been assigned its extraordinary role in the process of manumission.[3]

With the expansion of slavery into the New World and the heavy importation of African Negroes, the church continued to apply standard Castilian law and practice to both the religious and legal rights of the slave. If anything, the New World Negro stood in a better relationship to the Spanish church than his Iberian predecessor. For unlike his predecessor he was not a Moslem, since all Moslem slaves were prohibited by the crown from entering the New World. He was therefore considered to be of a primitive or prereligious state, identical in this to the Indian, and therefore also falling under the great evangelical zeal of the New World church. As religious primitives the African bozales fell into this same tutorial status, and although this meant the exclusion of Indians and Negroes from the priesthood for this period, it also meant that they were exempt from the jurisdiction of the Inquisition.

Although the majority of the Catholic clergy both in Spain and the New World had successfully attacked the legality and practice of enslaving the Indians, only a few exceptional clerics contested the right to Negro slavery. For the Negro was not originally a subject of the crown of Castile and his enslavement had occurred prior to his entrance into the Spanish realms. This gave the clerics no legal grounds and less moral will for denying the practice, since it was initiated, according to the thinking of the day, by the heathens themselves. But although the church never officially opposed the institution of Negro slavery, it deliberately interfered in the direct relationship between master and slave on the grounds that both were communicants in the church and that nothing must challenge this primary Christian right to salvation and the sacraments.

The crown specifically charged the New World clergy with the responsibility of caring for its Negro communicants, as well as of guaranteeing that every subject of the crown was a practicing Christian. In the very opening book of the *Leyes de Indias*, the famous compilation of colonial legislation, the crown demanded that the church take especial care in dealing with Negro slaves. It stated that:

We order and command to all those persons who have Slaves, Negroes and Mulattoes, that they send them to the Church or Monastery at the hour which the Prelate has designated,[3] and there the Christian Doctrine be taught to them; and the Archbishops and Bishops of our Indies have very particular care for their conversion and indoctrination, in order that they live Christianly, and they give to it the same order and care that is prepared and entrusted by the laws of this Book for the Conversion and Indoctrination of the Indians; so that they be instructed in our Holy Roman Catholic Faith, living in the service of God our Master.[4]

Nor was the church itself slow in meeting these demands, and in its earliest colonial synods it dealt long and extensively with the problems of its Negro members. Given the close tie that existed between civil and canonical law, the legislation that came forth from these synods became an essential part of the Cuban slave legislation.[5]

The first of these colonial church synods to meet in the Caribbean was the Dominican provincial synod that met early in the seventeenth century on the island of Hispaniola. Carried out under the auspices of the Archbishopric of Hispaniola, which included all of the West Indies, Cuba, Florida, and Venezuela,[6] this first Caribbean church synod spent a good part of its time considering the problem of its Negro communicants. With strong royal representation in the person of the

---

[3] See pp. 62–63.
[4] *Recopilación de leyes de los reynos de las Indias* (3 vols.; Madrid: D. Joaquin Ibara, 1791), I, 5, Libro I, Título I, Ley XIII. In the preceding law the crown had specifically ordered "that in each one of the towns of Christians a determined hour each day, be designated by the prelate in which all the Indians, Negroes and Mulattoes, free as well as slave, that are within the towns, be brought together to hear the Christian Doctrine." This same law also provided a similar arrangement for those who worked and lived in the countryside. *Ibid.*, I, 4–5, Libro I, Título I, Ley XII.
[5] Fernando Ortiz, *Hampa afro-cubana: Los negros esclavos, estudio sociológico y de derecho publico* (Havana: Revista Bimestre Cubana, 1916), p. 348.
[6] Ybot León, *La iglesia y los eclesiásticos españoles*, II, 55.

governor and president of the audiencia of Santo Domingo,[7] these leading bishops and clerics prepared, after much discussion, a series of laws and ordinances known as *sanctiones*.[8] Because of royal representation and support, these Latin codes were later translated into Spanish and became the official civil code within the audiencia and the binding canonical law for the ecclesiastical province.[9]

One of the very earliest of these sanctiones of the Provincial Dominican Council, and the first dealing with the Negro concerned the very basic task of determining if the Negro had been properly admitted into the church:

Since we learn from a certain experienced leader that Negroes have been transported from Africa and brought from other parts to these Indies without benefit of baptism, so if at some time it is claimed that these were besprinkled with holy water by traders when they are put ashore by us, it is recommended that they be questioned concerning their baptism: that is, if they have received the water of baptism before they left from Africa, or on the sea, or in any other place or whether they did not receive it at all . . . Also one may question them whether at the time they received the baptism they had obtained any knowledge, however imperfect, concerning the performance of this sacrament which was conferred upon them. . . . and also whether they willingly received this holy water at the time it was offered to them. If however, any of these conditions are found to be lacking in their baptism, they must be baptized anew.[10]

In the next section it was stated that redoing the baptism was essential if there were any doubts, because to the Negro "it is thus shown that the privilege of the sacrament is given to them, and the Negroes know themselves to be baptized equal to the others."[11] Thus it followed that no cleric of the province could "confer baptism upon Negro adults unless they have been imbued first with the Christian doctrine,"[12] which

[7] Fr. Cipriano de Utrera, "El Concilio Dominicano de 1622, con una introdución histórica," *Boletin eclesiástico de la arquidiócesis de Santo Domingo* (1938–39), pp. 8–9.

[8] The original Latin ordinances, or *Sanctiones Concilii Dominicani*, are reprinted in *ibid.*, pp. 23–81.

[9] *Ibid.*, pp. 10–11.

[10] Sanctiones Concilii Dominicani, Sessio Secunda, Caput I, Sectio vii.

[11] Sessio Secunda, Caput I, Sectio viii.

[12] Sessio Secunda, Caput I, Sectio ix.

education was to be undertaken as soon as they entered the province by a priest specifically designated for this task.[13] If Negroes refused to be baptized, they were given two to three months "during which the fear of the doctrine must be found." At the end of this time the cleric "may administer baptism to them, provided they are, one and all, sorry for their transgressions, they display the sign of this sorrow, and they realize the power of the sacrament of baptism."[14]

As for the sacrament of confirmation, it was demanded that the "priests ever warns the master of Negroes to place before them the means and the place to receive this divine sacrament, but if they do otherwise they may be punished with a judgement."[15] In the sacrament of marriage, it was required that at Negro weddings—as at Indian ones—that two special benedictions be given instead of the usual one, to impress them with the importance of this sacrament.[16] If an unbaptized Negro contracted marriage with someone already baptized, it was required that a new agreement be made and the marriage ceremony be repeated. And this was to be done as soon as possible, "so that the benefits of marriage may be rightfully enjoyed."[17]

Negroes were not to be granted absolution until they had overcome their ignorance and inexperience and had finally accepted the faith. It was also provided that every qualified confessor could hear the confessions of Negroes.[18] Again, with the administration of extreme unction—as with all other sacraments—it was demanded that the Negro be taught its meaning and accept its significance before it could be administered to him.[19]

It was required by these *sanctiones* that Negroes who lived at great distances from the churches and worked in the country should hear mass at least at six festive holy days per year. And if the master was not willing to allow his slaves to hear

---

[13] Sessio Secunda, Caput I, Sectio x.
[14] Sessio Secunda, Caput I, Sectio ix.
[15] Sessio Secunda, Caput II, Sectio iii.
[16] Sessio Secunda, Caput IV, Sectio iii.
[17] Sessio Secunda, Caput IV, Sectio vii.
[18] Sessio Secunda, Caput V, Sectiones i, vi.
[19] Sessio Secunda, Caput VII, Sectio iv.

mass at least these six times, then the prelate was to see to his legal chastisement.[20] The church council also demanded that "no master of Negroes may put slaves to any servile work on the festive days, nor may he hire others; under the penalty of ten silver pounds for the first transgression, for the second he will truly be implicated with excommunication."[21] For the Negroes on these days were to be taught by the priest "so that they may learn the articles of faith and reap the harvest of sacraments."[22]

Largely supporting the declarations and ordinances of the Dominican Provincial Synod of 1622 and also providing further clarifications of the rights of Christian Negroes were the *Constituciones*, published by the church synod that met for the Cuban diocese in June of 1680. Constitución IV repeated a proviso that had become an essential part of imperial slave code, that is, that all slaves be instructed in the Roman Catholic faith and be baptized within a year of their admittance into the Indies.[23]

It also provided that bozales could not be married by a priest until both parties were baptized.[24] In attempting to deal with this problem, the diocesan synod was forced to take into account the African background of the slave and adjust the Catholic atmosphere to the matrimonial customs brought by the slave from his native land. "Because there come many Indians . . . and Negro bozales, married in their infidelity: we order that wanting to live together in this bishopric, after being baptized, their marriage be ratified *in facie ecclesiae* [in the sight of the Church]." If either partner refused the faith, he or she was given up to seven months and six warnings to be baptized. If, after this time elapsed, they still refused baptism they could not continue their marital relations. And "if any of the said infidels come married with many wives," they were required to be baptized and married to the first

[20] Sessio Tertia, Caput I, Sectio iv.
[21] Sessio Tertia, Caput I, Sectio v.
[22] Sessio Quarta, Caput VII, Sectio ii.
[23] Fernando Ortiz, *Hampa afro-cubana: los negros brujos* (Madrid: Librería de Fernando Fe, 1906), p. 304.
[24] Constitución III, quoted in Ortiz, *Los negros esclavos*, p. 348.

one with whom "according to their custom and rites" they had contracted marriage. If the first one could not be so ascertained, then the male could marry the one he desired. And it was also required that if the male had married within the direct parental line (mother, sister, etc.), his marriage was declared invalid and they had to separate before baptism was administered.[25]

The diocesan synod also attempted to eradicate the continuing problem of unscrupulous masters who, for either personal reasons or those of economic expediency, tried to prevent their slaves from marrying or refused to honor these marriages. Thus Constitución V established that "marriage should be free" and ordered that:

no master prohibit his slaves against marriage, nor impede those who cohabit in it, because we have experienced that many masters with little fear of God and with serious damage to their consciences, proscribe that their slaves not marry or impede their cohabitation with their married partners, with feigned pretexts; . . .

In this same law, masters were prohibited from taking their slaves outside of Havana to sell them unless they took husband and wife together. Constitución VI added that masters could not sell their slaves overseas or in remote parts to impede marital cohabitation. If this was done, then the slaves sold in this manner should be brought back with the master paying the expense.[26]

Thus, the local church did all in its power to carry out the intent of the metropolitan slave codes and to guarantee to their Negro communicants their full rights. The churches met in powerful synods to deal with local conditions and the unique backgrounds of their particular colored congregants and always legislated in favor of the fullest freedom and rights that were permissible. While the upper clergy dealt with these problems in law, the lower clergy, especially at the parish level, effectively carried this law into practice.

This correlation between law and practice is abundantly

[25] *Ibid.*, pp. 349–50.
[26] *Ibid.*, p. 349.

supported by the local parish statistics available on the administration of the sacraments. What these materials indicate is that the slave and the free colored population had the same percentage and absolute figures of baptism as the white population. According to the census of 1827, for example, when whites represented 44% and the slaves 41% of the total population, each group had 12,938 and 12,729 baptisms performed, respectively, on the island in that year.[27]

Not only were slaves and free colored fully admitted into the church, but they also heavily participated in all the sacraments and most importantly in that of marriage. For example, in the four years from 1752 through 1755, the rector of the Cathedral Church at Santiago de Cuba reported 55 slave marriages to 75 free white marriages in his parish.[28] At this time the entire urban population of Santiago de Cuba consisted of 5,765 slaves and 6,525 whites,[29] which means that the slave marriages in that period represented 1 out of 104 slaves in the city, and the free white marriages 1 out of 87 whites. In short, despite the sharp differences in education, social status, and wealth, the slave marriage rate was close to the free white rate. This is all the more extraordinary given the fact that a large portion of the adult population, of all colors and social conditions, lived in free unions because of the high cost of clerical ceremonies.

That illegitimacy was strongly implanted in all classes, can be seen in the figures for the local parish of Santo Tomás, also within the jurisdiction of the church of Santiago de Cuba. Of its adult population in the parish census of 1824, only 44% of the whites over 16 were married, and only 42% of its free colored adults were.[30] Nevertheless, despite this high

---

[27] Ramón de la Sagra, *Historia económico-política y estadística de la isla de Cuba* (Havana: Imprenta de las viudas de Arazoza y Soler, 1831), pp. 7–8, 20. The free colored, who made up 15% of the total population in 1827, had 4,826 baptisms.

[28] Archivo General de Indias, Sevilla, Audiencia de Santo Domingo, leg. 516, no. 30, June 14, 1758 [Hereafter cited as AGI].

[29] Sagra, *Historia económico-política*, p. 3.

[30] The figure for slaves was only 29% of the adults, but this seems to be an exceptionally low percentage, for in almost all the total statistics for the island slaves consistently have higher marriage rates than free colored. For the parish statistics see: AGI, Santo Domingo, leg. 223, February 15, 1824.

incidence of illegal unions among all classes, the number of legitimate births seem to have been high. In the copper mining town of Santiago del Cobre, the parish records for a nine-and-one-half-year period (January, 1771–August, 1780) reveal that 170 out of the total slave births, or 58%, were legitimate, as opposed to 121 illegitimate slave births in the same period.[31]

As for the entire island, the total marriages performed in 1827 were: 1,868 white marriages, 1,381 slave marriages, and 385 free colored marriages. Dividing this into the total population figures for that same year, it means that 1 marriage was performed out of every 166 white persons, 1 out of every 207 colored slaves, 1 out of every 236 free mulattoes, the worst ratio being that of free Negroes, which was 1 out of 347 persons.[32] The high slave marriage rate as contrasted to that of the free colored population is apparently due to the fact that the slave population was accountable to a master, and through him to the local church, and was therefore more completely under the influence of the local parish priest.

Another remarkable fact revealed by the ecclesiastical statistics is the large number of marriages that legally occurred between free and slave persons. Thus, of the 702 colored marriages that took place in six selected parishes of Havana between 1825 and 1829, some 278 were contracted between two slave partners, 293 between two free partners, and an unusually large number, 131, between one slave partner and one free partner.[33]

All of these baptismal and marriage statistics reinforce the fact that civil and canonical law was the very essence of actual practice, and that the Negro slave enjoyed coequal status with his master before the sacraments of the church. That the church was so effective in carrying law into practice and constantly guaranteeing these rights is also due to the extraordinarily large number of priests on the island. Thus, the census of 1778, listed 1,063 practicing clergy in Cuba, exclusive of

---

[31] AGI, Santo Domingo, leg. 1630, auto 2.
[32] Sagra, *Historia económico-política*, pp. 20, 24. In France at this time, the figure was one married couple for each 134 persons. *Ibid.*, p. 24 n.
[33] *Ibid.*, p. 65.

nuns. This meant that for the island's total population of 179,484, there was one priest for every 168 persons, a figure not even approached in any country in the Americas today.[34]

Aside from its direct role in the sacraments and in carrying out Catholic education, the church also played an important auxiliary role in the vital process of manumission. The church encouraged this process by stressing to the masters that manumission of their slaves was an act beneficial in the eyes of God to their own good conduct. Thus on his special saint's day, or in honor of a marriage, or a birth, or a recovery from a severe illness, a master gave thanks to God by freeing some of his slaves. The crown greatly encouraged these procedures by making it possible to manumit a slave by a simple declaration from the master in a church before the local priest.[35]

That the work of the clergy in providing a moral climate conducive to manumission was successful can also be seen in the statistics. Thus, from the early days of slave importation, a large free colored class began to appear in Cuba, largely as a result of voluntary manumission by their masters. So rapid was the growth of this class that by the first government census in 1774, fully 41%, or 30,847 of the total colored population on the island were freedmen.[36]

The church was not only the most important factor in encouraging and maintaining the impetus to voluntary manumission by the masters, which created the vast mass of freedmen, but it was also instrumental in the extraordinary process, known as coartación, by which slaves purchased their own freedom. Throughout the whole process of coartación, which had been created by custom and fully guaranteed by the

---

[34] For the 1778 census breakdown, see AGI, Indiferente General, leg. 1527, December 31, 1778. For a clerical census of the Americas in 1959, see Donald S. Castro, *et al.*, *Statistical Abstract of Latin America, 1963* (U.C.L.A., Center of Latin American Studies, 1964), p. 22. The lowest figure for any contemporary Latin American country was Chile, with one priest for every 2,750 Catholics. The United States figure in 1965, is 1 priest to 778 practicing Catholics. *The Official Catholic Directory, 1965*, General Summary, pp. 1–2.

[35] Frank Tannenbaum, *Slave and Citizen, the Negro in the Americas* (New York: Alfred A. Knopf, 1947), pp. 53 ff.

[36] See below, chapter 9.

crown, the church played a vital role, for it was the prime guarantor of the free time and labor of the Negro outside his master's jurisdiction. To obtain funds, the Negro slave was permitted to work for himself in his own private truck garden, or *conuco*, on all holy days and Sundays. Income from these conucos was also exempted from tithe payments, which was an extremely unusual privilege in colonial society, where the *diezmos*, or tithes, were the most universal form of production and property taxes.[37] Finally, in seeking a reliable third party to hold his savings toward the initial down payment and also to help him present his legal case, the Negro slave sometimes relied on the local parish priest.[38]

Although the clergy tended to leave the actual functioning of the slave regime to the masters as much as possible, it was not adverse at times to attacking daily practice concerning housing and basic necessities. Thus the Bishop of Santiago de Cuba in the late seventeenth century bitterly complained that the masters were not properly clothing their slaves, and that the latter were often embarrassed to come to church service because of their poor dress. The bishop warned the masters that they were under obligation to provide the slaves with decent clothing and not force the slaves to provide for themselves in this matter.

Toward the Negroes themselves, the clergy was not always a sympathetic parent, especially on matters of laxity in church attendance and disinterest in learning their doctrine. This same bishop who concerned himself over the poor dress of his Negro communicants was also rather shocked at the indifference of some of the slaves to church service. He charged that many were not attending mass on holy days and Sundays before they began to work on their own properties, and that others were not seriously learning their lessons. In both situations he wanted the civil authorities to intervene and in the latter case even wanted to go so far as to incorporate physical

[37] AGI, Santo Domingo, leg. 152, ramo 2, no. 39, September 24, 1680.
[38] Such for example was the experience of the parish priest of the copper mining town of Santiago del Cobre in the seventeenth century with his 500 free and slave communicants. AGI, Santo Domingo, leg. 417, no. 15, December, 1709.

punishment for laxity. He proposed that instead of the present gentle method of instruction, the local clergy should adopt "the method by which the clerical teachers of New Spain and Peru teach their Indians," that is by using the whip on them in front of their fellow communicants if they forgot their lessons.[39]

But the stern attitude of this particular bishop was the exception rather than the rule, and most attempted to deal gently with both established tradition and with their Negro churchgoers. One who attempted to mold custom to the church—and who largely succeeded—was Bishop Pedro Agustin Morel de Santa Cruz who was bishop on the island in the middle of the eighteenth century. When he took up his diocese he found that in the city of Havana there were twenty-one Negro clubs or cabildos, each with its own house, where Negroes of both sexes gathered during holidays and Sundays to drink, dance "in extremely torrid and provocative dances," and commit other excesses too sinful to mention. Many told the bishop that it was better to leave these cabildos alone, for they provided a reasonable outlet for the slaves and freedmen without causing undue harm. But, he declared

not being satisfied with similar scruples, I attempted the gentle method of going by turns to each of the cabildos, to administer the sacrament of confirmation, and praying the Holy Rosary with those of that organization (*gremio*), before an Image of Our Lady which I carried with me. Concluding this act, I left the image in their houses, charging them to continue with their worship and devotion. . . .

After this initial assault, the bishop named a specific clergyman to each of the cabildos to go to them on Sundays and holy days to teach them Christian doctrine. He also appointed each cabildo in charge of a particular virgin that it was to venerate under the direction of a clergyman. This rather unusual and enthusiastic bishop even went so far as to propose that his clergymen learn the various African languages spoken by the slaves so that they might better teach them the Christian religion.[40]

[39] AGI, Santo Domingo, leg. 151, ramo 2, no. 22, February 22, 1682.
[40] AGI, Santo Domingo, leg. 515, no. 51, 1755.

Although this latter approach was never taken, there is no question of the successful syncretism of Catholicism with the African folk religions brought to Cuba by the Negro slaves. Bishop Morel de Santa Cruz's action was only one such attempt in a long chain of effort to construct a *cofradía* (or religious brotherhood) system by the church. So successful were these developments that the African cofradías played a vital role in the social life of both slaves and freedmen, with their own saints and special functions in various holy marches and carnivals. Usually organized along lines of regional African origins, with its members coming from the same *nación*, or geographic location, these associations were both of a religious and strongly benevolent nature.

The African cabildo was not indigenous to Cuba, but existed throughout the Spanish and Portuguese Indies wherever Negroes were congregated. The Spanish ones had their origins in medieval Seville, whose Negro cofradías and cabildos were active and fully recognized from as far back as the fourteenth century. Thus, the Havana municipal government as early as 1573 ordered that all the Negroes of the city present themselves for aid in the Corpus Christi processions, "the same as they assisted in the famous one of Seville." In the great religious processions the Negro cabildos played an increasingly important part. Although outright African fetishes were quickly prohibited from display, the local saints and virgins showed so much influence of African mythology and even of African costume that these displays often tended to perpetuate pre-New World patterns and beliefs.[41] One English traveler with a knowledge of African customs and beliefs who visited the island in 1820 described these cabildos in the following manner:

Each tribe or people has a *king* elected out of their number, whom, if they cannot enthrone in *Ashantee* glory, yet they rag out with much savage grandeur on the holidays on which they are permitted to meet. At these courtly festivals (usually held every Sunday and feast day) numbers of free and enslaved negroes assemble to do homage with a sort of grave merriment that one

[41] An excellent study of these cabildos is Fernando Ortiz, "Los cabildos afro-cubanos," *Revista Bimestre Cubana*, XVI (1921), 5-39.

would doubt whether it was done in ridicule or memory of their former condition. The *gong-gong* (christianized by the name of *diablito*), *cows-horns*, and every kind of inharmonious instrument, are flourished on by a gasping band, assisted by clapping of hands, howling and the striking of every sounding material within reach, while the whole assemblage dance with maniac eagerness till their strength fails. The only *civilized* part of the entertainment is— *drinking rum.*[42]

Probably the most important religious processional for these organizations was the famous Christmas festival of the Day of the Kings. This day was universally recognized throughout the island as a special day for the Negro cabildos and cofradías and almost unlimited license was permitted by the white authorities in the great dances, drinkings, and ceremonies. For the Negroes, both slave and free, it was the crowning event in their year and provided an unparalleled opportunity for individual and community expression for the entire Negro population.

Almost every traveler who viewed this great event was astounded by the license and the color of the spectacle. An American physician, Dr. Wurdemann, who visited the island in the 1840's described the day in the following manner:

The next day being *el día de los Reyes,* twelfthday, almost unlimited liberty was given to the negroes. Each tribe, having selected its king and queen, paraded the streets with a flag, having its name, and the words *viva Isabella,* with the arms of Spain, painted on it. Their majesties were dressed in the extreme of fashion, and were very ceremoniously waited on by the ladies and gentlemen of the court, one of the ladies holding an umbrella over the head of the queen. They bore their honors with that dignity which the negro loves so much to assume, which they, moreover, preserved in the presence of the whites. The whole

---

[42] Robert Francis Jameson, *Letters from the Havana during the Year 1820* (London: John Miller, 1821), pp. 21–22. For white-planter categorizations of these African groupings as to their differing qualities as workers and their intellectual ability see [J. G. F. Wurdemann], *Notes on Cuba* (Boston: James Monroe & Co., 1844), p. 257. This American physician noted that the Cuba planters of the 1840's had little difficulty telling whether a Negro was a congo, mandigo, etc., since "these different tribes are distinguished either by peculiar cuts and tattooing on their faces and bodies, or by their stature and habits. . . ." For the African geographic meanings of the Cuban *nación* designations see Ortiz, *Los negros esclavos,* pp. 25–52.

gang was under the command of a negro marshal, who, with a drawn sword, having a small piece of sugar-cane stuck on its point, was continually on the move to preserve order in the ranks. But the chief object in the group was an athletic negro, with a fantastic straw helmet, an immensely thick girdle of stripes of palm-leaves around his waist, and other uncouth articles of dress. Whenever they stopped, their banjoes struck up one of their monotonous tunes, and this frightful figure would commence a devil's dance, which was the signal for all his court to join in a general fandango, a description of which my pen refuseth to give. Yet when these parties stopped at the doors of houses, which they frequently did to collect money from the inmates, often intruding into the very passages, the ladies mingled freely among the spectators. Only three tribes paraded the streets of Guines [the small town in which the author was residing], but Havana is on this day in a perfect hubub, and the confusion that seems to reign among its colored population is indescribable. On all the plantations the negroes, also, pass the day in dancing to the music of their rude instruments; and the women, especially, are decked out in all the finery of tinsel and gaudy clothes. Songs are often combined with the dance, and in their native dialects they ridicule their owners before their faces, enjoying with much glee their happy ignorance of the burthen of their songs. Their African drums are then heard far and near, and their sonorous sounds, now falling, now rising on the air, seem like the summons to a general insurrection.[43]

Thus, between religious processions, annual *día de reyes* celebrations, and the daily conduct of their cofradías and cabildos, the Negro masses were provided by the church with a vast and crucial outlet for social expression and community development.

While providing a rich fabric of social existence for the masses within the canopy of the church, the Cuban clergy also aided the exceptionally able Negro to break through the rigid class-caste barriers of the white community by means of their control over the educational process. Since, at the pre-university level, education was exclusively in the hands of the church, primary and secondary education was available to

---

[43] [Wurdemann], *Notes on Cuba*, pp. 83–84. For a thorough analysis of this fiesta see Fernando Ortiz, "La fiesta afro-cubana del 'día de reyes,'" *Revista Bimestre Cubana*, XV (1920), 5–26.

the exceptional and upwardly mobile free Negro. And education was the only means by which a colored person could
break through from the lower economic classes to at least the
learned professions, and possibly higher. For sons of prosperous colored artisans and successful colored militia officers,
both mulattoes and Negroes, the open opportunity of the
schools run by the secular and regular clergy was their avenue
of mobility. And while the university consistently fought the
entrance of colored persons into its ranks, the large number of
petitions from colored persons to the crown demanding the
right to practice a profession for which they had already been
trained indicates that many succeeded in "passing" with little
trouble. This was achieved through the combination of light
skins and the crucial pre-collegiate training they had received
from the clerical schools.[44] Even though the majority of free
colored were denied university admission, their very possession of a secondary *colegio* education in the days of mass
illiteracy and nonprofessional university programs was more
than enough to break into the professional classes and the
upper social levels. To read and write at least, according to
the church, if not the colonial universities, was a right open
to all, and a right that held out almost unlimited opportunities for the few who could achieve it.

Concerned for his social existence, his freedom, his family,
and his soul, and even in a minority of cases for the training of
his mind, the church deeply and vitally committed itself to
its role as guardian of its Negro slave communicant. Because
it effectively controlled an important part of their lives, the
church was unquestionably the primary intermediary agent
between master and slave, and the only institution that daily
claimed its rights, as opposed to the property rights of the
masters.

Although the church could not abolish the rigors of harsh
plantation servitude, it could modify that life to the extent
of guaranteeing minimal periods of rest and independence
for the blacks. The church could also guarantee a degree of
self-expression for all slaves, which enabled them to escape

---

[44] For a full discussion of this problem, see chapter 9.

the 'close confines of bondage in many ways and thus to validate their human personalities and potential. Finally, it could create the panoply of mores and attitudes that permitted the Negro to be treated as a coequal human being and allowed him to merge fully into Cuban society when the harsh regime of slavery was destroyed.

6. The Negro and the Church
of England in Virginia.

Like Cuba, Virginia was settled by a dominant established church, in this case the Church of England. Both Spain and England at the times of colonization had a hierarchical metropolitan church that was closely tied with the royal government and was considered one of the major governing institutions of the realm. But whereas the Counter-Reformation church of Spain was able to suppress all opposition to its religious authority, the Anglican church found itself constantly struggling against Protestant dissenter groups who attempted to challenge its established authority. At the time of the initial planting of the Virginia colony, however, the crown and the church were fully united and the Anglican church was declared the established church of the colony. As early as 1606, the crown decreed that the Virginia Company ". . . should provide that the true word and service of God should be preached, planted and used, *according to the Rites and Doctrine of the Church of England.*"[1] In the first organization of the company, there was even a bishop of the realm, John King of the London diocese, who was a leading member.[2] Through these actions, Anglicanism was guaranteed as the religion of the colonists, and from then until the end of the colonial period, the Church of England was overwhelmingly the state church of Virginia, and its membership encompassed the majority of the population.

[1] Quoted in Arthur Lyon Cross, *The Anglican Episcopate and the American Colonies* (Cambridge: Harvard University Press, 1924), p. 10.
[2] George Maclaren Brydon, *Virginia's Mother Church and the Political Conditions Under Which It Grew* (2 vols.; Richmond: Virginia Historical Society, 1947–52), I, 40–42.

But while there was never any challenge to the religion of the metropolitan church in Virginia, the crown never established the leadership and organization whereby the church could function in its accustomed manner in the colony. In sharp contrast to Cuba, where this problem was never raised, the crown and the hierarchy simply made no attempt to fit the colony into the normal functioning of the church. Whereas Cuba had its first bishop appointed in 1516, just five years after the conquest, neither the Archbishop of Canterbury, nor the crown saw fit to establish a native bishop, or even more crucially, to place the colony within the jurisdiction of an insular diocese.

The Bishop of London, because of his connection with the company, originally helped to provide clergymen and some financial assistance in establishing the Virginia church, but this tenuous connection was destroyed when the company was dissolved by the crown in 1624. Thus, although the company provided land for church income, divided the colony up into parishes, and encouraged the migration of clergymen,[3] it made no effort to obtain the establishment of a native bishop, primarily because of the cost; nor was the church or the crown at this time the least bit interested in subsidizing such a venture or even in considering it.

Because of this amazing and gross neglect, the colonists within a few short years had completely usurped hierarchical authority and had transformed the centuries' old organization of English church government. In traditional English ecclesiastical organization, the local landowner or other outside body or institution had the power to nominate ministers for the parish within their jurisdiction. This meant that the landowner or institution could present his own candidate for the local parish office to the bishop for investiture. The bishop then had the power to certify or reject the nominee, but once invested with his office, the clergyman served for life. Throughout this process, the local parishioners had no say either in the nomination or investiture process and had no recourse but to accept their minister on a lifetime basis. The

[3] *Ibid.*, I, 10–11.

minister, in fact, was accountable only to the church, and only the bishop could control his work or chastize his actions. The local parishioners' vestry and churchwarden were subservient to the local clergymen, and what duties they performed were all determined by law.[4]

The church hierarchy also guaranteed religious uniformity, sanctified government action, and had extensive civil-ecclesiastical functions. Thus the bishops could appoint special courts to try and condemn heresy; they had full jurisdiction over marriages, the probating of wills, the collation to benefices, and the appointment of notaries; and they had extensive rights over tithes and other ecclesiastical taxes.[5]

Without the hierarchical structure, however, most of these functions could not be maintained; and, in fact, rapid erosion soon wiped out the complete edifice of the church as it was known in England. Although the company at first appeared to claim the right to nominate clergymen to Virginia parishes, it seems not to have exercised that right but simply sent out preordained clergymen, which left open the question of their initiation into their parishes. With the dissolution of the company and the failure of English authorities to claim their rights, the local colonists absorbed all power unto themselves. First the General Court of Virginia, consisting of the members of the upper house of the General Assembly, claimed that the right of nomination or presentation devolved on them from the company. They also proceeded to absorb a host of other juridical, administrative, and even ecclesiastical matters, which by tradition belonged to the bishop. This meant that the control over vital statistics, notaries, and wills; the establishment of parishes; the naming and defining of all ecclesiastical offices; the collection of tithes; the regulation of church conduct; and even the maintenance of the purity of the faith and the dogma were determined, not by the bishop, canonical law courts, and ecclesiastical officials as in England, but by the local General Assembly of Virginia.[6]

Although central authority now came to rest in a popular

[4] *Ibid.*, I, 42–44.
[5] *Ibid.*, I, 67; Cross, *The Anglican Episcopate*, p. 2.
[6] Brydon, *Virginia's Mother Church*, I, 67–68, 86 ff.

civil assembly, the local church came increasingly under the power of the parishioners themselves, rather than that of the ministry. Developing new institutions and adapting old practices to local conditions, the colonists began to establish their own distinctly unique form of church government, at the center of which stood the all-powerful locally elected board of governing parishioners known as the vestry.

With the devolution to the General Assembly of all matters pertaining to the church, the assembly in turn gave to each local parish vestry a multitude of civil and ecclesiastical rights and obligations and made it the prime institution of a new type of established church. As early as the 1620's, the Assembly was providing that local churchwardens and leading members of the parish should concern themselves with the maintenance of the church. From this simple maintenance task the evolving vestry organization quickly began to assume ever greater powers. A reflection of this occurred in 1643 when, in a formal legal enactment, the Assembly provided that each parish should have a vestry, and "that the most sufficient and selected men be chosen and joyned to the minister and churchwardens to be of that Vestrie." Among the tasks enumerated for the vestry was the crucial absorption of the right of nomination. The 1643 act declared "that the vestrie of evrie parish . . . shall henceforward have power, to elect and make choyce of their ministers. . . ."[7] The vestry was to present the candidate for minister of their parish to the governor, not to a bishop as in England, and the governor then made the formal induction and confirmation of that minister to hold the given office for life.[8]

The creation of the first vestries seems to have been by appointment of the General Court,[9] but by the 1640's the Assembly provided that the vestry was to be organized on the basis of election from among the parishioners. By the time the

---

[7] William W. Hening, (ed.), *The Statutes at Large: being a collection of All the Laws of Virginia from the first session of the Legislature in the year 1619* (13 vols.; Richmond: Samuel Pleasents, 1819–23), I, 241–42.
[8] Brydon, *Virginia's Mother Church*, I, 92.
[9] *Ibid.*, I, 93.

laws on the church were codified by the General Assembly in 1662, it was provided:

That for the makeing and proportioning the levyes and assessments for building and repayring the churches, and chappells, provision for the poore, maintenance of the minister, and such other necessary *duties* for the more orderly manageing all parociall affaires, *Be it enacted* that twelve of the most able men of each parish be by the major part of the *said* parish, *chosen* to be vestry-men out of which number the minister and vestry to make choice of two churchwardens yearly, as *alsoe* in the case of death of any vestry man, or his departure out of the parish, that the said minister and vestry make choice of another to supply his roome. . . .[10]

By this act, which abolished the electoral system, the vestries in fact became autocratic local bodies of the leading planters who exercised enormous control over social and economic conditions within the parish. After their initial establishment, members usually held their office till death or resignation, and elections never took place. When vacancies occurred, the vestrymen themselves proceeded to choose leading planters as members. So oligarchic and powerful did these vestries become that one of the constant themes of colonial Virginian history was the popular, and continually unsatisfied, demand for periodic elections and the breakup of this autocratic control.[11]

Given this entrenched self-perpetuating planter leadership in control of the church, the role of the transitory minister could be only a subordinate one at best. In complete contradiction to the entire organization of the Church of England, the vestry refused to present their ministers for induction. Since induction by the governor would have guaranteed the minister his parish for life, barring ill conduct, the vestries simply refused to present their ministers, and by this means made the minister's position completely dependent on the goodwill of his leading parishioners. While the royal governors had full power to force induction on the vestries, not one

[10] Hening, *Statutes at Large*, II, 44–45.
[11] One of the major reforms of Bacon's rebellion was the call for vestry elections every three years. Brydon, *Virginia's Mother Church*, I, 97.

governor in the entire history of the colony saw fit to exercise this right out of fear of vestry power.[12]

This entire system was bitterly attacked by regular Church of England clergymen. The mid-seventeenth century clergyman Morgan Godwyn, who served in Virginia and in the British West Indies, scornfully called this arrangement a "probational tenure" system,[13] and at the end of the century the bishops' representative in the colony, Commissary James Blair, was badly disturbed by what he described as this "Custom of making annual Agreements with the Ministers, which they [i.e., the vestries] call by a Name coarse enough, *viz.* Hiring of the Ministers; so that they seldom present any ministers, that they may by that Means keep them in more Subjection and Dependence."[14] In short, stated the commissary, "they are only in the nature of Chaplains" whose tenure of office was dependent on an annual agreement renewable at the option of a small body of men.[15] Thus any independence on the part of the clergymen was quickly suppressed by the planters, who by the very nature of their positions would naturally be the strongest representatives of the status quo in the community. As Godwyn noted, they "obstruct all designs for the good of those Churches, and to report all things already so well settled as not needing the least amendment or alteration."[16]

Because of these developments, the regular clergy of England by and large refused to come to Virginia. For as Blair lamented, "no good Ministers that were inform'd of it would come into the Country, and if they came ignorant of any such Custom, they quickly felt the Effects of it in the high

[12] Philip Alexander Bruce, *Institutional History of Virginia in the Seventeenth Century* (2 vols.; New York: G. P. Putnam's Sons, 1910), I, 136–39.

[13] Morgan Godwyn, *The Negro's and Indians Advocate, Suing for their Admission into the Church* (London: J.D., 1680), p. 168.

[14] Henry Hartwell, James Blair, and Edward Chilton, *The Present State of Virginia* (2d ed.; Williamsburg: Colonial Williamsburg, Inc., 1940), p. 66.

[15] *Ibid.*, p. 67.

[16] Godwyn, *The Negro's and Indians Advocate*, Preface, p. 1. According to Godwyn the Virginia colonists chafed at the cost of church tithes and quickly lost their interest in the Anglican creed because, he charged, Virginians "for the most part do know no other *God* but *Money*, nor *Religion* but *Profit*."

Hand wherewith most Vestries manag'd their Power, and got out of the Country again as soon as they could."[17] Until well into the eighteenth century, a goodly portion of the practicing clergymen in Virginia were in fact deacons, or as Morgan Godwyn called them, *"Lay-Priests* of the *Vestries ordination."*[18]

Even in his very vocation was the minister challenged by the vestry. Thus the Reverend Hugh Jones in 1724 warned that ". . . in several places the clerks [of the parish] are so ingenious or malicious, that they contrive to be liked as well or better than the minister, which created ill-will and disturbance, besides other harm."[19] Given the chance, he charged, they will usurp almost all of the clergymen's functions, even to the giving of sermons, and warned that they should have their functions carefully defined by law to prevent these abuses.

So all-embracing was parishioner influence and control that the clergyman had to win popular endorsement and constantly keep his congregation happy, which of course excluded all possibilities of giving independent thought or challenge to the existing moral and social situation, for this was the sure road to ruin. Their independence was so pervasive, in fact, that parishioners even went as far, in this era of nonconformity, as often to question and modify standard church dogma. Thus Reverend Jones noted in his analysis of contemporary Virginia that: "In several respects the clergy are obliged to omit or alter some minute parts of the liturgy, and deviate from the strict discipline and ceremonies of the Church; to avoid giving offence. . . ."[20]

The mother church soon became deeply aware of the heterodoxy and complete breakdown of the established church in Virginia, but it could do little to change the situation. Deeply involved in religious civil wars at home, it was not until after the Restoration that the Church of England could even begin

[17] Hartwell, Blair, and Chilton, *Present State of Virginia,* p. 66.
[18] Godwyn, *The Negro's and Indians Advocate,* p. 170.
[19] Hugh Jones, *The Present State of Virginia* (2d ed.; Chapel Hill: University of North Carolina Press, 1956), p. 96.
[20] *Ibid.,* p. 98.

to deal with the situation. It was only with the investiture of Henry Compton as Bishop of London, in 1675, that the church finally forced the crown to place the colony within a diocese. For a number of historical reasons, the Diocese of London was chosen; however, traditions were so entrenched that little real change in ecclesiastical matters was effected by this development. The bishop made no attempt to oppose vestry control or to retake possession of his normal ecclesiastical or civil functions, or even his right of investiture. His only concern was to maintain some kind of purity of dogma by guaranteeing minimal standards for clergymen. This he did by forcing the colonists to accept only accredited clergymen licensed by himself. Thus in the instructions to Governor Culpeper of Virginia, the bishop had the crown declare that "no Minister be prefrr'd by you to any Ecclesiastical Benefice in that our Colony *without a Certificate from the Lord Bp. of London, of his being conformable to the Doctrine of the Church of England.*"[21]

While the bishop eventually succeeded in sending a representative to the colony with the title of commissary, or vicar general, this clergyman could only exercise moderating influence and had to persuade rather than enjoin acceptance of church rules.[22] The first commissar, James Blair (1689–1743) created much heat but little concrete change,[23] and despite all attempts of several energetic London bishops, the vestries could not be forced to induct their ministers, leaving the majority of them to the arbitrary will of their congregations. Through the commissary rule of Blair and his successors, some positive results were attained toward providing a regular ordained clergy for all the parishes, but in the end, the commissaries had little or no effect in reforming the general structure of the Virginia church. When the metropolitan hierarchy realized this failure, it attempted to establish a resident bishop for the American colonies. But this was a potentially powerful challenge to local authority, and colonial

[21] Quoted in Cross, *The Anglican Episcopate*, p. 26.
[22] *Ibid.*, pp. 3–4, 44.
[23] *Ibid.*, pp. 78–80.

opposition was so constant and vehement against this idea that the matter was never carried to fruition, despite all the strenuous efforts made by the mother church.[24]

Not only was the church after the Restoration terribly concerned about the religion of the white colonists, but it also began to take an increasingly involved position on the status of the Negro and Indian heathens within England's American Empire. This concern with the plight of the Negro slave, especially, is heavily attested to by the growing movement among the lower and upper clergy for conversion, education, and even emancipation. This movement began as early as the end of the seventeenth century, and one of its first advocates was Morgan Godwyn, the angry clergyman who served in the British West Indies and in the colony of Virginia, and whose *The Negro's and Indians Advocate* (1680) created a good deal of sentiment. This growing awareness of the complete lack of impact of the church on the Negro slaves, in sharp contrast to that of the Catholic church in the Spanish and French islands, as many Church of England men noted,[25] caused the Bishop of London to put pressure on the crown.

In the royal instructions to Governor Culpeper of Virginia in 1681–82, the crown proposed that:

Ye shall endeavour to get a Law passed for the restraining of any inhuman severity which by ill masters or overseers may be used towards their Christian Servants or Slaves. And you are alsoe

---

[24] For the history of this struggle see Carl Bridenbaugh, *Mitre and Sceptre, Transatlantic Faith, Ideas, Personalities and Politics, 1689–1775* (New York: Oxford University Press, 1962).

[25] In his famous denunciation of West Indian slavery, for example, the Reverend James Ramsay constantly contrasted the British to the French treatment of slaves. "In the French colonies," he declared, "the public pays an immediate attention to the treatment and instruction of slaves. The intendants [government administrative officers] are charged with their protection, proper missionaries are appointed for the purpose of training them up to a certain degree of religious knowledge: and ample estates and funds are allotted for the maintenance of these ecclesiastics. . . . The respect in which marriage is held, brings a farther advantage to French slaves. The ceremony is solemnized by the priest, and the tie continues for life. This gives them an attachment to their families, . . . that is seldom seen among English slaves; where the connection between the sexes is arbitrary, and too frequently casual." Rev. James Ramsay, *An Essay on the Treatment of African Slaves in the British Sugar Colonies* (London: James Philipps, 1784), pp. 52, 54.

with the assistance of the Council and Assembly, to find out the best means to facilitate and encourage the conversion of Negroes to the Christian Religion, *wherein you are to leave a due* caution and regards to ye property of the Inhabitants and safety of the Colonies.[26]

The unusual restraint of this request indicates the royal government's recognition of the primacy of local law and custom over the humanitarian demands of the clergymen.

Nevertheless, despite the inaction of the local colonial governments, the English hierarchy was becoming deeply concerned over the failure of the colonials to Christianize the Negro slaves. Finding that little could be accomplished directly through regular church and governmental channels, the bishops decided that the only alternative was a missionary society, completely financed from England. Thus, in 1701, the hierarchy in England founded the famous Society for the Propagation of the Gospel in Foreign Parts (SPG).[27]

That one of the primary aims of the society was conversion of the slaves was understood by the bishops from the very beginning. Thus in the annual sermon given to the society in 1710, Bishop William Fleetwood bitterly attacked the masters of slaves who refused to permit their conversion to Christianity. He claimed the refusal to permit baptism and Christian education was:

A thing so common in all our *Plantations* abroad, that I have reason to doubt, whether there be any Exception of any People *of ours,* who cause their slaves to be Baptized. What do these people think of Christ? . . . That He who came from Heaven, to purchase to Himself a Church, with his own precious Blood, should sit contented, and behold with unconcern, those who profess themselves his Servants, excluding from its Gates those who would gladly enter if they might, and exercising no less Cruelty to their Souls (as far as they are able) than to their Bodies?

These People were made to be as Happy as themselves, and are as capable of being so; and however hard their Condition be in this

[26] *The Virginia Magazine of History and Biography,* XXVIII (1920), 43–44.

[27] H. P. Thompson, *Into All Lands, The History of the Society for the Propagation of the Gospel in Foreign Parts, 1701–1950* (London: S.P.C.K., 1951), chap. 1.

World, with respect to their Captivity and Subjugation. . . . They were bought with the same Price, purchased with the same Blood of Christ, their common Saviour and Redeemer; and on order to all this, they were to have the Means of Salvation put into their Hands, they were to be instructed in the Faith of *Christ*, to have the Terms and Conditions fairly offered to them.

Not only did Bishop Fleetwood attack the very Christianity of the masters, but also considered that this was probably their greatest sin, for he declared, "no Man living can assign a better and more justifiable Cause, for God's with-holding Mercy from a *Christian*, than that *Christian's* with-holding the Mercy of *Christianity* from an Unbeliever."[28] The radical bishop even went so far as to attack slavery itself, holding, as Adam Smith was later to proclaim, that hired labor was the far superior system of labor and that slavery should be abolished. He attacked the ideas of the colonists, which held that Christianity challenged the slave status, but instead of proclaiming the docility of slaves under Christian doctrine as some clerics did, he properly attacked the Christianity of the colonists who would refuse to treat fellow human beings with Christian brotherly love. Finally, he proposed that the society take up the crucial task of Christianizing the infidels, Negroes and slaves, and that this example would have a powerful impact on the masters, who apparently were unimpressed by "the Example both of *French* and *Spaniards* . . ., who all along have brought their Slaves to Baptism."[29]

This call appears to have been heeded, for in the annual sermon of 1740, Bishop Secker pointed to the work of the society in this special area. But the bishop noted the vast difficulty still faced by the church in this work, as only a few slaves had been converted and thousands yet remained outside the fold.

For it is not to be expected, that Masters, too commonly negligent of Christianity themselves, will take much Pains to teach it to their Slaves: whom even the better Part of them are in a great measure

[28] This sermon is reprinted in its entirety in Frank J. Klingberg, *Anglican Humanitarianism in Colonial New York* (Philadelphia: Church Historical Society, 1940), pp. 203–4.
[29] *Ibid.*, p. 211.

habituated to consider, as they do their Cattle, merely with a View to the Profit arising from them. Not a few therefore have openly opposed their Instruction, from an Imagination, now indeed proved and acknowledged to be groundless, that Baptism would entitle them to Freedom. . . . And some, it may be feared, have been averse to their becoming Christians, because, after that, no Pretence will remain for not treating them like Men.[30]

By the middle of the eighteenth century, both within and without the society, the upper clergy was beginning to put pressure on the colonies to change their local customs and laws on these subjects and to create a new panoply of beliefs that would permit the church to carry on the work of conversion in a positive atmosphere.

The Bishop of London in 1742 put great pressure on Commissary Blair to indicate to the local government his great zeal in converting Negroes to the Christian faith and to get that government to support a school for Negroes.[31] But incapable of even fully protecting standard dogma and church practice, Blair and his successors could accomplish little. As for the SPG, the demands on its resources were so great that it concentrated its efforts in the British West Indies, where the bulk of the New World slaves resided, and in the colonies in which the church was not yet established.[32]

This meant, in essence, that whatever might be the feelings of the hierarchy in England about the desirability of conversion of the slaves to Christianity and their participation in the sacraments, this desire had little, if any, impact on New World conditions. With no clergymen capable of opposing these assumptions and customs, the planters felt under no obligation to change their ways. Thus the religious life of the slave was wholly dependent upon the will of his master, and this was determined almost exclusively by local custom.

Unfortunately for the Negro slave, custom was indifferent, if not openly hostile, to the conversion of Negro slaves. In the early years of the seventeenth century, there had existed

---

[30] *Ibid.*, p. 217.
[31] *William and Mary Quarterly*, 1st Series, IX (1901), 225.
[32] Thompson, *History of the Society*, chap. 3.

the almost universal belief that conversion for the slave required his freedom, since Christians could not hold other Christians in bondage. But although the General Assembly eventually declared that this was not so,[33] the idea was hard to uproot, and it persisted throughout the colonial period. Even when this factor was resolved or admitted by the reluctant master, there was still the key fear of education making the slaves intractable. As the Reverend Hugh Jones reported, he constantly tried to assuage this fear among colonials:

As for baptizing Indians and Negroes, several of the people disapprove of it, because they say it often makes them proud, and not so good servants: But these, and such objections, are easily refuted, for Christianity encourages and orders them to become more humble and better servants, and not worse, than when they were heathens.

He did agree with the general opinion, however, that held that Negro slaves should not be taught to read and write, since this "has been found to be dangerous upon several political accounts, especially self-preservation."[34]

Although there could be found masters who sponsored the baptism of their slaves and encouraged them to learn the catechism, and some who even read to them from the Bible, these were usually the exception rather than the rule. The pattern, in fact, was quite haphazard, and in the majority of cases conversion was never properly undertaken. This is clearly revealed in a survey of the colonial church of Virginia carried out in the early eighteenth century. In 1724 Commissary Blair sent out an extraordinarily revealing and exhaus-

---

[33] The Virginia legislature itself seriously accepted the thesis that Christianity was incompatible with slavery and in its early definitions actually defined slaves as persons who were not Christians. In 1670 it enacted a statute that declared that "all servants not being christians imported into this country by shipping shalbe slaves for life." Hening, *Statutes at Large*, II, 283. This was finally rectified in 1682 when the Assembly decreed that: "all servants excepts Turks and Moores . . . which shall be brought or imported into this country, either by sea or land, whether Negroes, . . . Mulattoes or Indians, who and whose parentage and native country are not christian, although afterwards, and before such their importation . . . they shall be converted to the christian faith; . . . shall be judged, deemed and taken to be slaves. . . ." *Ibid.*, II, 490–91.

[34] Jones, *Present State of Virginia*, p. 99.

tive questionnaire to all the parishes of Virginia. Among the questions asked of all these clergymen was: "Are there any Infidels, bond or free, within your Parish; and what means are used for their conversion?" From the twenty-nine clergymen who answered the inquiry the overwhelming impression is that the clerics were only moderately interested in the problem, whereas the planters were generally indifferent, if not actually hostile. As the Reverend George Robertson of Bristol Parish reported, "I have several times exhorted their Masters to send such of them as could speak English to Church to be catechised, but they would not. Some masters instruct their Slaves at home and so bring them to baptism, but not many such."[35] In almost the same language the Reverend Henry Collings of St. Peter's Parish reported that of the Negro slaves in his parish, "Some . . . are suffered by their respective masters to be baptized and to attend on divine service but others not."[36] The Reverend John Warden reported that in his parish "some masters will have their slaves baptised and others will not, by reason that they will not be surities for them in Baptism,"[37] and Alexander Forbes reported in his parish that the local Negro slaves "as soon as they are capable they are taught and baptised by the care of some Masters, but this too much neglected by many."[38] The clergymen of Henrico and Southwark parishes, respectively, replied of the slaves that "their Masters, do no more than let some of them now and then go to Church for their Conversion," and that "there are some of their Masters on whom I do prevail to have them baptised and taught, but not many."[39] The Reverend John Brunskill of Wilmington Parish probably best summed up the problem when he concluded that:

The Negroes who are slaves to the whites cannot, I think, be said to be of any Religion for as there is no law of the Colony oblidg-

---

[35] William Stevens Perry (ed.), *Historical Collections Relating to the American Colonial Church* (5 vols.; Hartford: Church Press Co., 1870–78), I, 267.
[36] *Ibid.*, I, 269.
[37] *Ibid.*, I, 289.
[38] *Ibid.*, I, 295.
[39] *Ibid.*, I, 304, 306.

ing their Masters or Owners to instruct them in the principles of Christianity and so they are hardly to be persuaded by the Minister to take so much pains with them, by which means the poor creatures generally live and die without it.[40]

Even for the minority that were baptized, converted, and taught the Christian religion, there were no positive rewards. No matter how Christian, no master allowed his slaves to be married. For if the sacrament of marriage was not to be made a totally ridiculous right, then Negro slaves could not be admitted. For by this admission, it was recognized that human agencies had no right to separate the conjugal couple, and this was never accepted. For even when the best of masters died, the constant fluidity of fortunes meant that no slave community could remain intact beyond a few generations, and families were simply not sold together. This was uneconomical and therefore impractical. As the Virginia baptist chronicler John Leland noted in 1790, "the marriage of slaves, is a subject not known in our code of laws. What promises soever they make, their masters may and do part them at pleasure."[41]

[40] *Ibid.*, I, 277–78. Interestingly, the few surviving records of slave education and conversion carried out by masters came not from Church of England slaveowners but from Presbyterians and Quakers. Robert Pleasants, one of the wealthiest planters of Virginia in the eighteenth century, and a Quaker, not only converted his slaves but even educated and eventually freed them. Adair P. Archer, "The Quakers Attitude towards the Revolution," *William and Mary Quarterly*, 2d Series, I (1921), 168. For his part, the Presbyterian planter Colonel James Gordon, in his journal in 1761, noted that "Several strange negroes come to Mr. Criswell [the local Presbyterian teacher] to be instructed, in which he takes great pains." *William and Mary Quarterly*, 1st Series, XI (1903), 223.

Nevertheless, despite these and other efforts, the consensus of historical opinion is best summed up by Marcus W. Jernegan who declared that throughout the colonial period, "most of the slaves lived and died strangers to christianity" and that "with comparatively few exceptions the conversion of negro slaves was not seriously undertaken by their masters. On the contrary many of them strenuously and persistently opposed the Church of England, and the Society for the Propagation of the Gospel in Foreign Parts. . . ." Marcus W. Jernegan, "Slavery and Conversion in the American Colonies," *American Historical Review*, XXI, No. 3 (April, 1916), 504; also see Jerome W. Jones, "The Established Virginia Church and the Conversion of Negroes and Indians, 1620–1760," *Journal of Negro History*, XLVI, No. 1 (January, 1961), 12–31.

[41] John Leland, *The Virginia Chronicle* (Norfolk: Prentis & Baxter, 1790), p. 8.

As for the complex web of social organizations to which the Cuban slave had recourse, this simply did not exist under the established church of Virginia. There were no fraternal brotherhoods, no great processionals and special holidays, and absolutely no syncretism of Christian belief with the folk religion of African origin. After 1740, there did exist, for the Negro slaves on the frontier of Virginia, the possibility of being admitted into the mass evangelical movement that was known as the Great Awakening. From 1740 and especially after 1760, numbers of Methodist, Baptist, Presbyterian, and a host of other sect preachers began invading the frontier counties of Virginia above the tidewater.[42] Most of these preachers, like Wesley himself, were bitter opponents of slavery and welcomed the Negroes into the church. Thus John Leland in his Virginia Chronicle of 1790 reported:

The poor slaves, under all their hardships, discover as great inclination for religion as the free-born do, when they engage in the service of God, they spare no pains. It is nothing strange for them to walk 20 miles on Sunday morning to meeting, and back again at night. They are remarkable for learning a toon soon, and have very melodious voices.

They cannot read, and therefore are more exposed to delusion than the whites are; but many of them give clear, rational accounts of a work of grace in their harts, and evidence of the same by their lives. When religion is lively they are remarkable fond of meeting together, to sing, pray and exhort, and sometimes preach, and seem to be unwearied in the procession. They seem in general to put more confidence in their own colour, then they do in whites; when they attempt to preach, they seldom fail of being very zealous; their language is broken, but they understand each other, and the whites may gain their ideas. A few of them have undertaken to administer baptism, but it generally ends in confusion; they commonly are more noisy in time of preaching than the whites, and are more subject to bodily exercise, and if they meet with any encouragement in these things, they grow extravagant.[43]

But these camp meetings and nonhierarchical churches were not open for the majority of Virginia Negroes, who continued

---

[42] *Ibid.*, pp. 21 ff.; also see Wesley M. Gewehr, *The Great Awakening in Virginia, 1740–1790* (Durham: Duke University Press, 1930).
[43] Leland, *Virginia Chronicle*, p. 13.

to reside in the areas dominated by the Church of England. Nor were the masters too ready to permit them the openness of these great revivalist gatherings. As Leland himself notes: ". . . many masters and overseers will whip and torture the poor creatures for going to meeting, even at night, when the labor of the day is done."[44] As fear of insurrection developed in the period after independence, such church meetings became less and less common as public gatherings of slaves, even for religious purposes, were severely restricted. Even the evangelical churches themselves, after a brief period of strong support for Negro conversion and religious instruction, by the early decades of the nineteenth century had conformed to planter opinion and had kept slave conversion and participation to a minimum. They had even gone so far as to develop a special system of "religion without letters" for the special evangelization of free Negroes as well as slave.[45] When, in 1802, the Baptist church discovered that because of its leadership in the conversion movement it had the startling number of 9,000 colored communicants—mostly slaves, it decided to check the potential power of this group by ruling that only free persons could exercise authority within the Church.[46] By the time of the famous 1804 and 1805 laws on religious meetings of slaves, it became virtually impossible for the slave to participate freely in the revivalist meetings of the evangelical churches, and his role in these churches quickly declined to the same point as his role in the Anglican church and its successor.

Not only were these churches incapable of undertaking a general conversion of the slaves, but they were also unable to promote manumission. The common pattern of manumission inspired by the church, which was the accepted custom and practice in Cuba, was unknown in Protestant Virginia. Although the Methodists and Quakers early demanded that their members give up slave trading and emancipate their

[44] *Ibid.*, p. 9.

[45] C. G. Woodson, *The Education of the Negro Prior to 1861* (New York: G. P. Putnam's Sons, 1915), chaps. 7, 8.

[46] Joseph B. Earnest, Jr., *The Religious Development of the Negro in Virginia* (Charlottesville: Michie Co., 1914), p. 66.

slaves, and although several revolutionary leaders followed Enlightenment thought to its logical conclusion and freed their Negroes, no powerful undercurrent of emancipation ever occurred. Quaker emancipations were few and of little consequence, and the Methodist leadership was soon forced to condone the existence of slaveholding even among its traveling clergy and to give up its proposals for emancipation.[47] The Anglican hierarchy also developed a powerful commitment to emancipation at the end of the eighteenth century, but it took forceful Parliamentary legislation to carry out emancipation even in the West Indies. But in Virginia this emancipation movement was never reflected in the local episcopal hierarchy, when the latter was finally established in 1790.[48]

Unlike the clergy of Cuba, the clergy of Virginia was unable to convince the planters that emancipation was a good act in the sight of God and was to be considered a common and accepted form of pious action. Nor, on the other hand, could the morally aroused and committed clergy, of whatever denomination, convince the masters that slavery was essentially a moral evil and that on these grounds the slaves should be emancipated as expeditiously as possible. Since emancipation could not be forced on moral grounds from above, nor could it become a part of routine common practice from below, the whole emancipation movement in Virginia was at best a haphazard and distinctly minor affair. In fact, from the late seventeenth to the late eighteenth century, emancipation was for all intents and purposes outlawed by the state. Even when private emancipation was again permitted after 1782, the free

[47] On the failure of the Methodists see Gewehr, *The Great Awakening,* pp. 242–49; and for the Quakers see Thomas E. Drake, *Quakers and Slavery in America* (New Haven: Yale University Press, 1950).

[48] Although the Anglican church consecrated native candidates between 1784 and 1790, which enabled the Americans to establish the Protestant Episcopal Church in the United States, the new bishops were subservient to local interests, and vestry government was in no way changed. See Cross, *The Anglican Episcopate,* pp. 263 ff; Clara O. Loveland, *The Critical Years, The Reconstruction of the Anglican Church in the United States of America: 1780–1789* (Greenwich: Seabury Press, 1956); Edward Lewis Goodwin, *The Colonial Church in Virginia* (Milwaukee: Morehouse Pub. Co., 1927), pp. 127 ff, for the early bishops of the Diocese of Virginia.

colored were only a small part of the colored class, representing at the time of the first federal census in 1790 only 4% of the total colored population. Nor was any major change indicated in the half-century between the first federal census and the Civil War. While the percentage of freedmen slowly rose from decade to decade, it only reached 11% in 1860. With roughly the same number of colored, in both Cuba and Virginia in 1860–61, Virginia had only 58,042 freedmen (or 11% of the total colored) to Cuba's 213,167 (or 35%).[49]

As for the development of formal education for the free Negroes, this was informal and haphazard in the extreme, except for one short-lived experiment. In the late 1720's, Dr. Thomas Bray, who had been commissary in Maryland for the Bishop of London, helped found a group of missionaries known as Bray's Associates who directed considerable attention to founding schools for Negroes in the American colonies. A leading founder of the SPG, Bray received a private donation of £900 to found several schools in the North American colonies.[50] After setting up such a successful school with the aid of Benjamin Franklin in Philadelphia in 1759, Bray helped establish a Negro school in Williamsburg in 1764. Under the direction of Commissary Dawson, local clerics, and Mrs. Ann Wager, the school soon opened its doors to twenty-four Negro students and made progress in the area.[51] It appears to have won some local support, for a local printer, Mr. William Hunter, left in his will in 1761 some £7 for the support of Mrs. Wager.[52] But despite the initial success and support granted to the school, with the death of Mrs. Wager in 1774 the school ceased to operate. In fact, in the agitation of those years, all the Negro and Indian schools on the North American continent founded by Bray and his associates, as well as

---

[49] U.S. Bureau of the Census, *Negro Population 1790–1915* (Washington: Government Printing Office, 1918), p. 57, Table 6. It should be noted that Virginia had the largest number and percentage of freedmen to colored population in 1860 of any slave state in the Union except Maryland, which was a unique border state.

[50] Thompson, *History of the Society*, pp. 9–19, 42–43.

[51] Mary F. Goodwin, "Christianizing and Educating the Negro in Colonial Virginia," *Historical Magazine of the Protestant Episcopal Church*, I, no. 3 (September, 1932), 148–51.

[52] *William and Mary Quarterly*, 1st Series, VII (1899), 13.

by the SPG, also collapsed. The Williamsburg school was also the model for a school in Fredericksburg that lasted five years in the 1770's, but with the American Revolution the source of English enthusiasm and funds for these schools was destroyed, and local planter interest seems to have been exhausted.[53] It appears that aside from these schools, neither free nor slave Negroes were permitted regular education by the local county schools.

There was some attempt by the vestries, however, to provide for the free Negroes, orphans, and poor some type of apprenticeship in which they were also taught to read and write by the person to whom they were indentured. The vestry of Petsworth Parish in 1716, for example, required that for his indenture, Mr. Ralph Bevis was to

give George Petsworth, a mulattoe boy of the age of 2 years, 3 years' schooling, and carefully to Instruct him afterwards that he may read well in any part of the Bible, also to instruct and Learn him ye s[ai]d mulattoe boy such Lawful way and ways that he may be able after his Indented time expired to gitt his own Liveing, and to allow him sufficient meat, Drink, washing, and apparill, until the expiration of ye sd time &c. . . .[54]

But these indenture and apprenticeship programs were for only a few free Negroes, and aside from the temporary Negro school experiment on the eve of the American Revolution, there seems to have been almost no serious effort, or no successful one, by the church to educate the Virginia Negro. No Negro was admitted to William and Mary College, and none appears to have been trained by the church in local parish schools for the liberal professions, as in Cuba; and in the harsh reaction that took place by the early nineteenth century, even basic literacy was denied the freedmen.[55]

Thus the Virginia church, dominated by the planter elite, offered no educational escape opportunities for the free

[53] Thompson, *History of the Society*, chap. 4.
[54] *William and Mary Quarterly*, 1st Series, V (1897), 219; also see the case of Robert, son of the free Negro woman Cuba, who was bound out in Lancaster County in 1719 till his twenty-first birthday. *William and Mary Quarterly*, 1st Series, VIII (1899), 82.
[55] In 1800 the General Assembly specifically prohibited the local parishes from requiring the masters to teach the indentured free colored children to

Negroes, and none whatsoever for the slaves. It totally d
the right to slave marriages, and by and large in the colon
period did not even Christianize the majority of African
Negroes. Finally, the Virginia established church provided
no social appenditures that could enrich the community life
of the Negroes. Under Anglicanism there was no religious
brotherhood system, no great pageantry and processions, and
no folk religious syncretism, which was such an important
part of the fabric of Catholic Cuba. Although after 1740 the
dissenter groups in the Great Awakening provided some types
of compensation in the evangelical and revivalist meetings,
which gave birth to the future Negro church movement, this
activity was confined to the frontier in the colonial period
and involved only a few thousand Negro slaves. For the Great
Awakening in colonial Virginia was the work of only a handful of ministers, and it never penetrated into the Tidewater
parishes where the overwhelming majority of slaves lived
under Anglican masters. Even with the breakdown of the
established church in the 1780's and the tremendous growth
of permanent Methodist, Baptist, and Presbyterian church
movements, the slaves in the plantation areas still found themselves under the domination of Episcopalians. And by the
1840's, the great rendering of the evangelical churches into
northern and southern branches assured the planter's domination of Church attitudes toward the Negro by all sects
except the Quakers.

Thus despite the greater religious diversity of Virginia in
the nineteenth century, the customs and practices established
under the Anglican church of colonial Virginia persisted.
And in the nineteenth century, as in the two preceding centuries of Anglican control, the law remained glaringly silent
on the religious rights and needs of the African slave.

In reviewing the work of the Anglican church in the colonial period, it can be seen that despite all the efforts of the
Bishop of London and his commissaries, the few local clergy

read or write, and by the 1830's the state legislature was prohibiting all types
of schooling and education for free Negroes who were willing to pay the
costs. John H. Russell, *The Free Negro in Virginia, 1619–1865* (Baltimore:
Johns Hopkins Press, 1913), pp. 140, 144–45.

to maintain even the established church
olonists. Even as late as 1774, Virginia had
f England clergymen,[56] out of a total popu-
447,000 persons in the colony,[57] or just 1
298 colonists. Nor was this ratio unusual,
James Ramsay in his famous attack on
slavery ın ᴛʜᴇ ʙritish West Indies asked for an ideal of 1
clergyman per 3,000 inhabitants to carry out the needed
Christianization of the Negroes.[58]

Since it was few in number, operating on provisional contracts based on the consent of the congregation, completely
subservient to the planter-dominated vestry, and working
against ingrained opposition to conversion, it is surprising that
the Church of England did accomplish as much as it did.
Unfortunately, however, when moral pressure within the
church finally began to build up to the degree that the metropolitan hierarchy was willing to put full pressure on the
crown and Parliament to override local slave legislation, it
was already too late for Virginia. For the great antislavery
crusade did not fully get underway, despite the sentiments of
such early leaders as Bishop Fleetwood, until after 1783, when
the colonies were no longer a part of the British Empire.
Although this attack would have a profound impact on the
British West Indies and on the abolition of the slave trade,
the severance of political ties and the establishment of an
independent Episcopalian church in Virginia rendered the
North American colonies impervious to this great moral crusade. How different events might have been in such a case is
shown by the impact of the aroused church on the eventual
education, Christianization, and emancipation of the British
West Indian Negro slave.[59]

[56] Brydon, *Virginia's Mother Church*, II, 608–14.
[57] Evarts B. Greene and Virginia D. Harrington, *American Population before the Federal Census of 1790* (New York: Columbia University Press, 1932), p. 141.
[58] Ramsay, *On the Treatment of African Slaves*, pp. 265–66.
[59] For the history of this struggle see Reginald Coupland, *The British Anti-Slavery Movement* (2d ed.; London: Frank Cass & Co., 1964), along with Frank J. Klingberg, *The Anti-Slavery Movement in England, A Study in English Humanitarianism* (New Haven: Yale University Press, 1926).

PART IV. Slavery and the Economy

Introduction. In the creation of their slave regimes, both Cuba and Virginia would be most immediately influenced by local economic forces. And although, as the previous chapters attempt to show, Cuba would have to be highly sensitive to outside institutions jealous of their rights, its system of Negro slavery would be molded in important ways by the economic use to which it was put.

For the Negro, both slave and free, the question of his economic occupation would have a determining influence not only upon the level of social and economic power he might attain in the colonial community but in the development of his personality as well. No matter what the law did or did not create, the means of production demanded adjustments on the part of the Negro that might prove either harmful or beneficial to him, allow him room for personal development and expression, or destroy his individuality and dull his abilities. Moreover, his control over strategic economic crafts and industries provided him with a position of potential economic power by which he might greatly influence the attitude of the master class in its dealings and attitudes toward him. Thus the economic foundations of Negro slavery fixed certain limits to which all other developments of the slave regime had to adjust.

Crucial in determining this economic role would be the place of the Negro slave within the plantation systems of these two societies. Was the Negro confined only to unskilled plantation labor? Were nonplantation skills and occupations open to him? Were these nonplantation opportunities readily available and in large supply? What role did the Negro slave and also the colored freedman play in the labor market? Did he successfully compete with white labor in nonplantation jobs and skills? Was he permitted to determine his craft and opportunities as a slave and freedman by economic criteria alone, or by noneconomic standards? Could he transfer skills learned in slavery to his free status when this occurred? These are some of the crucial questions that determined the impact of the economy on the world of Negro slavery.[1]

7. Cuba and the Diversified

Economy. The sixteenth century for Cuba was a period of marked economic instability. The island at the time of its discovery possessed natural resources of great value and in what appeared to be unusual quantities, and so it became immediately involved in a period of rapid economic exploitation

---

[1] Of key importance in the following pages will be the discussion of the plantation, and it would be well at this point to clarify the term. Perhaps the most adequate definition of the plantation has been provided by L. C. Gray, who noted that: "the plantation was a capitalistic type of agricultural organization in which a considerable number of unfree laborers were employed under unified direction and control in the production of a staple crop." Lewis Cecil Gray, *History of Agriculture in the Southern United States to 1860* (2 vols.; Washington: Carnegie Institution, 1933), I, 302. Since the time of Gray's definition, which is perfectly applicable to the present historical analysis, social scientists have tended to broaden the definition to include all types of large-scale commercial crop agricultural systems, no matter whether the labor is free or slave, and they have tried to distinguish it from the feudal type of hacienda pattern, where production is not capitalistic in terms of management, nor in terms of producing a commercial export crop. For some of these problems, see the excellent study by the Pan American Union, *Plantation Systems of the New World* (Washington: P.A.U., Social Science Monographs, No. VII, 1959).

and prosperity. The early struggle for economic survival that played such an important part in Virginia colonization was never experienced by Cuba in its first years. In fact, its gold and its Indian labor supply soon made Cuba one of the most prominent, populous, and wealthy of Castile's overseas possessions.

This boom period quickly subsided, however, for the Castilian conquest had moved into the continental area of Central and South America and revealed new sources of wealth that made Cuba's resources appear insignificant by comparison. The island itself fell into a long period of economic stagnation because of the attraction of these newer regions, the depletion of its former staples—gold and Indians, and the exploitation of its remaining resources in futile attempts at Florida conquest. The island's fertile soil and climate and extremely strategic location soon brought it renewed economic activity and development, however, and during the middle decades of the century, there came a slow reestablishment of economic prosperity on the island, this time based on a far more diversified production of goods and with the institution of Negro slavery firmly established in place of Indian labor.

When the first Spaniards arrived in Cuba, they discovered gold in large quantities, as well as an Indian population estimated at 60,000.[1] The Indians were quickly and easily subdued and were immediately turned to mining—which assumed prime importance in the island's economy—and in a few short years appreciable amounts of gold were annually being mined on the island.[2] Seeking to establish a firmer economic base than a mining community would provide, the farsighted Velázquez was instrumental in seeing that agriculture was not ignored, and not only were the indigenous crops produced in abundance, but extensive attempts were made

[1] Ramiro Guerra y Sánchez, *et al., Historia de la nación cubana* (10 vols.; Havana: Editorial Historia de la Nación Cubana, 1952), I, 38.
[2] Irene Aloha Wright, *The Early History of Cuba, 1492–1586* (New York: Macmillan Co., 1916), pp. 69, 81. In the first four years, about 62,000 pesos of gold were produced and some 100,000 pesos were being mined annually by 1517.

to raise all the staple European crops and livestock. The wisdom of this policy quickly bore fruit, for in this agricultural activity, the island found an added source of revenue in the provisioning, especially with livestock, of the rising continental colonies.[3]

This first burst of economic prosperity, however, was blighted by the expansion of the Castilian empire into new frontiers, frontiers that held untold wealth in the commodities that had first brought the Spaniards to Cuba—Indians and precious metals. Ironically enough, it was the governor and conqueror of the island, Diego Velázquez, who first turned the island from its own development and subordinated it to further conquest. No sooner had settlement been completed than Velázquez was petitioning the crown for rights to further exploration under his management.[4] In 1516, a slave-hunting expedition off the coast of Yucatan happened upon Indians more civilized than any yet encountered by the Europeans, as well as upon quantities of gold. This discovery greatly stimulated Velázquez and in 1517 and 1518, he sent out two exploratory expeditions to the coasts of Mexico and Yucatan. The news they brought back allowed the Cuban governor to petition for the rights of conquest, and in 1519 he equipped an expedition of some 600 Castilians, along with numerous Indian auxiliaries, under his "friend" Hernando Cortés. This expedition, the largest ever organized from the infant colony, greatly strained its resources.[5]

Yet this was only the first of many such expeditions that would draw off men and supplies from Cuba into the vast continental empire. Because of the revolt of Cortés from the authority of Velázquez, another and larger expedition sailed from Cuba in 1520. It not only failed to subdue Cortés, but became instead his much needed reinforcement—and these provisions and colonists were a permanent loss to the island.[6]

[3] *Ibid.*, p. 82.
[4] Guerra y Sánchez, *La nación cubana*, I, 152–53.
[5] *Ibid.*, I, 153–54; Wright, *Early History of Cuba*, pp. 71–72, 85–86.
[6] Guerra y Sánchez, *La nación cubana*, I, 155. Arthur Percival Newton, *The European Nations in the West Indies, 1493–1688* (London: A & C Black Ltd., 1933), p. 37.

Not only did settlers leave the island by formal expeditions but by every means possible, for the wealth of the Aztec Empire soon caused a mass exodus from all the established colonies, including Cuba—a tide that even stringent imperial legislation could not hold back. The gold pouring out of the Mexican mines completely outweighed Cuban production, and at the same time the island's supplies of that metal began to give out.[7] Nor was Mexico's gold output the only competition Cuba faced, for the former was soon meeting all of her own agricultural and livestock requirements and even exporting food to the other colonies, thus reducing Cuba's role as a provisioning colony as well.[8]

The island's economy during this period of depression also experienced the near extinction of its other prime resource, the Indian. Aside from heavy labor that took its toll among the previously semi-nomadic natives, the inevitable European plagues struck the island in 1519, and again in 1528, and the impact of the pestilences on the Indians was devastating. The destruction of these Indians, the exodus of white colonials, the exhaustion of her minerals, and the exclusion of her agricultural products soon brought the island close to depopulation and exhausted the resources of those who were left.[9]

Despite this decline in her once prosperous colony, no help came from Spain. For in imperial thinking, Cuba was now to be used as a staging area for conquest and colonization of Florida. In 1538 Hernando de Soto sailed from Seville, having been appointed governor of the island as well as adelantado of Florida. This was done by the crown so that de Soto could more easily subordinate the island and its resources to his effort of conquest, an effort that would prove utterly disastrous.[10] The opening up of the long series of European wars

---

[7] In 1538, only 13,000 pesos of gold were mined on the island. Wright, *Early History of Cuba*, p. 203.

[8] Guerra y Sánchez, *La nación cubana*, I, 283. In fact, by the 1560's Cuba was herself importing maize from Campeche and Yucatan, Julio J. Le Riverend Brusone, *Los origenes de la economía cubana (1510–1600)* (Mexico: El Colegio de Mexico, 1945), p. 44.

[9] Wright, *Early History of Cuba*, pp. 86–87, 136; Newton, *European Nations in the West Indies*, p. 40.

[10] *Ibid.*, p. 43; Guerra y Sánchez, *La nación cubana*, I, 157.

between Charles V and Francis I had an equally damaging effect upon the island, for it soon brought French corsairs to the Caribbean to begin over a century of piratical depredations, which threatened not only the communications of the island with the outside world but the very existence of her cities.

While Cuba's prime export was declining by the 1530's, there was no decrease in her dependence on imports, for despite all her agricultural growth Cuba was still not agriculturally self-sufficient. Although it was rich in soil and in climate, the island could not produce the staple crops that had formed the base of the agricultural economy of central Castile. Attempts had been made to grow wheat, barley, grapes, and olives, but these had failed because of the tropical climate of the island, and while cattle throve, the all-essential sheep could not survive. Thus, the colony was forced to carry on a heavy import trade not only in the usual manufactured articles but also in agricultural products, and with the decline in their major export, there came a decline in the standard of living for the majority of Cubans.[11]

By the middle decades of the sixteenth century the prime native exports in goods were cattle products (undressed hides, tallow, and salted meats) and wood. The cattle and livestock industry had always overshadowed all other forms of agriculture, even in the days of greatest prosperity. The cattle and hogs brought to the island by the first conquistadores thrived mightily; so large did the herds become that the practice of public hunting was early adopted by the colonists. There were not only these wild herds but many private ones as well, and throughout the century, the largest agricultural holdings on the island were the cattle ranches, known as *hatos* or *fincas*.[12]

---

[11] *Ibid.*, I, 284–86.
[12] Wright, *Early History of Cuba*, p. 265; Le Riverend Brusone, *Origenes de la economía cubana*, pp. 38–42; Guerra y Sánchez, *La nación cubana*, I, 297. On the role of hides as the leading export commodity from Cuba in the sixteenth century see Huguette et Pierre Chaunu, *Séville et l'Atlantique (1504–1650)* (8 vols.; Paris: Institut des Hautes Études de l'Amérique Latine, 1955–60), Vol. VIII, Pt. 1, pp. 561–62.

Another nonperishable product that could reasonably be shipped to Europe was the assortment of fine woods found in the extensive forests of the island. At an early period the artisans of Europe were using Cuban woods in furniture making, and when late in the century Philip II began work on the Escorial, the island provided a large quantity of excellent woods for its construction.[13] But despite these concrete developments, the island's economic plight was still precarious, for these products by themselves could not absorb the trade deficit nor attract large numbers of colonists.

Although the products that would later become so essential to the Cuban economy were available at this time, they were of little economic value. Tobacco was an indigenous crop and was used by the Spaniards settled on the island; however, it had yet to develop a European market.[14] And while sugar cane was grown in small quantities throughout the century, there was not enough capital available for the construction of mills, so that refining and large-scale production did not begin until the last decade of the century.[15] This same lack of local capital hampered the full development of the rich copper deposits of the island until the seventeenth century.[16] These products, either for lack of capital or lack of a market, were thus not of commercial value at this crucial period in Cuba's economic history.

The island did possess, however, one resource that soon had to be recognized by all, and this was her strategic location. With her numerous and excellent habors, Cuba stood at the entrance to Spain's New World empire, and it was these geographic resources that would finally provide the island with a base upon which a firm prosperity could be built. As early as 1519, when Cortés' first treasure ship sought to bypass the

[13] Guerra y Sánchez, *La nación cubana*, I, 290. From 1579 to 1589 the various woods for the Escorial were cut in Cuba; Wright, *Early History of Cuba*, p. 307.

[14] Guerra y Sánchez, *La nación cubana*, I, 286.

[15] *Ibid.*, I, 283. Also Fernando Ortiz, *Cuban Counterpoint, Tobacco and Sugar*, trans. Harriet de Oñis (New York: Alfred A. Knopf, 1947), p. 281.

[16] H. E. Friedlaender, *Historia económica de Cuba* (Havana: Biblioteca de Historia, Filosofía y Sociología, 1944), p. 24.

usual exit from the Caribbean, the Mona Channel (between Hispaniola and Puerto Rico), the excellence of the Florida or Bahama Channel was discovered by the Spaniards. Because of the rapid Gulf Stream that ran through it and that led into the favorable antitrade (southwest) winds, the Bahama Channel between the Florida peninsula and western Cuba proved to be the best route out of the Caribbean.[17] The treasure vessel of Cortés made the trip from Vera Cruz to San Lucar in the then impressive time of a little more than two months, and soon the majority of ships leaving the Caribbean for Spain were regularly using the Bahama Channel, and the conveniently located harbor of Havana on the western end of the island became a prominent watering and provisioning place before heading out to sea.

Cuba thus stood at the gateway to the Caribbean empire, and her development as a strong bastion would be indispensable for the maintenance of Spain's Atlantic trade routes. But imperial thinking would not recognize the strategic nature of the island until the military threats of her warring European rivals made it dangerously clear. First seen in the years following the opening of the continent as a mere "way port" to be exploited for the further expansion of the frontiers of Spain, the long years of piratical raidings and military expeditions forced imperial thinking to regard Cuba as a bulwark of its Indies empire and the key to her imperial lifeline.[18]

The long series of wars between Charles V and Francis I brought the French privateers into New World waters for the first time in 1536 and 1537. Operating at first off the Bahamas, they soon grew bolder, and in 1537 struck at isolated communities on Hispaniola and succeeded in taking the Cuban capital of Santiago de Cuba. In that same year, they effected the first successful strike against the fabulous treasure galleons, and nine gold-laden ships were detached by the French from the Peruvian treasure fleet. Peace in 1538 brought only a temporary cessation of hostilities, and with the outbreak of

---

[17] Newton, *European Nations in the West Indies*, pp. xii–xiii, xv, 39–40.
[18] Wright, *Early History of Cuba*, p. 370.

the third Franco-Spanish war in 1543, the crown, in fear of having its trade routes with the New World completely severed, ordered that the convoy system be established.

Under the convoy system two fleets (the *flotas*) were to sail yearly from Spain for the New World, with all merchant vessels being required to proceed only with these fleets and never alone. The port of Nombre de Dios on the Panama peninsula was to serve as the entrepôt for all goods going to South America and Vera Cruz as the entrepôt for Mexico, while the Greater Antilles and Tierra Firme (the northeast coast of South America) were allowed to receive a few ships directly once the convoy had entered the Caribbean. The escorting vessels were usually required to station themselves at Havana, and once they reached the Caribbean the ships for the return voyage were also required to collect at that port. This arrangement was sporadically followed until the 1560's, when it was rigorously put into permanent effect and was to rule Spain's trade relations with her empire until the end of the Hapsburg era in the eighteenth century.[19] For while the European wars might end, there was to be no peace for the Spanish Indies, which were considered "beyond the line" until the end of the seventeenth century.[20]

Havana, under this arrangement, became the last port-of-call before the Atlantic crossing and was therefore the prime supplier to the fleets for stores of fresh fruits, vegetables, and salted meats. With the fleet gathering in the harbor for the return voyage, the size of the town would often swell overnight, for the ships sometimes remained in port as long as three or four months while awaiting favorable weather. Thus shipyards, truck farms, and slaughter houses, along with taverns, eating houses, lodgings, laundries, and a host of other service industries sprang up to provide for the needs of the

[19] Charles H. Haring, *Trade and Navigation between Spain and the Indies in the Time of the Hapsburgs* (Cambridge: Harvard University Press, 1918), p. 207; Newton, *European Nations in the West Indies*, pp. 51–55.

[20] As Newton points out, prior to this time no European peace treaty was binding on the actions of respective nationals in the New World, and any incidents occurring in this area in the years of peace would not be considered grounds for war in Europe. *Ibid.*, p. 122.

fleets—industries in which the Negro, slave and free, would play a dominant role.[21]

To provide entertainment for the travelers and crews of the fleets in the harbor, gambling and prostitution flourished in the city.[22] Vices such as tobacco smoking were taught to the sailors and returning *indianos*,[23] and through them it spread to Europe and the other colonies, finally awakening a demand for the excellent Cuban tobacco.[24] During this time the shrewd *habaneros* would send their prices skyrocketing, but their customers seldom complained for they were well supplied with gold. In 1581, Gabriel de Lujan reported to the Castilian crown that

. . . this place [Havana] is the most expensive in all the Indies; this is because of the great number of ships that pass through here, and the people traveling on them who cannot refrain from spending even if they wanted to.[25]

Thus the invisible exports of Havana began to greatly augment the available capital on the island, finally securing for the Cubans that margin of profit they had lost with the exhaustion of the island's gold resources.

So important was Havana becoming in relation to the rest of the island that in 1550 Governor Angulo on his own initiative moved his residence there from Santiago de Cuba, thus changing the capital of the island for the third time in its brief history.[26] The crown, however, did not fully perceive its dependence upon the port until foreign aggression destroyed it.

A new war with France in 1554 again brought large-scale concentrated attacks on the West Indies, but this time in an intensity that Cuba had not previously experienced. Not only isolated communities, but principal ports were attacked as well, for in 1554 Santiago de Cuba was sacked, and in 1555

---

[21] Guerra y Sánchez, *La nación cubana*, I, 95; Friedlaender, *Historia económica*, p. 22.

[22] Newton, *European Nations in the West Indies*, p. 56.

[23] Those white colonials who secured their fortune in the New World and returned home to spend it.

[24] Ortiz, *Cuban Counterpoint*, p. 287.

[25] Quoted *ibid.*, p. 286.

[26] After some delay the audiencia finally backed Angulo's move in 1553, thus officially sanctioning Havana as the capital; Wright, *Early History of Cuba*, p. 229.

Jacques de Sores took Havana. After overcoming its meager defenses, the Frenchmen held the city and its environs for over a month, and when they were through, there was little left. A month later a small group of Frenchmen made another raid on the city with impunity, this time seeking the areas untouched by the previous destruction.[27]

This sudden blow dramatically awakened imperial thinking to the strategic position of the harbor and to the need to fortify it heavily if Spain were to hold her Caribbean empire intact. Beginning in 1556, the first of a long series of professional military men were appointed to the governorship (replacing the *licenciados* who had monopolized this office since the days of Velázquez), and soon men, money, and materials were flowing into Havana to make of it an impregnable fortress. This program of construction was largely financed by specie from Mexico and was carried on for the rest of the century and well beyond, especially after the famous Drake cruise of 1586. Havana was now provided with a permanent professional garrison, and the fortress of St. Augustine was constructed on the Florida peninsula to assist Havana in maintaining control of the channel.[28] It was this construction along with the provisioning and servicing of the fleets, that provided the needed capital for the growth of established industries as well as the development of new ones at the end of the century.

As the Cuban economy had undergone a dramatic change over its first century, so had the composition and characteristics of its labor market. The conquistadores had opened up in their conquest a rich reservoir of Indian labor, which they were quick to exploit. As compensation for their expenditure of money and labor they demanded these native Cubans for personal service, and this the crown was forced to allow, but they also demanded that they themselves be made into a colonial landed nobility. The conquistadores thus sought to possess the Indians and their lands in perpetuity (i.e., independent

[27] *Ibid.*, pp. 235–41; Newton, *European Nations in the West Indies*, pp. 57–58.
[28] Wright, *Early History of Cuba*, pp. 369–71; Guerra y Sánchez, *La nación cubana*, I, 95–97; Newton, *European Nations in the West Indies*, p. 75.

of the crown); this the crown refused to grant. For Castile and later all of Spain were being wrought into a modern, centralized monarchy, and to create a new feudal order overseas after debilitating the one at home would have reversed this whole trend and brought decentralization to the empire.

Thus the encomienda was a grant of the labor of a specified group of Indians to an individual settler and did not involve the land of the Indians nor judicial, political, or religious control over them. And even when the crown had gone farthest in appeasing the demands of the colonials, it allowed the grant of the encomienda to pass automatically only to the next generation, and no more. The whole system rested on the feudal justification that the Indian owed the crown tribute for his conversion, education, and protection, and the crown through its officials granted this tribute to specified colonials for services to the crown. The crown, however, often collected the tribute itself, especially when an encomienda had gone the full time or when an encomendero (holder of the grant) died without issue. Once the system had been reasonably established, the crown was able to place the Indians in their villages under the political control of their own *cacique* (or chief) and a priest, and the encomendero was not allowed to live among them.[29] But as long as the Indians were required to pay their tribute in personal service, the system differed little from outright slavery.[30]

These Cuban Indians were employed in the arduous tasks of washing and mining for gold, and their numbers were quickly depleted by the harsh labor extracted from them. The evils of this system of control were vigorously questioned by the Dominicans, and especially by one of their number who had been among the first to hold an encomienda in Cuba—Bartolomé de Las Casas. They attacked the very legality of the conquest, and although they were not successful in con-

[29] Silvio A. Zavala, *New Viewpoints on the Spanish Colonization of America* (Philadelphia: University of Pennsylvania Press, 1943), pp. 69–72, 75, 80–81; Charles H. Haring, *The Spanish Empire in America* (New York: Oxford University Press, 1947), pp. 60, 63.
[30] Lesley Byrd Simpson, *The Encomienda in New Spain* (Berkeley and Los Angeles: University of California Press, 1950), p. xiii.

vincing the crown on this point, they were able to destroy the encomienda as it was first created. Las Casas and the others fought for complete abolition of the colonials' control over the Indians and their labor, and in the famous New Laws of 1542, the crown accepted their position and decreed the abolition of the encomienda.[31] But the opposition from the colonials was too powerful, and the most controversial of these New Laws were revoked within four years.[32] The crown did not accept complete defeat, however, for it struck at the roots of the system when, in 1549, it effectively outlawed the right of the encomendero to require personal service from the Indians, requiring instead that the tribute be paid in goods and/or specie. So important was this change that by the end of the first century, after a long and bitter struggle, the crown had succeeded in converting the system from disguised slavery into a mere pension system for the white colonials with the Indians under direct control of the crown through the *corregidores de indios* system.[33]

But for the Caribbean Indians, these measures had come too late. Suicide, overwork, and plague had literally destroyed the pre-Columbian population of the island.[34] Seeing the rapid decline in the number of native Cubans, the Spaniards in Cuba followed the common practice of abducting Indians from unconquered areas and pressing them into slavery. Under the pretense of making "just wars" (i.e., against these Indians who were in supposed rebellion to his majesty's authority), slaving expeditions soon denuded the Bahamas and other areas of their Indian populations. For many years the crown openly encouraged and taxed these slaving expeditions, but eventually moral indignation in Spain proved overwhelming

---

[31] Lewis Hanke, *The Spanish Struggle for Justice in the Conquest of America* (Philadelphia: University of Pennsylvania Press, 1949), pp. 83, 92–95.

[32] Haring, *The Spanish Empire*, pp. 57–58.

[33] *Ibid.*, pp. 73, 142–43; Zavala, *New Viewpoints*, pp. 85, 97.

[34] By 1544 there were only about 1,000 left from the original 60,000 Cuban Indians. See Wright, *Early History of Cuba*, p. 194. In 1550 all the native Cubans who were left were freed from all services to the Spaniards, and were established in communities of their own, isolated from the whites, *ibid.*, pp. 185–186.

and the crown changed its position. In its usual fashion, it abruptly outlawed Indian slavery completely in 1530, only to revoke its stand under colonial pressure four years later. But the crown had made its extreme position known to the colonials and could then proceed by less rigid steps to destroy the foundations upon which the whole system of Indian slavery rested. It first carefully circumscribed the definition of "just war," and then proceeded to examine the titles of ownership held by all masters for their slaves in the light of this new definition, and, of course, those who could not produce the proper evidence that their Indian slaves had been taken in a "just war" had to free them. In 1538 the crown outlawed caciques from selling their Indians into slavery, and in 1548 all women and children under fourteen were emancipated.[35] Thus when full abolition, including the return of enslaved Indians to their place of origin, finally came to Cuba in 1552–53, it was carried out with relative ease.[36] Yet even as the Indian slave was being freed, he was already being replaced by the African Negro slave.[37]

As we have seen, the African slave trade in its modern version, which began with the opening up of West Africa by the Portuguese after 1444, brought in large numbers of colored slaves to the Iberian Peninsula. From here it was inevitable that slaves would be taken to the New World, and the crown early permitted and encouraged this development. Thus in the instructions to Nicolas Ovando, governor-elect of Santo

---

[35] Zavala, *New Viewpoints,* pp. 60–63.

[36] Wright, *Early History of Cuba,* pp. 229, 232.

[37] As Silvio Zavala has pointed out, there is a direct correlation between the survival of Indian peasant masses and the importation of Negro slaves. Where—because of their weak social structure and of decimation by disease —the Indian masses were totally destroyed, they were replaced by Negroes. In areas where the pre-conquest societies rested on a firm peasant agricultural base, as in Peru and Mexico, the Indian masses survived the shock of conquest, and their labor was sufficient to maintain the Spaniards in their prosperity. The Negro was to be found in the Antilles and in the coastal Caribbean and Pacific regions where the less stable Indian cultures had been destroyed. Zavala, "Relaciones históricas entre indios y negros en Ibero-américa," *Revista de las Indias,* No. 88 (April, 1946), pp. 53–54. For the standard typology of pre-conquest cultures, see Julian H. Steward and Louis Faron, *Native Peoples of South America* (New York: McGraw-Hill Book Co., 1959).

Domingo, who was gathering a tremendous fleet of New World colonists in 1501, the crown forbade him to carry to the Indies, either "Jews, Moors, or new converts; but allows the introduction in them of Negro slaves who were born in the power of the Christians."[38] But the high cost of these ladino slaves (Christian and Spanish speaking), their apparent corrupting influence on the Indians, and ability to escape Spanish control easily led to the adoption of the bozal only rule. But even with bozales the Spaniards experienced great difficulties in controlling them, and beginning in 1532, excluded a good number of rebellious Negro *naciones*, primarily Mohammedan, from importation.[39]

Thus, even before the opening up of Cuba, Negro slaves and the institution of slavery were already functioning in the New World. When Velázquez landed on the shores of the island, he in all probability carried with him the first Negro slaves as well as the first white colonists. In these early years of free enterprise in the slave trade, Negroes were brought in both by Portuguese traders who soon arrived on the island and by masters who brought their slaves with them. In 1515 the crown first introduced a dozen of its own Negro slaves from Hispaniola for work on the fortifications of Santiago de Cuba, a practice that was to continue for the rest of the century.[40] All of these importations were augmented finally by the large numbers of Negroes introduced under the several *asientos*, which began in 1518 and under which the island was usually assigned a quota.[41]

Cuban Negroes were among the followers of Cortés in his Mexican conquest in 1519, and many followed on the sub-

[38] José Antonio Saco, *Historia de la esclavitud de la raza africana en el Nuevo Mundo y en especial en los paises Américo-Hispanos* (Barcelona: Jaime Jepús, 1879), p. 61.

[39] Fernando Ortiz, *Hampa afro-cubana: los negros esclavos, estudio sociológico y de derecho publico* (Havana: Revista Bimestre Cubana, 1916), p. 343 n.

[40] Saco, *Historia de la esclavitud*, pp. 73, 82–83.

[41] For the asientos, see Fédéric Mauro, *Le Portugal et l'Atlantique au XVIIe siècle (1570–1670)* (Paris: S.E.V.P.E.N., 1960), pp. 157 ff.; and Georges Scelle, *Histoire politique de la traite négrière aux Indes de Castille* (2 vols.; Paris: L. Larose et L. Tenin, 1906).

sequent expeditions.[42] But this exodus did not impede the growth of the Negro population on the island, for in 1532 there were some 500 African slaves, and by 1535 close to 1,000 were reported to be on Cuba.[43] Throughout the rest of the century there was a steady importation of Negroes, both legal and illegal, so that by 1606 there were said to be some 20,000 on the island.[44] So quickly did they replace Indian labor in importance that as early as 1542, the procuradores of the island declared that "Here the principal property are the Negroes."[45] Thus within thirty years of his introduction into Cuba, the Negro had become a major factor in the economic and social life of the island, whereas in Virginia it would take close to a century before Negro slave labor would begin to dominate the economic scene.

The major reason for this early predominance of coloreds in the labor market was essentially due to the initial lack of heavy white migration into the island in the first two centuries of colonization. In the history of Spanish migration to the Indies in this two-hundred-year span of time, the system of white indenture was never carried into effect. The careful exclusion of large numbers of "new Christians" and (in the first years) non-Castillians, did not allow for unrestricted immigration, and those who could meet the qualifications were required to pay for their own passage.[46] Although large numbers were transported free under particular expeditions supported either by the crown or by private funds, they were primarily soldiers rather than peasants or laborers. At various times, the crown did support the migration of groups of farmers, and it always maintained a small stream of artisans to the Indies. Under Charles V and Philip II various industrious merchants and farmers from imperial countries—especially Portugal—were allowed to settle in limited numbers in

[42] Mauro, *Portugal et l'Atlantique*, pp. 113–14.
[43] *Ibid.*, pp. 156, 160–61.
[44] Irene Aloha Wright, "Rescates: With special reference to Cuba, 1599–1610," *Hispanic American Historical Review*, III (1920), 358.
[45] Ortiz, *Los negros esclavos*, pp. 68–69.
[46] Not only religious and territorial restrictions but a whole series of technical requirements greatly restricted immigration. See Haring, *Trade and Navigation*, pp. 102–3.

the depopulated Antilles.[47] But when all these sources of white migrations are added together, they are of little significance, especially when compared to the English migrations under the indenture system whereby thousands of industrious laborers were indiscriminately allowed to cross the ocean. Without passage money of their own, countless numbers sold their labor to the colonials for a specified number of years to emigrate to America. But even if a large number of Spanish peasants and workers had wished to emigrate, the Spanish vessels of the sixteenth century were incapable of carrying such a volume of free white passengers profitably, especially under the fleet system.

The reintroduction of free trade within the empire in the eighteenth century and the tremendous growth of Cuba in the nineteenth drew in large numbers of white immigrants from the Canary Islands and the Basque countries, and thus turned the balance back to the whites; but this did not change already established patterns. The majority of migrants who came still sought the golden riches and a rapid return to their homes, and often they came with less skills than the long-established Negroes, free and slave, who inhabited the island. Although the unskilled white immigration labor competed successfully with the skilled artisans on the North American continent and succeeded in driving the skilled blacks out of numerous occupations, this did not occur in Cuba.[48] Faced by a financially prosperous free artisan class and a very skilled slave labor market, the newcomers simply adapted to the system and complemented the colored work force. No skills, as we shall see in the study of the free colored class, were preempted by the whites from the blacks, who in fact maintained their dominant, or proportionally greater, majority

[47] Silvio Zavala, "Los trabajadores antillanos en el siglo xvi," Part II, *Revista de Historia de América*, No. 3 (September, 1938), pp. 73–76. Writing of the period from 1555 to 1607 when these foreign introductions occurred, Guerra y Sánchez states that "the number of these foreigners was so reduced, that they were consequently an almost insignificant factor of the population." Guerra y Sánchez, *La nación cubana*, I, 232.

[48] For an excellent survey of this problem in the southern United States see Richard C. Wade, *Slavery in the Cities, The South 1820–1860* (New York: Oxford University Press, 1964), pp. 273–75.

in almost all the major artisanal and labor activities on the island. The poor white immigrants in their turn, occupied many of the unskilled lower ranks, even below the free and slave blacks. The reason for this accommodation is probably due to the fact that economic considerations predominated over all others and that the immigrants neither thought to, nor would they have succeeded in, making a sharp distinction of occupational skills based on the color line, as they did in North America.

Aiding this development was the strong desire, at least in the first two centuries of colonization, of whites to give up manual labor. Driven to the Indies for economic betterment and inbred with the classic *hidalguismo* ideals of the ignobility of manual toil, large numbers of poorer white immigrants gladly deserted their skilled callings for the lure of a lifetime of living off the land. Status in Cuban society came from the possession of land, and the trades marked a man, even of the upper merchant classes, as a person of distinctly lower status.[49] Because of this hidalguismo ideal, master craftsmen gladly taught their skills to their Negro slaves, and as soon as they had accumulated enough capital, they willingly removed themselves from their occupations altogether. This left all the skilled trades open to Negro labor, first as slaves, and then quite rapidly, as freedmen. Thus when massive white peasant immigration got underway in the nineteenth century, the unskilled European peasants found the labor market already heavily controlled by the Negroes, and this control was never broken. Thus the lack of a large white immigration for the first two-hundred years and the wholesale abandonment of the artisanal occupations to the Negroes, slave and free, set a pattern of unchallengable Negro power in the Cuban labor market.

Because of this the Negro came to be employed in almost every branch of industry and commerce on the island. Negroes were employed deep within the island in all the stages

[49] For the concept of hidalguismo see Americo Castro, *The Structure of Spanish History*, trans. Edmund L. King (Princeton: Princeton University Press, 1954), pp. 628 ff.

of cattle raising and slaughtering.[50] They were, as in almost every other Spanish colony, the principal miners, first in gold and later in the copper deposits near Santiago de Cuba.[51] In the 1540's Negroes first opened these deposits, and in 1546 a German expert was teaching, in apprenticeships lasting a year and a half, copper mining and smelting to Negro slaves belonging to the settlers.[52]

In this early period of Cuban history, however, the Negroes were most heavily concentrated in and around the major cities, where the heart of Cuban civilization lay.[53] The *estancias*, or small produce farms—which were located in the environs of all the major cities, and which supplied the urban areas with their food and the fleets of Havana with their fresh fruits and vegetables—were largely operated by the Negro, either by free colored on their own lands or by slaves working for their masters.[54] Within the towns, the Negro worked at an infinite number of nonagricultural occupations. In Havana for instance, the Negresses, both slave and free, owned and operated almost all the taverns, eating houses, and lodgings. The taverns and inns with their sale of wines and tobacco soon proved so lucrative a trade that in 1557 the cabildo prohibited Negresses from owning them, and they largely fell under the ownership of the whites.[55] The colored women had no competition as the laundresses of Havana, the domestic laborers, and the prostitutes of this, the greatest port in the New World.[56] And in time of emergency, such as in 1555,

[50] Negro vaqueros, or cowboys, seem to have been an important group, for in 1574 when Negro slaves were prohibited from carrying arms, they were specifically exempted from this proviso. Ortiz, *Los negros esclavos*, p. 445.

[51] Possibly the first Negro slave revolt on the island occurred in 1533 at the new Jacabo mines. Wright, *Early History of Cuba*, p. 151.

[52] *Ibid.*, p. 206. For the history of this mining community of Santiago del Cobre (or Santiago del Pardo), see e.g. Archivo General de Indias, Sevilla, Audiencia de Santo Domingo, legs. 1627–31. [Hereafter cited as AGI.]

[53] By 1606 half of the island's total population was located in and around Havana. Guerra y Sánchez, *La nación cubana*, I, 316.

[54] *Ibid.*, I, 298.

[55] Ortiz, *Cuban Counterpoint*, pp. 286–87. The Negresses must still have had a good deal of control over the ownership of these establishments, however, for in 1574 these prohibitions were reiterated. See Ortiz, *Los negros esclavos*, p. 445.

[56] Friedlaender, *Historia económica de Cuba*, pp. 31–32.

they were even employed in defense of the city.[57]

Negro males, again both slave and free, were the prime construction workers on the island. As we have seen, as early as 1515 the crown was sending in a steady stream of Negroes to be employed specifically in heavy masonry construction, and throughout the colonial period, all the massive fortifications built on the island, and especially at Havana, were built by Negro labor.[58] Nor was heavy construction the only type of creative labor performed by the Negro, for he was early employed in ship construction and repair, as well as in numerous other trades and skills essential to an urban community.

Under urban slavery, unlike a rural system, the most common method of labor distribution was through the hiring-out or renting of slave labor from the crude bozales to the most highly skilled artisans. Although crude bozal laborers were rented by their masters to third parties and usually worked in a gang labor force, the skilled Negro slave hired himself out and controlled his own income, typically paying his master a fixed sum at stated intervals.[59]

In practice this usually meant complete freedom for the slave to live where he chose and to set up his business the way he wished—renting space, making contracts, and so forth—in short to be a free artisan in all but name.

The pattern of urban slave rentals is well illustrated by the announcements of the daily press of Havana at the beginning of the nineteenth century. Typical rental notices ran as follows:

Seek a Negro woman cook for service in a house.[60]

Wish a Negro man or woman who knows how to sell any type of goods that are given to them, under the responsibility of their master or of a known person, and equally wanted, a master shoemaker who wishes to work for a private person.[61]

Seek a Negro for selling, and whom his master will guarantee. . . .[62]

---

[57] Wright, *Early History of Cuba*, p. 237.
[58] E.g., see *ibid.*, pp. 249, 275, 288–89.
[59] Ortiz, *Los negros esclavos*, p. 312.
[60] *La Cena*, October 24, 1814.
[61] *Noticioso, Diario del Comercio*, October 18, 1814.
[62] *Ibid.*, October 25, 1814.

Seek a good coachman and of good qualities. . . .[63]

Wish to rent Negro field hands for one year or each six months; the master wishing to assure himself by this means of the salary of his slaves should come to casa 39. . . .[64]

Seek eight Negroes to hire, either for six months or a year, who are good for labor in the countryside, some four leagues from the city.[65]

This pattern of domestic urban growth and diversified small-farming agriculture that was established by the end of the sixteenth century would set the pattern for the Cuban economy until the twentieth century. But the initial growth of the colony in the first century of its establishment began to level off in the seventeenth century under the combined impact of the disastrous decline of the colonial fleet system and the general state of war in the Caribbean, which constantly disturbed the local and regional economy. Because of this, the internal capital of Cuba was insufficient to pay for the importation of large numbers of slaves, and by the end of the seventeenth century, the total colored population on the island probably did not exceed 40,000 persons.[66] This sluggish growth was in sharp contrast to the phenomenal importation of Negro slaves into the French and British West Indian islands, where sugar production was creating a legendary wealth. By the mid-eighteenth century, when Cuba probably had no more than 50,000 Negroes and mulattoes, tiny Barbados had 60,000 slaves, Haiti over 450,000 Negroes, and even Virginia had well over 300,000.[67]

---

[63] *Ibid.*, October 28, 1814.

[64] *Diario Civico*, May 21, 1814.

[65] *El Observador de la isla de Cuba*, January 28, 1821. The above Havana newspapers can be found in AGI, Santo Domingo, legs. 1635, 1637.

[66] For a survey of the seventeenth century economy, see Guerra y Sánchez, *La nación cubana*, I, 322–27. The first formal census in Cuba was not undertaken until 1774, and then the total colored population had risen to 75,180, or only some 50,000 in 168 years. Humboldt estimated that only 60,000 African Negroes were imported into Cuba between 1521 and 1763. Alexander von Humboldt, *The Island of Cuba*, trans. with notes by J. S. Thrasher (New York: Derby & Jackson, 1856), p. 217.

[67] Ramiro Guerra y Sánchez, *Sugar and Society in the Caribbean, an Economic History of Cuban Agriculture* (New Haven: Yale University Press, 1964), p. 46.

Although the seventeenth century was one of economic depression, it nevertheless witnessed the growth of the first of the modern agricultural commercial crops—tobacco. Unlike Virginia, where tobacco would be developed as a plantation crop with intensive use of slave labor, the Cuban tobacco industry from the beginning was uniquely a small farm, individually cultivated, largely free labor crop. Spreading down the rich alluvial lands along the banks of the major rivers of the island, the tobacco planters reached deep into hitherto unexploited regions of the interior. Because of the nature of the crop land, and the preemption of almost all the island's territory by cattle *latifundios*, the tobacco farm, or *vega*, tended to be a small property, or *minifundio* system. A good percentage of the tobacco farmers, in fact, rented their lands either from the towns or the cattlemen and produced a relatively small crop on their natural or alluvial vegas. A large number of slaves were employed in the cultivation of tobacco, but these were scattered in small lots among numerous families, and it was often common for the poor white tobacco farmer to work alongside his slaves in the field. It also appears that some slaves even rented vegas on their own and paid their masters a fixed sum. The bulk of the workers, however, were poor whites and a fair number of free colored. Because of this labor and land pattern, the tobacco industry had a sharply democratic flavor to it.

Since tobacco growing was labor intensive and required little initial capital, it attracted poor white colonists from the Canary Islands and Spain and was the major drawing power for white immigration to the islands. Although its rapid growth at the end of the seventeenth and beginning of the eighteenth centuries seemed to promise that the industry would develop into a more capital intensive one, this did not occur. Beginning in 1717, the crown created a monopoly and fixed price structure for the product of the industry. The resulting governmental fiscal policies prevented planters from making major profits, and this worked against the large-scale introduction of slave labor. This governmental stifling of industrial growth and profitability quickly put a ceiling on the continued expansion of the industry, despite the tremendous growth of European demand. Thus, although Cuban tobacco farmers produced 8 million pounds of tobacco in 1717, at the end of the century, production was at almost the same position, being some 9 million pounds in 1788. Nevertheless, while the tobacco industry tended to level off in the eighteenth century, its position within the economy became entrenched, and it continued to maintain an important place in Cuban agriculture for the rest of the colonial period.[68]

With the new administration in Spain in the eighteenth century, the opening up of greater commercial contacts, and the important destruction of Haitian industries toward the end of the century, a whole new era of economic growth occurred in Cuba. First in importance of the new crops of the eighteenth century was coffee. Although it was introduced into Cuba in the early part of the century, coffee production did not become commercially important until the 1790's. From that date, however, its growth was phenomenal. Unlike tobacco, coffee immediately became a plantation crop. It did not require as great an initial outlay of capital as sugar production, but the pattern of plantation slave labor required major investment of capital. In this case, most of the capital seems to have been provided by French planter emigrees from Santo Domingo who quickly made Cuba a major world producer of coffee, and for a time, an effective competitor of the infant Brazilian industry.[69] Thus production rose from 7,000 *arrobas* (a twenty-five pound measure) in 1790 to 900,000 in 1815,[70] with the industry at this latter date employing some 28,000 slaves.[71] But despite government protection, the industry suffered a major setback after the middle of the nineteenth century, and thereafter went into a slow but steady decline.[72]

The final major commercial crop that became of prime importance in the closing years of the eighteenth century was,

---

[68] Guerra y Sánchez, *La nación cubana,* II, 140–42, 170–73.
[69] *Ibid.,* II, 180.
[70] Friedlaender, *Historia económica,* p. 121.
[71] Humboldt, *The Island of Cuba,* p. 283.
[72] Note by Thrasher, *ibid.,* p. 284.

of course, sugar. Sugar had been one of the first crops brought by the Spaniards to Cuba in the sixteenth century and had been steadily cultivated for the next two centuries, but it remained a relatively minor crop until the closing decades of the eighteenth century. Through the combination of the investment of foreign capital, the growth of European markets, and the disastrous decline of Haitian production, the industry began to acquire a new importance. Large numbers of slaves were now imported and heavy expenditures were made for refining machinery. Thus production by the 1780's was up to 1 million arrobas per year, by the 1790's to 2 million, and practically doubled every decade until by the 1850's the island was producing close to 30 million arrobas a year.[73]

Sugar rapidly gained a predominant influence on the foreign trade of the island, and both the economy and the institution of slavery came to be judged by the operation of the sugar plantation system. Of all forms of slave labor, the contemporary chroniclers of Cuba qualified sugar plantation labor as the worst. Since it required more time for production and harvesting than other crops—the cutting and harvesting of the cane being one of the most toilsome of occupations—sugar work was exacting and grueling. Hours were long, work harsh, *mayorales*, or overseers, extremely cruel, and mortality quite high by the island's standards. In the early days, especially, the new sugar planters tended to use only raw bozal males, to discourage family life by refusing to purchase females, and deliberately to overtax their slaves. Because of this, many later commentators, including Fernando Ortiz, tended to see Cuban slavery as an unmitigated harsh system by New World standards, at least compared to North America. But despite this belief, it should be kept in mind that sugar did not become the all-encompassing mono-production industry of Cuba until *after* the end of slavery, and that even at the height of slavery in the nineteenth century, it did not control a majority of the Negro slaves on the island.

Thus despite the fact that the sugar industry was one of

[73] Jacobo de la Pezuela, *Diccionario geográfico, estadístico, histórico de la isla de Cuba* (4 vols.; Madrid: Imprenta Mellado, 1863–66), I, 62–63.

the prime importers of African slaves after 1800, the overwhelming bulk of the Negroes on Cuba neither lived nor
worked on the great sugar plantations during the entire period
of Cuban slavery. So diversified had the Cuban economy
become that despite its importance sugar employed only a
minority of the slaves, even in the 1860's. For throughout the
period of the rise of the new commercial export crops of
coffee and sugar, there had also occurred the steady growth
of such classical agricultural industries as cattle and hides,
truck farming, and a host of diversified agricultural crops
from a huge bee industry to cotton production. And all this
was beside the steady growth of a major industrial complex
in the key urban centers of the island.

Thus in 1825, when coffee was reaching its peak and
sugar just beginning to take over its dominant position, Humboldt estimated the number of slaves engaged in the production of sugar at over 66,000 and in all staple crops at some
140,000, with another 45,000 or so rural slaves completely
outside this staple crop production engaged in a tremendously
diversified rural economy. Out of the total of about 260,000
slaves on the island at this time, 28% or over 73,000 of the
slaves were located in the cities and larger towns engaged in
an infinite variety of urban occupations.[74]

These estimations were fully supported by the studies of
Ramón de la Sagra in 1830. Table 1 shows the estimations
made by this famous botanist and demographer concerning
the value and distribution of slaves in rural industry in 1830.[75]
In the census of 1827, the government listed a total slave
population for the island at 286,942, which meant that according to the above estimation, a good half of the slaves were not
even engaged in rural agriculture but were in the cities in
urban occupations, and this was completely exclusive of the
large urban free colored population.[76]

While the tremendous growth of slave labor on the sugar

[74] Humboldt, *The Island of Cuba*, pp. 242 n. 275. In 1811, *ca.* 32% were
urban slaves.
[75] Ramón de la Sagra, *Historia económico-política y estadística de la isla
de Cuba* (Havana: Imprenta de las viudas de Arazoza y Soler, 1831), p. 123.
[76] *Ibid.*, p. 7 for the census of 1827.

plantations between 1830 and 1860 modified these percentages, and overcame the temporary urban slave predominance, sugar slavery itself never consumed a majority of Negro slaves even at its height. The American, J. S. Thrasher, in his later com-

TABLE 1

THE VALUE AND DISTRIBUTION OF SLAVES BY RURAL INDUSTRY (CUBA, 1830)

Type of Agriculture	Number of Slaves	Value of Slaves
Sugar plantations	50,000	$15,000,000
Coffee plantations	50,000	15,000,000
Small farms and cattle ranches	31,065	9,319,500
Tobacco farms	7,927	2,378,100
	138,992	$41,697,600

mentaries on Humboldt, points out that in the census of 1846, an estimated 116,735 slaves worked on the sugar estates, and this represented only 18% of the total colored population.[77] For his part Pezuela, in 1860, estimated that there were some 150,000 sugar-plantation slaves on the island, probably the very peak figure.[78] Even at this high point, and despite the fact that it occurred when the total slave population was already going into serious decline, slaves engaged in sugar still represented only 38% of the slave population and but 24% of the total colored population.

Admittedly, for the important minority of slaves who did work on the sugar plantations, life was neither pleasant nor productive. In the early years, that is from the 1790's until the 1820's or so, the tendency was to buy only raw males just off the boat and to exclude women completely. Under these first planters, the bozales were usually confined to a barracks and locked in at night. Aside from the barracks atmosphere, daily labor in the harvesting season was long and difficult, and it appears as if many of these pioneer planters deliberately purchased less slaves than they needed and overworked their gangs. It was the accepted pattern during the harvest season for slaves to work six days a week, with only four or five hours

[77] *Ibid.*, p. 214 n.
[78] Pezuela, *Diccionario*, I, 61.

of sleep a night. Because of this exhausting labor, many contemporaries believed that the life expectancy on these estates was extremely short for these Negro slaves.[79] But despite these beliefs, the actual life expectancy of bozales was entirely different. If seasoning is excluded, and it is estimated that large numbers of raw blacks in all types of labor died within the first year, it appears that the sugar slave had a potential life-span not too dissimilar from other slaves, especially after the first years of harsh exploitation.[80]

For after the initial boom period, from the late eighteenth century to the early decades of the nineteenth century, it seems that sugar planters greatly modified the earlier harsh conditions. By the 1830's and 1840's the introduction of steam mills, the adoption of generally superior management techniques, and the deliberate encouragement of female slave labor greatly changed the daily pattern on the great estates and largely terminated the previous uneconomic over-exploitation of slave labor.[81] These changes were well described by an American physician who visited the sugar estates of western Cuba in 1840.

A sugar-plantation, during the manufacture of sugar, presents a picture not only of active industry, but of unremitting labor. ... The negroes are allowed but five hours of sleep, but although subjected to this inordinate tasking of their physical powers, in

[79] R. R. Madden, *The Island of Cuba: Its Resources, Progress, and Prospects* (London: Charles Gilpin, 1849), p. 159; David Turnbull, *Travels in the West: Cuba; with Notices of Porto Rico and the Slave Trade* (London: Longman, Orme, Brown, Green & Longmans, 1840), chap. 14.

[80] Many commentators, without checking its validity, took the figure of life expectancy for a bozal on these early sugar estates to be about seven years. Thrasher, however, who subjected this current belief to scientific investigation, noted that if this was the case, then the slave class "must have diminished eighty-five percent from 1835 to 1852," even despite the heavy importations, and this obviously did not occur. He pointed out that these estimates were based on sugar plantation data, and that the majority of slaves were not even engaged in sugar and were multiplying rapidly. He challenged these estimates and declared that "the supposed rate of loss has greatly diminished during the last twenty years, by the improvements in the system of conducting the sugar plantations, and a greater equalization of sexes upon them." Humboldt, *The Island of Cuba*, pp. 208–9.

[81] On the new developments in the sugar industry, which began in the middle decades of the nineteenth century, see Guerra y Sánchez, *La nación cubana*, IV, 198 ff.

general preserve their good looks. Before the introduction of the steam engine and the example of a milder treatment of the negro by foreign residents, the annual loss by death was fully ten per cent, including, however, new slaves, many of whom died from the changes of climate. At present the annual loss in Limonar [a sugar and coffee district near Matanzas], I was informed by an intelligent English physician, does not exceed two and a half per cent, even including the old. On some plantations, on the south side of the island the custom still prevails of excluding all female slaves, and even on those where the two sexes are well proportioned in number they do not increase. . . . That this arises from mismanagement is proved by the rapid increase on a few estates where the negroes are well cared for. . . .[82]

Not only did new management and new technology ease the lot of plantation slaves, but the traditional protective barriers of custom, church, and state also succeeded in preventing the complete dehumanization of the newly imported African. Thus even at the height of the grinding season, though slaves might work right through Saturday night, all work ceased on Sunday and all church holidays. Also, on every plantation the slaves had their own conucos, or gardens, and sometimes cows and chickens, from which they often supplied part of the produce needs of the plantation itself. When the masters wanted slaves to work on holidays, they had to pay them for their labor and had to make a free contract with them.[83] Nor was contact with the outside world at all cut off. Not only did the priest make weekly visits to the given plantation and the government síndico a yearly one, but equally important the slaves themselves engaged in daily commerce with rural merchants. Many planters bitterly complained that Catalan vendors were buying stolen plantation property from the slaves, aside from the produce from their own gardens. By these methods, it seemed possible for the extraordinary plantation slave even to become a *coartado* like his urban fellow slave. Nevertheless, this was a more difficult process on the plantation, and simple cruelty and barbarism of the worst

[82] [J. G. F. Wurdemann], *Notes on Cuba* (Boston: James Monroe & Co., 1844), p. 153.
[83] Demoticus Philalethes (pseud.), *Yankee Travels Through the Island of Cuba* (New York: D. Appleton & Co., 1856), pp. 25–26.

kind was not uncommon on the sugar estates. In fact, most urban slaves seemed to have been corrected more by the threat of being shipped to the plantation than of being whipped in town.[84]

Yet even if a slave could not buy his way to freedom, or live enough of his own life in the confines of the holidays and Sundays, he still had a major area left to him, independent of the masters' control. For those incapable of adjusting to the plantation system, which included a large percentage of the slaves, there was readily available the simple expedient of escaping. Runaway Negro slaves, in fact, seemed to have been an extraordinarily common occurrence in Cuba, far out of proportion to anything experienced in Virginia. Operating in a tropical climate where self-survival was quite simple, on an island that still had vast unexplored regions, as the powerful survival of cimarrones and palenques attested to, and where a large percentage of the colored population was free, the obdurate Negro slave could simply and often successfully run away.

So endemic, in fact, was the runaway problem, especially on the plantations, that most masters seem to have treated running away as a temporary lapse of duty and nothing more, so that they might easily reabsorb an outlying slave without having to sustain a total loss by forcing him into full-scale flight. To give reality and function to this convenient myth, planters resorted to the curious *padrino* (godfather) system, whereby runaway slaves could use third parties to intercede in their behalf before the master. The system took its name from the famous institution of godparenthood, common to the Spanish kinship system, in which the godparent usually defended the interests of the child. An American physician, who in 1840 observed the padrino system in practice, described it in the following manner. "The delinquent gives himself up to a neighbor of his master, who becomes his *padrino*, and intercedes for him. Unless his offense is very grevious he is forgiven, and returns to his work unpunished."[85]

---

[84] Ortiz, *Los negros esclavos*, chap. 14.
[85] Wurdemann, *Notes on Cuba*, p. 261.

That the masters allowed this process was probably not due to any kindness but simply to the fear of serious loss. Opportunity for successful escape seemed readily available, and slaves seemed to have left at the slightest excuse. Thus this same physician noted that "during the winter, when the labor on the sugar estates is very great, many of the slaves abscound, and lead a roving life in the woods. They often make extensive depredations on the hogs and plantains of the coffee planters, and are sometimes hunted by bloodhounds." He also told of a particular case he knew about where "on an adjoining sugar estate [which stood next to the coffee plantation on which he was staying], through the negligence of the guards at night, several hogs were stolen. The four negroes on duty discovered the loss, and to avoid punishment of their carelessness ran away." These four stayed close to the sugar estate, and after a few days used the local estate doctor successfully to intercede for them, and they returned to work without any punishment being applied. He also reported that on his own coffee estate "ten runaways were caught in a few months."[86]

Not only did these Negroes escape at the slightest excuse, but there was the chance that they would leave the vicinity altogether and become full fledged cimarrones. Also, if the master resorted to legal action to obtain the return of his tired, frightened, or temporarily depressed slaves, he involved himself in huge costs and risked the possibility of having his slaves permanently injured by the professional slave hunters. Not only did the professional hunters get a reward, but the crown charged a government tax and also billed the master for lodging the slave until he was returned to his rightful owner. It also confiscated all slaves not legally imported and paid for, which probably consisted of about one-third to one-

[86] *Ibid.*, p. 262. The problem of runaways and the whole pattern of cimarron communities for the island of Santo Domingo is brilliantly explored in a pioneer sociological study by Y. Debbasch, "Le marronnage: Essai sur la désertion de l'esclave antillais," *L'Année Sociologique*, 3d series (1961), pp. 3–161; (1962), pp. 120–95. See also Roger Bastide, "Nègres marrons et nègres libres," *Annales. Économies-Sociétés-Civilisations*, Année 20, No. 1 (1965), pp. 169–74.

half of the slave population before free trade in slaves was declared in the late eighteenth century.

So burdensome did this system become that the planters did everything possible to get around resorting to official intervention. Not only did they offer liberal pardons for temporarily running away by means of the padrino system, but they used their own slaves to hunt their Negroes or even hunted them themselves. But even these arrangements were not enough, and finally in the 1790's, the major sugar planters appealed to the crown to allow the local commercial guild, or consulado, to handle the entire system and keep it out of the hands of government officials. Claiming that high costs and excessive cruelties rendered the whole system useless, they convinced the governor at Havana to adopt this new system for a year. The consulado, through a special tax on all masters, would pay a reward for the captured runaways and lodge them in their own headquarters and hospitals to keep them in good health until their masters retrieved them. The consulado applied no punishment whatsoever to the runaways, promised them good treatment, and left all punishment up to the individual master.[87] So successful did this new method prove that in the year 1797–98 the governor of Havana reported that the local consulado had handled some 569 captured runaways in that one-year period, and this seems to have been only those caught in the western part of the island.[88]

For the plantation Negro, then, even under the harshest system, there existed innumerable avenues for escaping from the full rigors of the closed world of the master-slave relationship and from the degrading toil of unskilled sugar production. And it should be stressed that even in the plantation system, sugar was but one pattern of organization. Compared to work on the sugar plantations, all contemporary commentators noted that the work on the coffee plantations was mild in the extreme. Their harvesting schedule and daily labor was entirely different and required far less physical labor.

[87] AGI, Papeles del Estado, leg. 8, ramo 4, August 7, 1796.
[88] AGI, Papeles del Estado, leg. 8, ramo 4, July 5, 1798.

The coffee estates also provided better food, lodging, and management and were generally considered to be equivalent to European patterns of free agricultural labor.[89]

Thus, within even the two industries of the island that used the plantation system a large minority of the slaves were operating under a mild form of plantation labor. And to the vast majority of slaves during the entire history of slavery on the island, the whole concept of plantation slavery was unknown since they were never employed in these systems. Instead, a good one-quarter to one-half of the rural slave population lived and worked on small tobacco farms or on the great cattle estates as *vaqueros*. In fact, despite the dispersal of its estates and the relatively quiet role it played in international trade, the Cuban cattle and hides industry was one of the most important on the island, and even as late as 1830 cattle and cattle products had about the same value as the total sugar production.[90]

And even at the height of the sugar industry in the mid-nineteenth century, some 20% to 35% of the Negroes still worked in nonrural occupations in the cities and towns of the island. Employed mainly as artisans, factory workers, day laborers, tradesmen and domestics, these slaves were the skilled leaders of the slave community and from their ranks came the bulk of the coartados. The factory and shop workers were an especially important group. In 1855, for instance, it was estimated that there were 20,000 urban slaves employed in manufacturing (i.e., artisanal shops and factories), and this was compared to 32,500 free industrial workers (white and colored).[91] These 20,000 urban industrial slave laborers represented an extraordinarily high 42% of the adult urban slave work force.[92]

---

[89] Even the overly critical English abolitionist and antislavery propagandist David Turnbull saw coffee as a relatively mild labor plantation crop, especially when compared to sugar. Turnbull, *Travels in the West*, pp. 293–94.

[90] Sagra, *Historia económico-política*, p. 125.

[91] José García de Arboleya, *Manual de la isla de Cuba. Compendio de su historia, geográfia, estadística y administración* (2d ed.; Havana: Imprenta del Tiempo, 1859), p. 186.

[92] The above percentage is taken from the calculations of urban adult (ages 12 to 60) slaves given in *ibid.*, p. 116.

These industrial, or artisanal, workers were employed in everything from shipyards to tobacco factories. The shipyards of Havana after 1723 were especially important, and a fantastic amount of tonnage was built in the eighteenth century. Humboldt estimated that between 1724 and 1796 some 114 ships, of which fully 51 were the gigantic ships-of-the-line carrying 60 or more guns, were built.[93] In tobacco manufactures, when the royal factory was established in 1765, it employed an average of 120 slaves, and when the royal monopoly was disbanded in 1821 and free manufacturing permitted, even more slaves were used.[94] Thus in the 1850's, of the 14,000 workers employed in Cuban tobacco factories, 4,000 were slaves who either worked for themselves or were directly hired out by their masters.[95] There also existed in the 1850's numerous tanning and leather industries employing large numbers of free and slave workers, and it was estimated in 1850, for example, that over 400 slaves were engaged in shoe manufacturing in Havana.[96] And, of course, the great fortification construction never ceased until the end of the eighteenth century. Especially after the English captured Havana in the 1760's, large numbers of new forts and walls were constructed by royal slaves, by hired day laboring slaves, and by a large body of what the Cubans called *forzados*. These were foreign prisoners of war, captured pirates, and other whites who were used as prison labor.[97] Finally, in the urban centers were slaves who performed all types of domestic labor, from cooking and laundering to nursing and riding in livery. It seems that a good number of freely operating laundresses who washed for many families were slaves, and many masters hired out their slaves as professional cooks and so forth.[98]

Not only were employment opportunities entirely different

---

[93] Humboldt, *The Island of Cuba*, pp. 119–23.
[94] *Ibid.*, p. 287. On the Royal Factory of Tobacco and its production see Grupo Cubano de Investigaciones Económicas, *Un estudio sobre Cuba* (Miami: University of Miami Press, 1963), pp. 146–47.
[95] García de Arboleya, *Manual de la isla de Cuba*, p. 180.
[96] *Ibid.*, p. 183.
[97] See AGI, Santo Domingo, leg. 1223.
[98] On the renting out of slaves see e.g. the advertisements in *Noticioso, Diario del Comercio*, October 18, 25, and 28, 1814.

for urban and rural slaves, but there was also a sharp difference in the pattern of slave ownership. In contrast to the concentration of large holdings of slaves by one master found in the countryside, there was a large spread of slaves and slave owners in the cities. Thus in the census of 1855, there were 283,625 rural slaves, and 25,947 rural slave owners, or one owner for each 10.9 slaves. In the urban centers, however, there were 20,947 slave owners for some 65,121 urban slaves, or only 3.1 slaves for every urban slave master. This "democratic" slaveholding pattern was obviously due to the artisanal nature of the urban work force and to the frequent employment of slaves by artisan masters who owned one or two slave apprentices.[99]

Along with enjoying more economic opportunity and the semi-free privileges associated with living out and hiring out, the urban slaves also maintained an active social commerce with freedmen and other slaves in their own taverns and cabildos and in other social activities. Life was indeed rich and varied for the urban slaves. But even here the bonds of slavery could chafe harshly, and the number of fugitive slaves among the urban colored was probably as high as among the rural plantation slaves. But while escaping for a plantation Negro meant giving up many comforts and reverting to a more primitive and dangerous life, just the opposite seems to have been the case with runaway urban slaves. For given the vast numbers of freedmen, coartados, and of slaves who lived and worked away from their masters, it was simple for these fugitives to melt into these other urban classes. For the skilled Negroes this could mean continuing their own professions and claiming to be freedmen. Even for the raw bozal, it was possible simply to be absorbed into the faceless mass of the urban lower classes and to have little difficulty claiming that one was free or simply a self-employed slave. Old and young, men and women, Negro and mulatto, *criollo* (native born) and bozal (imported African), skilled and

[99] García de Arboleya, *Manual de la isla de Cuba*, pp. 116–17. The resulting average for the entire island, both rural and urban, is 7.7 slaves per master, which is a smaller slaveholding pattern than existed in Virginia.

unskilled, the urban slaves successfully fled from their masters' homes.

The diversity of this flow can be seen in the fugitive notices printed in the papers of Havana in the early nineteenth century. For example, in the Havana newspapers of the 1810's and 1820's appeared the following notices:

. . . a *crillo moreno* [Cuban-born Negro] named José María Andrade, occupation tailor, of tall stature, with cataracts, . . . makes false papers claiming that he is looking for a master and renting rooms, when he does not outrightly claim that he is free.[100]

. . . a Negro woman named Narcisa of around 40 years of age, who speaks good English, and makes her livelihood in general domestic service, [also] has a free mulatto son by the name of Miguel Calderon.[101]

A Negro girl *bozal*, who already speaks some Spanish, of the Carabali nation, named María del Carmen, of around 9 years of age. . . .[102]

Has been a fugitive slave for 11 months, a criollo Negro, named Marcos Ramón, of 19 years of age, robust, of regular stature. . . .[103]

A Negro *bozal* of the Mandiga nation, named Carrion, somewhat corpulent, with yellow teeth and an intense aspect, of around 30 years of age. . . .[104]

A criollo Negro named Eusebio de la Cruz, of regular stature, robust . . . friend of dancers, accustomed to going about in filthy condition, with the occupation of shoemaker, who although he may have a license, is a fugitive slave. . . .[105]

A *criollo* Negro named Vicente Estrada, occupation of carpenter, who was a slave of the master carpenter Augustin Vargas . . . and fled eight months ago.[106]

. . . a Negro boy of eight or nine years of age, height of four feet, beautiful teeth, thin lips, fat, . . . he does not speak either French or Spanish, who answers to the name of Valentine.[107]

[100] *Noticioso, Diario del Comercio*, June 7, 1814.
[101] *La Cena*, May 27, 1814.
[102] *Noticioso, Diario del Comercio*, August 4, 1814.
[103] *La Cena*, July 31, 1814.
[104] *Ibid.*, July 9, 1814.
[105] *Café del Comercio*, October 9, 1814.
[106] *Noticioso, Diario del Comercio*, December 9, 1814.
[107] *El Observador*, March 4, 1821.

... a mulatto Manuel, shoemaker, tobacco worker, produce and pig farmer, ... of 40 years of age, without teeth, ... who presents himself as a well to do man, [after listing rewards for his capture, the desperate owner also declared] and if he presents himself to me, with whichever *padrino*, I will pardon him for running away.[108]

There were even cases of rural skilled slaves migrating to the cities and there escaping to freedom. The crown especially had this problem with its royal slave community in the copper mining town of Santiago del Cobre. Since copper production was often in suspension, the crown hired out large numbers of these slaves as daily laborers for work in the cities, both in nearby Santiago de Cuba and in Havana. Once in these towns, large numbers of these slaves escaped, set themselves up as freedmen, and·to the crown's astonishment, even succeeded in having local parish priests register their children as freeborn.[109]

Employed in every conceivable industry and profession in the urban centers and heavily engaged in a multitude of rural activities, from produce farming to cattle raising and bee keeping, the African Negro slave lived in a rich world of economic opportunity. Wages for skilled labor were high throughout the colonial period, and this coupled with the great demand for skills and the possibilities for private and self-employment allowed a large amount of private wealth to accumulate in the hands of slaves. From this wealth came the capital for self-purchase and for a multitude of amenities that relieved the daily burden of slavery. Even in the remotest rural areas, Catalan innkeepers kept the rural slaves well supplied with a host of products for their ready cash, including hard liquor,[110] and in the urban areas, entire sections of the

---

[108] *Ibid.*, August 19, 1822. The above Havana newspapers will be found in AGI, Santo Domingo, leg. 1635, 1637.

[109] AGI, Santo Domingo, leg. 358, no. 28, 1704. In a census of Santiago del Cobre (also called Santiago del Pardo) taken in 1796, it was discovered that there were 129 fugitive slaves missing out of a community of around 1,500 slaves. The average time that these slaves had been fugitives from the community was almost 5 years. See AGI, Santo Domingo, leg. 1627, November 24, 1796.

[110] D. Philalethes, *Yankee Travels*, p. 27.

town were filled with canteens and taverns that catered primarily to the monied slaves.

This abundance of economic opportunity not only provided a large reserve of private capital for slaves, but it also left them with a rich industrial heritage. The master's investment in the training and education of his slaves of course gave the master a large return on his capital, but it also left the slave endowed with assets that would last him a lifetime. All of this made for an easy transfer from slave status to free. Working in every industry as freedmen, the slaves—once emancipated or having purchased their own freedom—simply continued in the same economic occupation as before, often even in the same factories and shops.

All of this was in sharp contrast to Virginia. Here, unskilled rural labor from a plantation economy would dominate the labor market, and even for the skilled artisanal slaves, there would be heavy and, eventually, completely overpowering competition from free white workers, which would drive them out of the labor market. As for those slaves who were freed, a host of racial laws and anti-education restrictions deprived them of the opportunity to compete with white labor, to learn a skill, or often even to practice the few skills that they did acquire.

The economic heritage and opportunities of the Cuban Negro slave were thus crucially different from those of the Virginia slave. Because of this rich industrial heritage, the Cuban Negro occupied a vital place within Cuban society, which racial opposition denied him in Virginia. For even with the influx of white peasants from Europe, the Negro easily retained his economic leadership in most artisanal professions and thereby retained his extremely important place in Cuban society. Without the Negro, the island would have been deprived not only of a major part of its unskilled labor force, but of its entire complex of urban and rural skilled labor upon which the entire economic life of the community rested. In short, in the urban areas, as well as on the rural plantations, the Negro was a vital economic element of society, and this economic importance procured for him a host of privileges that even the benevolent crown could not have granted him.

8. Virginia and the Plantation

System. The success of self-government in Virginia and the emergence of an entrenched planter leadership freed from imperial control forms the prime background for the discussion of the role of the Negro in the Virginian economy. For when the planters' attention was focused upon the establishment of the institution of Negro slavery, it was economic considerations, to the exclusion of all others, that operated most decisively upon the entire structure of statutory law and custom that made up the slave regime.

It is the history of tobacco, the mass migration of laboring whites, and the rise of the plantation system that more than anything else, determined the character of slave institutions in Virginia. These and other economic factors were the prime catalysts rather than the interests and attitudes of a distant monarchy and an all-powerful church—which in the case of Cuban slavery were of such positive importance.

Whereas Cuba sought economic stability and development through a diversified economy heavily influenced by urban organization, Virginia was overwhelmingly dominated by a rural plantation system and tobacco. With little exaggeration it has been claimed that the colonial history of Virginia is merely the story of tobacco, for it was tobacco more than any other single factor that came to dominate the Virginia scene.[1]

Throughout the years of early settlement, the need to find a commercially profitable crop had been the dominant theme. For until a commercial product of some kind was found, the colony proved a constant drain on the ever dwindling resources of the company, and the latter had to resort to all

---

[1] "In no similar instance," wrote the most eminent historian of seventeenth-century Virginia, "has an agricultural product entered so deeply and extensively into the spirit and framework of any modern community." Philip Alexander Bruce, *Economic History of Virginia in the Seventeenth Century* (2 vols.; New York: Macmillan Co., 1896), II, 496.

kinds of subscriptions, lotteries, and new issues of stock to survive financially.[2] From the beginning the company was forever seeking the desperately needed commodity, especially as precious metals and a northwest passage failed to appear. At first considering Virginia as a semi-tropical area, it experimented with all the crops that had proven successful in such areas previously, and hence the company's stress on silk and grapes, as well as on a host of other commodities not produced in England.[3] Yet for one reason or another, all these attempts failed, all except the attempt to grow the phenomenal tobacco leaf, which seemed to have been the first plant that successfully prospered in all of England's early New World possessions.[4] The tobacco experiments were initially carried out by the colonist John Rolfe in 1612, and within a few short years the Virginia leaf had been brought up to acceptable standards. So quickly did Virginia leaf find a profitable market that by the end of the third decade of the seventeenth century, tobacco had achieved its position of dominance over the Virginia economy that was thereafter never seriously challenged.[5]

The early returns on tobacco, based as they were on the prevailing luxury rate that was then being asked in England for Spanish tobacco, were indeed fantastic.[6] It has been estimated that during this early period a man's labor in tobacco yielded six times the return that might be secured from any other crop.[7] The high profits of these bonanza years gave the

---

[2] Wesley Frank Craven, *The Southern Colonies in the Seventeenth Century, 1607–1689* (Baton Rouge: Louisiana State University Press, 1949), pp. 110–11, 114, 116–17, 121.

[3] *Ibid.*, pp. 45–46, 108–9.

[4] In the 1620's tobacco was planted by the English on the Guiana coast of South America and on the islands of St. Christopher and Barbados. Arthur Percival Newton, *The European Nations in the West Indies, 1493–1688* (London: A. & C. Black Ltd., 1933), pp. 142–43, 158. Nor was Bermuda far behind Virginia in this production. Craven, *The Southern Colonies*, p. 119.

[5] Lewis Cecil Gray, *History of Agriculture in the Southern United States to 1860* (2 vols.; Washington: Carnegie Institution, 1933), I, 21–22.

[6] *Ibid.*, p. 259. Between 1600 and 1613 Spanish tobacco cost an average of forty shillings per pound. Among the Virginia planters, three shillings per pound was considered an excellent price.

[7] Avery Odele Craven, *Soil Exhaustion as a Factor in the Agricultural History of Virginia and Maryland, 1606–1860* (Urbana: University of Illinois Press, 1926), p. 30.

colony the appearance of a boom town, for many came from England to seek a quick profit in tobacco and returned to enjoy their wealth in England.[8]

No wonder then that it was early reported to the company that in Virginia "Tobacco was the business, and for ought that I could hear every man madded upon that little thought or looked for anything else," a fact that was to hold true for the rest of the century.[9] So absorbed were the colonists in the production of the golden leaf that in 1617 it was reported of Jamestown that even "the market-place and streets, and all other spare places [were] planted with Tobacco."[10] There was even the threat of starvation in these first crazed years because the cultivation of foodstuff was neglected in the rush to plant tobacco.[11] Tobacco so thoroughly dominated the economy that it became the prime means of exchange instead of specie. Fines, taxes, salaries, and bills were all evaluated and paid in pounds of tobacco throughout the seventeenth century.[12]

The rapid expansion of tobacco production, begun under company rule, continued with few interruptions throughout the seventeenth century and did not seriously level off until the war period of 1703–13.[13] As the crown, through its exclu-

[8] Gray, *Agriculture in the Southern U.S.,* I, 206–61. T. J. Wertenbaker, *Planters of Colonial Virginia* (Princeton: Princeton University Press, 1922), p. 64.

[9] Quoted in Gray, *Agriculture in the Southern U.S.,* I, 23.

[10] Quoted *ibid.,* I, 22.

[11] *Ibid.,* I, 29.

[12] Bruce, *Economic History,* II, 495–98. In 1696 it was claimed that: "Of Grain and Pulse they commonly provide only as much as they expect they themselves shall have Occasion for, for the Use of their Families, there being no Towns or Markets where they can have a ready Vent for them, and scarce any Money to serve for a common Exchange in buying and selling. The only Thing whereof they make as much as they can, is Tobacco; . . ." Henry Hartwell, James Blair, and Edward Chilton, *The Present State of Virginia, and the College,* ed. H. D. Farish (Williamsburg: Colonial Williamsburg Inc., 1940), p. 9.

[13] Gray, *Agriculture in the Southern U. S.,* I, 213. By 1627 Virginia's tobacco exports were about 500,000 pounds. *Ibid.,* p. 22; Wertenbaker, *Planters of Colonial Virginia,* p. 25. For the years 1637–40 inclusive, yearly receipts of Virginia tobacco in London averaged about 1,400,000 pounds and this was exclusive of the amounts carried to Holland. During the next decade-and-a-half production increased fivefold—in 1663 London imported over 7,000,000 pounds and in the period 1697–1701 average yearly exports from Virginia were about 22,000,000 pounds.

sive control over the tobacco import duties, profited almost as much as the Virginians, the former did all in its power to support the latter's control over the home market. As early as 1619, royal law forbade production of tobacco in England and Ireland, and in 1624 the superior Spanish leaf was taxed out of competition in the English market.[14] Equally important to the Virginia planter was the crown's attitude toward emigration to its New World possessions, for this made possible an expanding white labor market that was unknown in the Spanish Indies.

Long influenced by the belief that the British Isles were overpopulated, the English crown saw the New World primarily as a dumping ground, rather than thinking of it as an area carefully to be preserved from the heresies of the Old World.[15] Political prisoners, debtors, economic discontents, laborers, and religious dissenters were gladly shipped off from Bristol and other ports to infest the New World with their heresies, and also, conveniently, to fill up its empty spaces. With no Indian purity to concern itself about and with a desire to relieve home tensions, the English were allowed to pour out of their home country as the Castilians were never able to do. Thus a flood of white emigrants left England in the great migrations of the seventeenth century, a torrent that was never impeded by such noneconomic factors as a fanatic church or jealous crown.

The first major financier of this migration was the Virginia Company of London, but by the time of its fall, the private planter had come to supply the chief financial impetus for the migration. Once the colony had been firmly established, the monopolistic company, with its impediments to the free flow of nonmember capital and its accumulated debts, became a burden to the thriving colonists and to the majority of English merchants, and it was their opposition that was largely instrumental in preventing the company from being rechar-

[14] Gray, *Agriculture in the Southern U. S.*, I, 235, 237.
[15] Bruce, *Economic History*, I, 583; Marcus Wilson Jernegan, *Laboring and Dependent Classes in Colonial America, 1607–1783* (Chicago: University of Chicago Press, 1931), p. 47.

tered.[16] For the English mercantile wealth not involved in the company, the private plantation seemed to offer the most effective agency for uniting capital and labor in the mass production of a staple commodity. Thus, through the private planter rather than the commercial company, the capital of the English mercantile classes and the labor of the indentured servant and slave became effectively organized for the production of tobacco.[17]

Both the company and the smaller corporations that organized the hundreds had attempted to create an effective plantation system and had brought English indentured laborers over to work their "quasi-public" plantations.[18] These all failed to make any progress, however, because of absentee ownership and the lack of interested supervision, and in the massacre of 1622 they were almost all destroyed. The private plantations, which had developed when individual colonists at the expiration of their stock issue had taken up their dividend of 100 acres of land from the Company, were of a far more permanent nature. This permanency resulted because the planters could more easily solicit capital than the heavily indebted company and were considered a good risk. So powerful had they become at the close of company rule in 1624 that the two largest holders of indentured servants were private planters; and so crucial had this type of labor become to the colonial economy and, more especially, to the development of the plantation system, that the servile class already constituted forty per cent of the total colonial population.[19]

With the capital made available by the high returns from tobacco and with land in unlimited supply provided at nominal cost, the colonial planter, backed by English mercantile wealth, was able to bring about the mass importation of servile labor for the increase of his own production. The steady arrival of the yearly merchant fleets for the Virginia

[16] Philip Alexander Bruce, *Institutional History of Virginia in the Seventeenth Century* (2 vols.; New York: G. P. Putnam's Sons, 1910), II, 259–62.
[17] Gray, *Agriculture in the Southern U. S.*, I, 311.
[18] "Quasi-public" is the term used by Gray to define these company-managed plantations to distinguish them clearly from private plantations.
[19] *Ibid.*, pp. 315–21.

tobacco crop provided a quick and cheap mode of transportation for shipping servants. And the colonists were easily provided with the means for the wholesale importation of whites,[20] since tobacco instead of specie was readily accepted as payment for their transportation.

To these economic and physical aids to importing English laborers, the leaders of the company and later the colonial and home governments lent active and meaningful support. To get the movement started and to insure its continued flow, they created the unique reward of the "head-right." By this means, anyone transporting a person—including himself—to the New World was entitled to receive fifty acres of land free for each individual taken across. This head-right could be obtained not only by contracting in Europe for an indentured servant and sending him over, but merely by paying for the passage of someone who had already arrived by ship in Virginia without prior contract.[21]

The colonials evolved a full legal code that gave ample protection to the rights of the servant, just as much as to those of the master. Their system of indentured labor was in fact based on English apprenticeship and vagrancy laws and was clearly recognizable to all and was respected by all parties.[22] It was a system easily understood by the English laborer, and one to which he was perfectly willing to adapt himself, especially given the possible opportunities of advancement in Virginia as compared to the miserable economic conditions in England.

England during this period was stricken by severe unemployment and economic dislocations brought on during the Elizabethan period. Under Elizabethan laws an apprenticeship was needed for the practice of any trade, and all not so employed were required to labor in husbandry. With the dislocations of large numbers of yeomen under the enclosures and with the development through these apprenticeship laws of a small and jealous artisan class, the vast majority of workers was thrown into a perpetual and degrading enslavement to

[20] Bruce, *Economic History*, I, 620–21.
[21] *Ibid.*, I, 512–16.
[22] Gray, *Agriculture in the Southern U. S.*, I, 342–43.

agriculture. Nor did the wages of these agricultural laborers keep pace with rising food prices in the seventeenth century. Given these harsh economic conditions, only aggravated by the stringency of the poor and vagrancy laws, the rural population of England represented a ready pool of emigrant labor for the New World.[23] In fact, for the English laborer, thus able to sell his labor in a sellers' market such as Virginia and be immediately transported as well, it was indeed a bargain of which he quickly took advantage. It has been estimated that by the fourth decade of the century 1,500 to 2,000 indentured servants were coming to Virginia annually—a rate that was maintained for most of the century.[24]

As some authorities have noted, the system that developed— of transporting thousands of laborers across the Atlantic to be sold on the local labor market for whatever they might bring—much resembled the slave trade in its harshness.[25] And the complete surrender of the bondsman's labor to the individual master for a specified number of years and his employment during that time appeared similar to the conditions of the subsequent slave regime. But in reality nothing could be more inaccurate than equating these two labor systems. The underlying assumptions of the indenture system were that a wilderness needed populating by Englishmen, that a trained group of tobacco cultivators were needed to insure large scale production, and the quickest and cheapest way for this to be accomplished was for the English laborer to sell freely his labor for a number of years and to serve a kind of apprenticeship. Although he was forced to act as a bondsman with no control over the use of his labor, the indentured servant was learning the trade of tobacco cultivation. The main assumption was that when this apprenticeship was over, he would become a coequal member of the white society with the possibility not only of owning land but also, if he was economically successful, of rising to a prominent position in the

[23] Bruce, *Economic History*, I, 576–81; Jernegan, *Laboring and Dependent Classes*, pp. 46–47.
[24] Wertenbaker, *Planters of Colonial Virginia*, pp. 32, 35.
[25] See especially Jernegan, *Laboring and Dependent Classes*, pp. 50–51.

colonial society; then he in turn could act the master craftsman and employ indentured servants.[26]

The Virginia legislature, partly conscious of these goals but more clearly concerned with maintaining an adequate supply of laborers, had to make many concessions to these incoming indentured Englishmen, for this was labor contracted by free choice in the majority of cases and to challenge their rights would be to threaten the free flow of servants. Thus from 1619 on, it created a clear and impartial code to insure the indentured white from all kinds of fraudulent dealings and to protect him and his traditional rights as an Englishman before Virginia law.[27] Except for the rights others possessed to his labor, the indentured servant was considered a legal personality equal in almost all respects to a freedman of the colony, and his relationship to the master was one of a contract between equals.[28] Thus a contract was assumed, no matter what the circumstances of entrance into indenture were. The courts and custom thus guaranteed that one's labor could be sold only for a specified number of years—usually five—either by written contract in England or upon arrival in Virginia without prior indentures. The master was required by law to provide certain minimums of food, clothing, and shelter, and at the expiration of the term of servitude he had to provide "freedom dues." The whole basis of these freedom dues was that the indentured servant was to be provided with the most elementary necessities, aside from anything he might

---

[26] John Codman Hurd, *The Law of Freedom and Bondage in the United States* (2 vols.; New York: D. Van Nostrand, 1858–62), I, 218–20.

[27] Oscar and Mary Handlin, "Origins of the Southern Labor System," *William and Mary Quarterly*, 3d Series, VII (April, 1950), 210–11.

[28] James Curtis Ballagh, *White Servitude in the Colony of Virginia* (Baltimore: Johns Hopkins Press, 1895), pp. 44–45. It is interesting to note that in later years, when he did not form as important a part of the labor scene as previously, the indentured servant actually lost some of his rights and privileges. Ballagh claims that "the relation of master and servant was first a relation between legal persons, based on contract, and that such property right as existed consisted in the master's right to the labor and services of his servant, while the servant enjoyed a reciprocal right to support and, to some extent, to protection and instruction from his master. . . ." The conception of property gradually grew at the expense of that of personality, however, and many rights of the indentured servant came to be restricted, although he still was not reduced to the status of a slave. *Ibid.*, pp. 67–68.

previously have possessed or acquired, for undertaking life as a freedman in the colony. Thus the dues, which were liable to the indentured by law, usually consisted of clothing, corn, a gun, and sometimes fifty acres of land.[29]

While the price of tobacco remained high, there was always the strong likelihood that the indentured servant could hope to achieve some type of economic prosperity and land ownership in the colony. Although the Virginians were unable to maintain the luxury prices that had been paid for Spanish tobacco and the price continued to drop despite all attempts at upholding the market, the margin of profit, prior to the Restoration, was large enough to enable the new freedman to establish his economic independence.[30] A strong yeomanry easily developed during the period from the close of the company rule to the enthronement of Charles II, for during this entire period the price of tobacco never fell below a profitable rate, save in the depression years of 1638–39.[31] But while this Virginia white yeomanry played a part in the economic life of the colony, the political and economic control was almost exclusively vested in planter leadership—only a few of whose members ever sprang from the ranks of the indentured.

The colonial leadership had its roots in the very groups in England that had always had the greatest stake in the colony, the English mercantile classes.[32] Almost all of the major planter

[29] *Ibid.*, p. 46; Jernegan, *Laboring and Dependent Classes*, pp. 46, 54. It also seems to have been common practice for masters to allow their indentured servants—who never lost their property rights as did slaves—to acquire property for their freedom even while in their service. Thus, wrote John Hammond in 1656, "there is no Master almost but will allow his Servant a parcell of clear ground to plant some Tobacco in for himself, . . . which in time of Shipping he may lay out for commodities, and in Summer sell them again with advantage, and get a Sow-Pig or two, which . . . his Master suffer him to keep them with his own . . . and with one year's increase of them may purchase a Cow-Calf or two and by that time he is for himself." John Hammond, *Leah and Rachel, or the Two Fruitful Sisters Virginia and Mary-land* (London: T. Mabb, 1656), as reprinted in Peter Force, *Tracts and Other Papers, Relating Principally to the Origin, Settlement, and Progress of the Colonies in North America* (Washington: Printed by W. Q. Force, 1836–46), Vol. III, No. 14, p. 14.

[30] Wertenbaker, *Planters of Colonial Virginia*, pp. 72, 75.

[31] *Ibid.*, p. 82; Gray, *Agriculture in the Southern U. S.*, I, 263.

[32] Thomas J. Wertenbaker, *Patrician and Plebeian in Virginia, or the Origin and Development of the Social Classes in the Old Dominion* (Virginia: By the author, 1910), pp. 2–3.

families who had such extensive control over Virginia life derived from English merchants and traders or were intimately connected with them. The famous Byrd family came from humble artisan and trader beginnings, and its noted Virginia members throughout the century were not only prominent planters but active traders as well. Another leader of the Virginia "aristocracy" was William Fitzhugh, who was a trader of longstanding before becoming a planter.[33] "In fact there was hardly a family of social and political importance in the first century of the colony which did not have some kind of a connection with commerce."[34]

A good many additions to the colonial aristocracy came from English merchants who emigrated, especially during the periods of conflict at home. With their capital and their connections in the colony, such Englishmen quickly found themselves justices, burgesses, or even councilors, and firm members of the economic and political elite.[35] The absence of family connections or even of a mercantile background, however, never really impeded any individual who could make a "success in creating a plantation," which was the universally recognized standard for admission into the colonial leadership.[36]

The wealth attained by this class during the seventeenth century was indeed impressive. Robert Beverley, who died about 1686, left an estate valued at £3,700, and the first William Byrd achieved an even greater fortune. P. A. Bruce has estimated from county records that there were fifty to one-

---

[33] John Spencer Bassett, "The Relation between the Virginia Planter and the London Merchant," *American Historical Association, Annual Report, 1901,* I (Washington: Government Printing Office, 1902), 556–58.

[34] *Ibid.,* I, 561.

[35] Wertenbaker, *Patrician and Plebeian,* pp. 60–61.

[36] Stanley Elkins and Eric McKitrick, "Institutions and the Law of Slavery: The Dynamics of Unopposed Capitalism," *American Quarterly,* IX (Spring, 1957), 14–15. One irate gentleman reported around 1680 that: "Many who were of mean education and obscure original beggars in their native soil, have by their drudging industry since their arrival in this country attained to something of estate. The gross fancies of such cloudy-pated persons will by reason of their invincible ignorance misplace their esteem on a tailor, smith, shoemaker or the like necessary handicraftsmen, courting such a one with their utmost art and skill, when a scholar shall but be condemned and happily set at naught." From the *Life of Thomas Hellier,* quoted in Bruce, *Economic History,* II, 410 n.

hundred planters at the close of the century whose estates equalled, if they did not exceed, $50,000.[37]

As early as 1696, in his report to the Board of Trade, Edward Randolph claimed that almost all the valuable land of the colony had been preempted, often illegally, by the colonial planter leadership.[38] William Fitzhugh alone possessed some 50,000 acres of land, and there were many others who possessed equal and greater amounts of the choicest virgin soil. It has been estimated that members of this planter aristocracy possessed at the very least 5,000 acres of land each.[39] Nor was there any dearth of planters who possessed that other means of wealth, which after the middle of the century became so essential to success—the Negro slave. In the last decades of the century Mrs. Elizabeth Digges owned 108 Negro slaves—an impressive figure in any period of antebellum Virginia—while John Carter had 106, Ralph Wormely 91, and Robert Beverley 42.[40]

Although by the end of the seventeenth century the African Negro slave made up the bulk of the labor force on the Virginia tobacco plantations, his position for many years after his admittance into the colony was of an ambiguous nature, and his number remained few for some time. Whatever may have been the desire of Virginians for Negro laborers, the source of supply for a good part of the century was under the control of the rival Portuguese and Dutch, who held almost all the factories along the West African coast and excluded the English altogether. The first Negroes brought to Virginia in 1619 were in fact actually pirated from the Spanish in the West

[37] *Ibid.*, II, 254–55, and this is in 1896 U. S. currency.
[38] He claimed: ". . . the members of the Council and others, who make an interest in the Government have from time to time procured grants of very large Tracts of land, so that there has not for many years been any waste land to be taken up by those who bring with them servants, or by such Servants, who have served their time faithfully with their Masters, but it is taken up and ingrossed beforehand, whereby they are forced to hyer and pay a yearly rent for some of these Lands, or go to the utmost bounds of the Colony for Land, . . ." Quoted in Wertenbaker, *Planters of Colonial Virginia*, pp. 141–42.
[39] Bruce, *Economic History*, II, 252–53.
[40] *Ibid.*, II, 88 n.

Indies by a Dutch privateer who was probably in league with Englishmen.[41]

Because of this outside control of the slave trade, the importation of Negroes into Virginia got off to a slow start. Between 1619 and 1624, only twenty-three were brought into the colony. The first Negroes to come directly from Africa were brought in about 1630 by the English privateer, the "Fortune," which had intercepted a slaver just off the Angola coast and had brought the cargo directly to Virginia. In 1623 came the first head-right made out for the importation of a Negro, and by 1640 there were some 300 in the population. From the 1640's to the Restoration, the Dutch had been able to acquire a very large share of the carrying trade of the colony, and they also became its chief supplier of Negro slaves.[42]

It was to break this near monopoly, both in the carrying trade of slaves and in the control over African sources of supply, that the Royal African Company was formed in 1662.[43] But then individual adventurers took over the slave trade, excluding the Dutch, and thus the African Company's influence was not felt until the last decades of the century. By 1671 there were 2,000 Negro slaves in the colony with yearly importations rising steadily.[44] The disturbances in the last years of this decade, however, brought the trade almost to a standstill.[45] With internal peace and prosperity returning to the colony in the 1680's, the slave population mounted to 3,000 Negroes out of a total population of close to 70,000.[46] The New Englanders became increasingly involved in the trade at this time, but after 1682 the Royal African Company finally came to dominate the scene. With regular dispatch,

---

[41] Wertenbaker, *Planters of Colonial Virginia*, pp. 66, 125–26.
[42] Bruce, *Economic History*, II, 70, 73–76.
[43] *Ibid.*, II, 77.
[44] Quoted from the report of Governor Berkeley in William W. Hening (ed.), *The Statutes at Large: being a collection of All the Laws of Virginia from the first session of the Legislature in the year 1619* (13 vols.; Richmond: Samuel Pleasents, 1819–1923), II, 514.
[45] Bruce, *Economic History*, II, 79.
[46] Evarts B. Greene and Virginia D. Harrington, *American Population before the Federal Census of 1790* (New York: Columbia University Press, 1932), p. 137, taken from an estimate of Governor Culpepper.

slaves now began arriving from the British West Indies and from Africa, and by the 1690's they had become the most important single group listed for head-rights.[47]

So numerous had the slave population become by the last years of the century that planters were no longer solely dependent upon foreign importations, and the beginnings of an internal slave trade can already be noted before the end of the century. By the 1680's a stock of Negroes had finally been built up who were native-born Virginians, and William Fitzhugh in 1688 maintained that almost all of the Negro slaves who cultivated his plantations had been born in Virginia.[48] As their numbers and importance in the economy had increased during the seventeenth century, so had their value; a prime Negro hand in the middle decades cost about £20, but by the last years of the century the price had risen to £30 and, in some instances, even as high as £50.[49] This price rise continued almost uninterruptedly for the next two centuries. By the middle of the eighteenth century the prices for imported Africans were averaging from £30 to £35 and those for prime domestic slaves from £40 to £60. By the end of the colonial period, the prices for raw blacks had risen to an average of £40 to £50, and for prime domestic field hands, to an average of £50 to £80. Thus by the time of the American Revolution slave prices had tripled. By the 1850's, prime male slaves were selling in Virginia for $1,200 to $1,300, or for almost five times their late seventeenth century prices.[50]

Under the impact of these prices, slave importations were constantly expanding. Thus the tempo begun by the last part of the seventeenth century was not only maintained, but was strongly increased in the eighteenth century. For not only was tobacco now bringing in the needed capital to finance slave importation, but British expansion into the slave trade now made England the prime supplier of slaves, and the number of Negroes imported became dependent only upon the ability of the market to absorb them. Given the rapid increase of the

[47] Bruce, *Economic History*, II, 82–83, 85.
[48] *Ibid.*, II, 87–88.
[49] *Ibid.*, II, 87–92.
[50] Gray, *Agriculture in the Southern U. S.*, I, 369, II, 665.

tobacco industry, despite a rather severe series of depressions in the eighteenth century, the number of Negroes in Virginia rose at an extraordinarily rapid rate. By 1700 there were 6,000 slaves reported in the colony. By 1708 the figure had risen to 12,000, and it was reported that 3,000 of these had been imported between 1705 and 1708. Within another seven years the number of slaves had almost doubled, and by 1742 there were 42,000 slaves in the colony. This figure was more than doubled in the next decade, for by the late 1750's there were well over 100,000 Negroes in Virginia. By the 1780's this figure had phenomenally doubled again, and by the first federal census of 1790, there were over 292,000 slaves in the newly created state of Virginia.[51]

Along with this tremendous increase in absolute numbers, the eighteenth century had also seen the very rapid percentage increase of the colored population. Representing 24% of the total population in 1715, the Negroes accounted for 41% of the total by 1756.[52] But this percentage growth quickly leveled out, despite the tremendous expansion of slave importations, with an equally heavy importation of free white colonists. Thus by 1790 the total was still 41% of the population, and this figure never rose higher than 43% in 1820–30 throughout the rest of the nineteenth century. In fact, the percentage actually declined, despite the growth in absolute terms of the colored class, to a low of 34% in 1860.[53]

Without question, the major occupation of the overwhelming majority of Negro slaves in the colonial period was tobacco production. Virginia had, in this period, a truly exploitive monoproduction economy, which produced little beyond the most elemental needs and devoted all its time and energy to the production of one raw material, tobacco.[54] What skilled

[51] Greene and Harrington, *American Population*, pp. 139–41, 154–55.

[52] Gray, *Agriculture in the Southern U. S.*, I, 355.

[53] U.S., Bureau of the Census, *Negro Population 1790–1915* (Washington: Government Printing Office, 1918), p. 51, Table 5.

[54] The Virginia planter Robert Beverley wrote in 1705 of the complete lack of home manufactures of even the most elemental kind despite an abundance of natural resources: "They have their Clothing of all sorts from *England*, as Linnen, Woollen, Silk, Hats, and Leather, Yet Flax, and Hemp grow no where in the World, better than there; their sheep yield a mighty increase, and bear good Fleeces, but they shear them only to cool

labor was performed in this plantation-dominated economy was done largely by white artisans who had been imported in large numbers into the colony from the very first years and who continued to dominate the skilled trades right through the colonial period.[55] Thus to labor in tobacco, for which reason they had been enslaved in the first place, was the lot assigned to the mass of Virginia Negroes, and what a monotonous task it was.

The cultivation of tobacco, either orinoko or sweet-scented, involved a long, painstaking routine. The seed had to be sown in early winter, around the middle of January, in specially prepared beds of mould, while the fields themselves were broken and laid off by shallow furrows into hills some four feet apart. When the carefully prepared seedlings had reached a certain height they were taken from the mould beds, usually during or just after an April, May, or June rain, and transplanted in the fields. Once laid out in these hills, the plants needed a steady repetition of hoeings and plowings to keep them free from weeds and to keep the soil loose. Then came the even more tedious jobs of topping each plant when a specified number of leaves had been grown to prevent further growth; removing the sucklers growing at the base of the leaf stems; and examining the leaves periodically for horn worms. When the crop began to turn yellow it was necessary to cut the stalks close to the ground, to wilt the leaves, and finally to cure them in tobacco houses. In the curing, each stalk with its leaves had to be pegged at a specified distance from its neighbor. The pegged tobacco was then air cured for a period of five to six weeks or more, and on an appropriately moist day, the leaves were stripped, made into "hands," and

them. . . . The very Furrs that their Hats are made of, perhaps go first from thence; and most of their Hides lie and rot, or are made use of, only for covering dry Goods, in a leaky House. . . . Nay, they are such abominable Ill-husbands, that tho' their Country be over-run with Wood, yet they have all their Wooden Ware from *England;* their Cabinets, Chairs, Tables, Stools, Chests, Boxes, Cart-Weels, and all other things, even so much as their Bowls, and Birchen Brooms. . . ." Robert Beverley, *The History and Present State of Virginia,* ed. Louis Wright (Chapel Hill: University of North Carolina Press, 1947), p. 295.

[55] Bruce, *Economic History,* II, 400–405.

put into hogsheads. Often by this time a new crop was being prepared for planting, and the routine began again. What spare time was left to the Negro work gangs in this year round routine was given to clearing new fields. This was especially important and difficult since a field was planted in tobacco on an average of only once in three years, and new fields had constantly to be hacked out of the heavily forested tracts that surrounded the old fields. The gangs were also put to tending subsidiary crops, building hogsheads, mending fences, and so forth.[56]

The plantation worked primarily by Negro slaves was already in existence by the last decades of the seventeenth century. There were the Negro quarters, the work gangs, and the white overseers.[57] With a ready pool of white labor available to the planter, there was no need to rely upon the Negro for either plantation management or for work in the skilled trades. The overwhelming number of overseers were drawn from the class of newly freed white indentured servants. As a rule, they were paid a percentage of the tobacco produced, a system that the Virginians eventually found to be hard both on the land and on the Negroes. For the larger the volume the greater the overseer's return, and there was no need or desire for him to conserve anything. In spite of the obvious evils of this system, however, it was not until the 1830's that the salary scheme was finally adopted by tobacco planters.[58]

Before the 1830's, the Negroes were worked in both the gang and task systems. For preparing the fields and planting, the Negroes usually worked in gangs of ten or more with a driver who set the pace. For specialized labor, such as stripping and prizing tobacco, the task system was adopted. This was a type of piece work whereby a slave was assigned a given

[56] Ulrich Bonnell Phillips, *American Negro Slavery, A Survey of the Supply, Employment, and Control of Negro Labor as determined by the Plantation Regime* (New York: D. Appleton and Co., 1929), pp. 82–83; Bruce, *Economic History*, I, 438–42. For the nineteenth-century modifications of these planting and harvesting patterns see Joseph Clarke Robert, *The Tobacco Kingdom, Plantation, Market, and Factory in Virginia and North Carolina, 1800–1860* (Durham: Duke University Press, 1938), chap. 3.
[57] Bruce, *Economic History*, II, 106.
[58] *Ibid.*, II, 47, 429–30; Robert, *Tobacco Kingdom*, p. 23.

amount to accomplish in a day depending on his ability. To help determine the ability of the field slaves, they were divided into such categories as full-hands, three-quarter hands, half- and quarter-hands, and an appropriate task was assigned to each.[59]

Although the drivers apparently worked with the gangs and set the pace, rather than standing behind and whipping them on, all failures to complete a task or fully to participate in the gangs would be punished by whipping at the end of the day. Nor were hours particularly shorter than on the Cuban plantations, for it has been estimated that at harvest time the average plantation slave worked from 15 to 16 hours, sometimes including Sundays.[60] Although tobacco labor was not as onerous as sugar production, the Virginia field laborer was in a far inferior position even to the toiling cane cutter of Cuba. For unlike the Cuban fieldworker, he worked a heavier schedule with far less diversions. By and large field Negroes did not accompany their masters to religious services; this was a privilege primarily for house servants. Instead, they used their Sundays as a day of total rest.[61] For aside from these Sundays, the Virginia slave had only three to four other holidays in the entire year—three days for Christmas and usually one day after the harvest.[62] In contrast, the Cuban field hand had 23 holidays other than Sundays, many of which were occasions for heavy feasting and drinking. And without private produce plots guaranteed them nor the right to sell their resulting production to local merchants, the field hands in Virginia were denied the power to obtain a host of private possessions that might enable them to evade the rigidity of plantation diet and regimented existence. Nor, of course, had they the legal right to buy their freedom.

Even the possibility of escape was severely limited for the

---

[59] Gray, *Agriculture in the Southern U. S.*, I, 550 ff. It seems that the nineteenth-century wheat plantations adopted a modified form of the gang labor system for working their slaves.

[60] *Ibid.*, I, 557.

[61] Philip Vickers Fithian, *Journal and Letters of Philip Vickers Fithian 1773-1774* (Williamsburg: Colonial Williamsburg, Inc., 1957), p. 203.

[62] Gray, *Agriculture in the Southern U. S.*, I, 557.

plantation slave. Virginia was densely forested like Cuba but, unlike the latter, it had a cold and harsh climate and was largely infested with hostile Indians who made no distinctions between slave or freedman. With the coast heavily populated and with the Indians and the frontiersmen controlling the forests, the plantation slave was in a true sense landlocked. It was virtually impossible for him to form fugitive slave villages in Virginia, and without these villages, which could provide shelter, he was incapable of surviving a winter in the forest. Here were no wild fruits to pick off the trees, or cattle and hogs to capture easily. Here was no semi-tropical climate the year round that allowed a fugitive to survive successfully even without shelter. Because of this, the slaves who did escape usually remained in the immediate vicinity of their plantations and lived by simply stealing their necessities from the stores of the local estate. For this reason, the records of Virginia time and again speak of escaped slaves as "Outlying Slaves," that is escaped slaves who were pilfering from and maintaining themselves near the white settlements and plantations. Typically, a law of 1705 claimed that "many times, slaves run away and lie out, hid and lurking in the swamps, woods and other obscure places, killing hogs and committing other injuries to the inhabitants. . . ."[63] A typical case history of a fugitive slave in Virginia was that of a Negro named Billy

[who] has severall years unlawfully absented himselfe from his masters services, lying out and lurking in obscure places supposed within the countys of James City, York and New-Kent, devouring and destroying stocks and crops, robing the houses of and committing and threatening other injuryes to severall of his majestyes good and liege people. . . .[64]

There was no mention of slave communities, of cimarrones, or of other than outlying slaves and simple runaways in the records of Virginia. Nor could the rural slave find haven in the cities or among the free colored classes. For major towns did not develop until late in the slave period, and the free

[63] Hening, *Statutes at Large*, III, 460.
[64] *Ibid.*, III, 210.

colored class was small and conspicuous and was carefully isolated and thoroughly controlled through a tight registration and pass system. Thus because of the two inhospitable barriers of forest and the seacoast, the lack of towns, and the isolation of the free colored community, the problem of runaways and fugitive slaves never approached the magnitude that it did in Cuba nor was the same impact felt on the normal functioning of the slave regime.

Thus the Virginia field hand saw the world in a vertical hierarchy—a precise hierarchy consisting of field hands, drivers, artisans, house servants, and finally overseers and masters. Rewards, punishments, and opportunities all came from above. Although this pattern also existed for the Cuban plantation slave, there was in addition another dimension, extending horizontally, that encompassed the church, towns, local merchants, holidays, private property, and even the cimarron villages. And there was as well the awareness of the existence of a majority of coloreds, both slaves and free, who were not even bound by the rigid plantation—big house complex. For sugar estates were interspersed with coffee plantations and were surrounded in the outlying regions by cattle ranches, and near the towns were a great variety of produce farms, and everywhere along the rivers were the small tobacco farmers. Virginia on the other hand, tended to aggregate its tobacco plantations in one area, primarily because of the special soil conditions. And even when small farms were scattered among the great estates, they were farms of poor whites whose attitude, if anything, tended to support the isolation of the plantation Negroes. There were no other major occupations for the Negro, and almost two-thirds would be found on the plantations from the development of the system until 1860.

√ Although opportunity for the non-field hands was somewhat greater, it was not significantly different from that of the field hands. Any skills that the Negro was allowed to acquire were intimately tied up with tobacco production, and although as early as the seventeenth century records show numerous Negro mechanics, these were primarily carpenters and coopers —the trades essential for making hogsheads. That the train-

ing received by these Negroes fitted them merely for the
crudest and most elemental tasks is seen from the fact that
large slaveholders like Byrd and Fitzhugh continued to
import English artisans at very heavy expense right through
the seventeenth century, men whose skills were similar to
those in which some of their own slaves had been trained.[65]
Nor did the colony as a whole ever lack a white artisan group.
Although the majority of them, unlike their English compa-
triots, devoted themselves to the production of tobacco and
became planters as well as artisans, this class of free artisans
survived and prospered despite the influx of cheap Negro
labor.[66]

In the period between the American Revolution and the
War of 1812, many plantations were temporarily forced into
becoming self-sustaining economies, but the post-1812 period
saw an even greater return to the simple monoproduction of
a staple crop and the wholesale importation of manufactured
goods for all the luxuries and many of the necessities of
plantation life, including the clothes and food for the slaves
themselves.[67] Thus the skilled plantation artisan, between the
competition of local white artisans and the importation of
manufactured goods, was left only a small area of skills, these
being associated with house construction and the immediate
packaging and handling of the staple crop.

In fact, only the house servants, who were associated closely
with the white family's separate economic and social life, had
the possibility of breaking out of the confined world of the
plantation. In the big house, skills were often well rewarded,
and faithful service could lead to substantial improvement
in daily living. Here, too, there was the possibility for an education, for better food, clothing, shelter, and religion. Here,
too, was the possibility for manumission. It is interesting to
observe in all the records of manumission how often a planter
on his death would free only a half-dozen or so of his several
hundred slaves, and these were almost always house servants.

[65] *Bruce, Economic History,* II, 403, 405.
[66] *Ibid.,* II, 410, 418.
[67] Gray, *Agriculture in the Southern U. S.,* I, 453 ff.

Thus for example, in the will of William Byrd, dated February 5, 1777, the planter declared:

Tis my earnest desire that my faithful servant Jack White, be set free on the Death of my beloved wife, for he has not only been the best of servants to me but on different occasions saved me from the grave.[68]

And in 1740 the widow Judith Butts requested that her executors "sett free a female Slave named Lilly, on Account of several very acceptable Services done by her Said Judith."[69]

But despite all of these rewards and possibilities, the house servant had to conform to the pattern established by the master, and in this pattern initiative and self-reliance were not the rewarded qualities. Whereas these qualities in a Cuban Negro could easily lead to escape from the system, in a Virginia slave they led to whipping and worse, if they were not curbed. For in the world of the plantation, the master and his conceptions dominated, and conformity to them was the only hope of survival.[70]

This pattern of North American plantation life was neither confined to tidewater Virginia nor to tobacco production. Once fully established in the late seventeenth and eighteenth centuries, the pattern, with minor adjustments, was repeated throughout Virginia and the rest of the South, for cotton and sugar as well as for tobacco. Thus, while the geographic settlement and the particular patterns of the plantation system and tobacco production began to change at the end of the eighteenth century, the basic patterns described above remained the same.

The changes that occurred within the Virginian economy in the late colonial and early national period were primarily due to geographic expansion and soil exhaustion. As the frontier moved beyond the navigable rivers and settlement

---

[68] *Virginia Magazine of History and Biography,* IX (1901–2), 88.
[69] *Ibid.,* XV (1907–8), 130.
[70] For a fuller discussion of these issues of planter-servant relationships see Kenneth M. Stampp, *The Peculiar Institution, Slavery in the Ante-Bellum South* (New York: Alfred A. Knopf, 1963), pp. 337–38; and Stanley M. Elkins, *Slavery, A Problem in American Institutional and Intellectual Life* (Chicago: University of Chicago Press, 1959), pp. 133 ff.

proceeded beyond the mountains, the Tidewater pattern of settlement and communication was balanced by the growth of a vital hinterland. The terminal ports of the rivers now became distribution and trading centers for the upland planters who could not ship directly from their own docks. Along with the development of the upriver ports came the growth of the crucial intermediate Piedmont region, which after the creation of the republic achieved great economic and social importance in the economy and society of Virginia. Finally, beyond the Piedmont stood the frontier, which rapidly spread beyond the western mountains. Settled largely by native-born Americans or immigrant farmers coming south from Pennsylvania, the tramontane frontier had an entirely new economy based on corn, wheat, and other general agricultural non-plantation crops. But the intermediate Piedmont region tended to reproduce the plantation system of the Tidewater, and in almost all respects it tended to merge into the previously predominant region.[71]

Soil exhaustion in the Tidewater and the continued fall of tobacco prices encouraged the growth of corn and, especially, wheat, and furthered the general diversification of crops even on the plantations, but neither the plantation system nor tobacco production was abandoned or lost its dominant position in the state. The tobacco-growing center was shifted to the Piedmont; and after a temporary setback around the period of the Revolutionary War, tobacco completely recovered its former position and by the last decades before the Civil War was a thriving industry. This new growth was due

[71] On the social and economic cohesiveness of Piedmont and Tidewater society, see Carl Bridenbaugh, *Myths and Realities, Societies of the Colonial South* (Baton Rouge: Louisiana State University Press, 1952), chap. 1. For its contrast to frontier society, see *ibid.*, chap. 3. On the political cohesiveness of the new Piedmont area and its adoption to the planter oligarchy that had been established in the Tidewater in the seventeenth and early eighteenth century see Charles S. Sydnor, *Gentleman Freeholders, Political Practices in Washington's Virginia* (Williamsburg: Institute of Early American History and Culture, 1952). Although Brown and Brown have recently challenged the picture presented by Sydnor, his position is still essentially a correct one. See Robert E. Brown and B. Katherine Brown, *Virginia 1705–1786: Democracy or Aristocracy?* (East Lansing: Michigan State University Press, 1964).

both to a more scientific attitude toward soil management
and to the introduction of new strains of tobacco. Thus
despite the spread of tobacco production to several western
states and the turning of many fields to corn, wheat, and other
crops, Virginia was still the largest producer of tobacco in the
nation right through the nineteenth century until the Civil
War.[72]

The Tidewater planters, even though they had often
switched to corn and wheat, still maintained the large plantation slave-labor system.[73] That the plantation system remained
intact is indicated by the distribution and ownership of slaves
in Virginia. By the 1770's, slavery was largely centered in the
Tidewater and Piedmont regions,[74] and this pattern remained
unchanged up to emancipation. If anything, the plantation
system had been further entrenched as the size of the slave
labor force constantly increased and the number of slave owners constantly decreased in the years between 1790 and 1860.
In 1790 there were 292,627 slaves in Virginia—more than
double the number of slaves in any other state of the union—
and 34,026 slave owners, who represented 7.6% of the white
population. In 1860, Virginia still had the largest number of
slaves in the union, this time 490,865, but the number of slave
owners was now 55,063, and they represented only 0.5% of
the white population.[75]

This seventy-year period also showed an actual increase of
the number of slaves involved in the plantation system. Thus,
according to L. C. Gray, slaves were considered to be part of

[72] Gray, *Agriculture in the Southern U. S.*, II, 757–58, 919–20; Robert,
Tobacco Kingdom, chaps. 2, 8.
[73] Gray, *Agriculture in the Southern U. S.*, II, 921–22. There are strong
grounds for belief that aside from raising non-tobacco crops like wheat and
corn, the Tidewater plantations also carried on a thriving business of slave
breeding and were able successfully to maintain their economic advantage
and the large plantation pattern. See Frederic Bancroft, *Slave-Trading in the
Old South* (Baltimore: J. H. Furst Company, 1931), especially chap. 4; and
Alfred H. Conrad and John R. Meyer, *The Economics of Slavery and Other
Studies in Econometric History* (Chicago: Aldine Publishing Co., 1964),
pp. 43 ff.
[74] For the geographic distribution of slaves in the eighteenth century, see
the population map drawn by Brown and Brown, *Virginia 1705–1786*, p. 73.
[75] U. S. Bureau of the Census, *A Century of Population Growth* . . .
1790–1909 (Washington: Government Printing Office, 1909), p. 135.

the plantation system if they were held in lots of ten or more under one owner.[76] By this definition, some 72% of the slaves in 1790 were thus involved in the plantation regime. In 1860 this figure had risen to close to 73%, and the median average slaveholding was 18.8 slaves. That is, approximately one-half of the slaves were held in parcels of 18.8 slaves or over! And in the tobacco regions of the Tidewater and Piedmont, median holdings were even higher. Thus in 1860 in the middle-Virginia tobacco region, the median holding of slaves was 24, and in the south central tobacco area, it was 28.[77]

All of this is in sharp contrast to the Cuban experience. Here it appears that the vast amount of slaves were held in small parcels and that no more than half of them, even in the middle decades of the nineteenth century, were held on large gang-labor plantations. In 1830, for example, only some 17% of the Cuban slave force was engaged in sugar plantation agriculture, the figure rising to only 18% in 1846, and even in 1860, a peak year for sugar production, the percentage of slaves in sugar was only some 38% and about 40% to 45% in all plantation crops.

That the plantation system was so predominant in Virginia was probably due not only to the continued dominance of commercial crops like tobacco, but also to the essential lack of urban growth and the lack of alternative economic opportunities for the use of slave labor. Without urbanization there was not only the lack of major urban industries and trades, but also of allied agriculture, particularly truck and produce farming which was an essential industry in Cuba. This is not to say that urban slavery or industrial slave labor did not exist in Virginia, but that its importance was minimal compared to the rural economy and almost negligible compared to plantation slavery. Even despite this minority position of urban and industrial slavery, Virginia was probably unique in the South in the extent of its manufacturing and the use of slaves in industry.

Around the early decades of the nineteenth century, Vir-

[76] Gray, *Agriculture in the Southern U. S.*, I, 481.
[77] *Ibid.*, I, 530–31.

ginia finally turned to the direct manufacture of tobacco products. From very small beginnings, the industry, by the 1850's, had become the most important single industrial complex in the state, which made Virginia the leading tobacco manufacturing state of the union and Richmond the leading city. From the initiation of the industry the tobacco manufacturers wholeheartedly adopted slave labor in their largely urban factories. As the industry rapidly increased, so did its number of slave employees. Thus some 3,342 were employed in 1840, with the number rising to 11,382 by 1860. Of this number, half were hired slaves and about half were owned directly by the manufacturers.[78] At variance with the basic mores of the plantation system, the tobacco manufacturers were uninterested in slave control and discipline and were primarily concerned with production and efficiency. Therefore, they allowed Negro slaves to hire themselves out, and to all hired-out Negroes they paid directly, in cash, the amount needed for their room and board, letting them locate their own housing and food. Slaves were also offered bonuses and other inducements for overtime work and worked under an extremely relaxed form of discipline.

But this pattern was hotly opposed by the majority of whites in Richmond and in the other tobacco-manufacturing towns, who time and again interfered in the relationship between the hired slave and his employer to bring about greater control of the Negroes. In 1858 laws were passed prohibiting the direct payment of room and board money to slaves, and there also occurred several recorded instances in which municipal authorities stepped in to discipline slave employees whom factory owners refused to condemn. In fact, these outside governmental authorities often deliberately interceded between manufacturing owner and slave to maintain the black-white standards that these owners had allowed to slacken in the name of economic efficiency. By the last years of the slave regime, free colored, and even more importantly, free white females, successfully began to compete with

[78] Robert, *Tobacco Kingdom*, pp. 161–64, 199.

slave labor in tobacco manufacturing.[79]

Furthermore, the famous slave ironworkers, especially those in the Richmond company of the Tredegar Ironworks, represented only a small percentage of the industrial slaves, and most of these colored workers were under skilled white artisanal direction, making the crews half slave and half free white. Nor were their total numbers very great, for Tredegar employed only 60 or so slaves in 1860. There was also heavy use made of slaves in the western coal mines and in all the coastal shipping and fishing trade.[80] But all of these areas of slave labor were constantly opposed by immigrant and native white workers, who placed strong pressure on the community to oppose industrial slave labor, and who more often than not succeeded in driving slave labor from their fields of competition.

Finally, and most importantly of all, urban slavery, even at its height in 1860, accounted for only 7% of the total slave labor force of the state. Even compared to the Virginia whites, some 12% of whom were found in Virginia's towns and cities, this was a very small percentage. Equally important was the fact that even within the cities of the state, the colored population was quite small. Thus Richmond, the heaviest manufacturing town and the largest city of the state, being twice the size of its nearest rival, had a colored population which represented only 38% of the total urban population. Of the four other towns in the state with populations over 10,000, Norfolk had only 30% colored, Alexandria 22%, and Wheeling, a town of over 14,000, had only 97 colored persons. Only Petersburg, with some 18,000 population in 1860 had a large colored population, being in this case half of the total population.[81] In Cuba, on the other hand, the colored

[79] *Ibid.*, pp. 203–8.
[80] Kathleen Bruce, *Virginia Iron Manufacture in the Slave Era* (New York: The Century Company, 1930), chap. 6.
[81] The comparative urbanization of the two societies is clearly revealed by the statistics. Using the data from 1855 (Cuba) and 1860 (Virginia), respectively, the number of persons living in towns of over 1,000 in Cuba was 309,384, or 30% of the total population, as opposed to only 166,128 persons, or 10% of the total for Virginia. As for major cities, Cuba had four cities over 20,000, the largest being Havana with a very conservatively

population, slave and free, made up 62% of the population of Havana in 1846,[82] and Santiago de Cuba, Bayamo, and the other cities of eastern Cuba had an even larger percentage of colored.

This meant that in every town of Virginia, the white urban classes were able to single out and isolate the urban colored population, to break down their social cohesion, and to control their nonworking habits—in short to control their actions as much as possible and make them conform to the more accepted pattern of rural slavery. Hiring out, living out, the right to self-purchase, religious brotherhoods, and a vigorous social existence were all accepted as the inevitable consequences of skilled urban slavery in Cuba, but in America the environment proved hostile to these conditions.

Time and again, masters found that slaves in the cities were difficult to handle and to control in the same manner as they had been in the countryside. In the cities they sometimes lived outside the home of the master, consorted with other slaves and colored freedmen, drank to excess, and were open to all types of outside influences. Nor could constant whipping and other restraints be used as readily in the cities as in the rural sections, and this made it difficult for the masters to enforce discipline and, in general, to prevent the emergence of an independence of spirit that was simply intolerable in preabolitionist Virginia.

Because of the inability of the urban masters to force their slaves into the dominant mold, the Virginia authorities took

estimated 134,952 persons. Virginia in 1860, which had half a million more persons in its total population than Cuba, had only one city of over 20,000, and this was Richmond with only 37,910. Whereas Virginia had only 7% of its slave population in the cities, Cuba in 1855 had 19%. And this percentage for Cuba is unquestionably the lowest in the slave period, since this was the peak of the plantation slavery era and a period when total slave population seems to have been seriously declining. These figures are compiled from José García de Arboleya, Manual de la isla de Cuba. Compendio de su historia, geografia, estadística y administración (2d ed.; Havana: Imprenta del Tiempo, 1859), pp. 120–30; and U. S. Bureau of the Census, Population of the United States in 1860 (Washington: Government Printing Office, 1864), pp. 518–20, Table 3.

[82] Alexander von Humboldt, The Island of Cuba, trans. with notes by J. S. Thrasher (New York: Derby & Jackson, 1856), p. 191.

the unusual step of interfering in the direct relationship between master and slave, a bond that was considered sacred and beyond government interference in the countryside. Thus the municipal governments more and more found themselves whipping and policing the slaves and, in short, controlling their daily lives. A good example of this was the "Ordinance concerning Negroes," which was passed in Richmond in 1857. This urban government ordinance gave the local police powers to curb colored and slave social gatherings, drinking, living out, and in fact every action considered to add independence to the existence of the slave or in any way allow him options unavailable on the plantation.[83]

But even despite these harsh municipal government actions, the urban condition was too liberal for chattel slavery, and in almost every southern city of the nation from 1820 to 1860, slavery seriously declined both in terms of percent and often in absolute numbers. For urban slavery, which was such a recognized and accepted part of the Cuban scene, was totally incapable of surviving in the closed world of the chattel-slave plantation system of North America.[84]

Thus the prime characteristics of Virginia slavery were the dominance of the plantation system and the lack of economic diversity. Faced by the hierarchical and closed system of the plantation and largely confined to unskilled labor, the Virginia Negro was denied self-expression and creativity in every facet of his life. Opposed by white labor and denied the opportunities of an economically diversified economy, the domination of this plantation system left the majority of slaves with abilities and a level of education commensurate only with the unskilled labor of the staple crop economy. A vigorous yeomanry or artisan class was extraneous to this system and was, in fact, a serious danger to the stability and docility of the plantation worker. For the planters, the primary objective was to maintain a docile and efficient labor force. If they often grumbled about slave inefficiency, the planters never-

---

[83] For the code see Richard C. Wade, *Slavery in the Cities, The South 1820–1860* (New York: Oxford University Press, 1964), pp. 106–9.
[84] See *ibid.*, pp. 243 ff.

theless never went out of their way to change the system, to increase the slaves' skills, or to create incentives. As Frederick Law Olmstead observed in the last years of southern slavery, "I begin to suspect that the great trouble and anxiety of Southern gentlemen is—How, without quite destroying the capabilities of the Negro for any work at all, to prevent him from learning to take care of himself."[85]

[85] Frederick Law Olmstead, *A Journey in the Seaboard Slave States, in the Years 1853-1854* (2 vols.; New York: G. P. Putnam's Sons, 1904), I, 64.

PART V. The Freedman as an Indicator of Assimilation

Introduction. Probably the best indication of a society's attitude toward the enslaved peoples within its ranks is the role that the freedman plays within the predominantly slave regime. Is his free status considered a natural occurrence, in no way jeopardizing the status of slavery; is he permitted the economic, social, and even political opportunities afforded men who were born free; is he, in short, accepted into society? How a society treats these problems, will affect not only the number of slaves permitted to escape bondage, but it will also indicate the extent to which a society is willing to integrate the former slave when total emancipation comes for the whole slave population. For the community of freedmen under slavery is a microcosm of what the post-emancipation freedmen society will be. Attitudes and responses built up by the white population towards the community will early determine and condition the response that these upper classes will have toward all freedmen from the day of emancipation onward. In short, the position of the freedmen under slavery is a prime indicator of the pattern of assimilation and the attitude of the white classes to the African Negro within their midst.

9. An Integrated Community:
The Free Colored in Cuba. The most remarkable

aspect of the Cuban slave regime was undoubtedly the tremendous size and importance of the free colored population. As Baron Alexander von Humboldt noted at the beginning of the nineteenth century, the free colored population of Cuba alone was greater than the entire free colored population of all the slave islands of the British West Indies.[1] Even more striking in this respect would be the sharp contrast between the size and role of the free colored community in Cuba and Virginia, despite the fact that by the time slavery ended in both areas, the size of the total colored population was roughly the same.

From the very beginning of the colonial period, in fact, a large and vital free colored population was developed on the island. Probably the most important reason for this rapid growth was the climate of opinion in Cuba, which regarded manumission as a natural part of slavery and something that was to be expected for the majority of slaves. This attitude was deeply imbedded in traditional custom and law and was fully promoted by the church. It was also supported by the economic and even military dependence of the larger white population on the colored slaves.

For the free colored community in Cuba was essential to the economy of the colony. Involved in every skilled profession, and controlling many, the free colored performed every economic task on the island from the most unskilled to the most skilled and professional services. The free colored community, which was often the largest single sector in many of the island's cities, was also extremely important in the military defense of the island. In fact, from the founding of the first militia companies in the late sixteenth century until the

[1] Alexander von Humboldt, *The Island of Cuba*, trans. with notes by J. S. Thrasher (New York: Derby & Jackson, 1856), p. 185. Not only did Cuba have more freedmen than any other European colony in the West Indies in 1800, but it had some 30,000 more free colored than *all* of the slave states in the United States. U. S. Bureau of the Census, *Negro Population 1790–1915* (Washington: Government Printing Office, 1918), p. 57.

1800's, the free colored community contributed even more than the free whites to the defense and military security of the island.

Not only was the colored community an essential economic and military component of Cuban society, but equally as crucial it was a natural and accepted part of that society. It was an unusually large and heavily urban community that easily fitted in with the pattern of slavery. At its edges were the half slaves, or coartados, and the large group of slaves who hired themselves out; these often led identical lives to those of the freedmen. The freedmen were therefore neither conspicuous nor exceptional, but blended equally into slavery without challenging that institution and into a free class society, forming a natural and fluid connection between the two.

In the atmosphere of urban, small farm, and skilled slavery that prevailed in Cuba, there was no sharp break between slave and free, or between colored and white freedmen. All three groups performed the same work and often shared the same social existence in the urban centers, and in the rural areas they worked side by side in truck farming, cattle raising, tobacco growing, and a host of other rural industries. Finally, the blending of the population into a complex racial amalgam with an ever increasing intermediate mulatto group in which intermarriage at the lower social ranks was high, created a fairly fluid social system in which racial criteria for social ranking of freedmen began to be replaced by socioeconomic ones.[2]

---

[2] In Cuba, as in the rest of Latin America, there quickly developed a three-fold color system in predominantly Negro regions between white, Negro, and mulatto. Very early in the slave era a mulatto grouping was formed and it became a separate, self-conscious group between the white and the Negro, blending into each at either end. Whereas socioeconomic criteria were to predominate in the developing system of social stratification, physical features were still an important element in defining a person's role, although not the primary one. In this racial classification, mulattoes were thought to form a distinct middle ground, having even their own separate character and intellectual makeup. It therefore became possible for a person to raise his status by lightening his skin, by "marrying up" in terms of color. Given the dark complexion of most Spaniards, it was often enough to be a moderate mulatto to be considered physically white, especially when the cultural and economic roles demanded such a definition. This system was still in its incipient stages under slavery, and would, like the normal ranking

Because of this acceptance of the free colored community, and the full expectation of manumission and emancipation, the free colored community grew at a rapid and accelerated pace from its initiation to the termination of slavery in the nineteenth century. The processes by which this growth was maintained were several. As has been seen in the study of the impact of the Catholic church on slavery, there existed a tremendous moral force on masters to free their slaves as good works having major value in the moral affairs of men. This religiously inspired policy of manumission was probably the chief source for freedmen over the long run.

There existed other means for freeing Negro slaves, however, and the most important of these was the famous institution of coartación, a uniquely Cuban development that placed the initiative for liberation on the slave. Although the right of a slave to purchase his freedom had existed in peninsular practice and in other systems of New World slavery, it seems that the process was never so important or so fully elaborated in customary practice as it was in Cuba. Developed as a customary institution in Cuba by the late seventeenth century, coartación was the process whereby the slave had the right, at any time, to purchase his own freedom on an installment basis. As fully developed and eventually codified by royal enactments in the eighteenth century,[3] coartación, meaning to limit or cut off, was the right of a Negro slave to demand that his price be publicly announced by a court of law and that he have the right to pay off this price in several installments. Basic to the coartacion's functioning was the slave's absolute right to property of his own, his *peculium*, which dated back to Roman law. This *peculium*, or private fund, could be

system, become fully developed in post-emancipation society. Nevertheless, it should be stressed that this unique area of color mobility was never even remotely approximated in North America. For here mulattoes of any hue were defined and treated as Negroes, no matter how the Negro community itself might define straighter hair or lighter skin.

[3] Coartación was first mentioned in metropolitan law in 1712. Fernando Ortiz, *Hampa afro-cubana: Los negros esclavos, estudio sociólogico y de derecho publico* (Havana: Revista Bimestre Cubana, 1916), pp. 317–18.

secured by a slave in innumerable ways—by working for himself on Sundays and religious holidays, by hiring himself out, by keeping anything above the fixed return demanded by the master, or by selling produce from his conuco.[4] With this property the slave could, after having his price determined, pay it off in installments. The first required payment was usually $50, which was around one-fourth of his original value. Once a slave had paid such an installment he acquired many more rights, the principal one being the right to change masters at will so long as he could find another who was willing to buy him in his coartado or limited status as opposed to an *entero* (that is, a whole or unlimited) slave.[5]

The coartado could come from either the urban or rural environment, although much more likely he came from the former. For urban wages for skilled labor seemed to have been extraordinarily high throughout the colonial period, and the opportunities for profit-making were numerous for skilled artisans. These were permitted by church and custom to work on holidays and Sundays for their own account and keep the income so derived. That these opportunities were abundant can be seen from the fact that Cuba officially had only some 290 work days per year, the rest being sanctioned holidays and Sundays. Although farm labor did not as readily offer high wage opportunities, there existed even on the most harshly run sugar plantations, private plots and grazing grounds for the slaves. Here the slaves could work their individual conucos, or plots—usually in produce, chickens, and dairy cattle—the products of which they often sold to the plantation owners. In some cases these slave producers seem to have been the chief suppliers of fresh produce for the plantations on which they worked.

At any time throughout the functioning of coartación, there were bound to be large numbers of Negroes who had partly

[4] Hubert H. S. Aimes, "Coartación: A Spanish Institution for the Advancement of Slaves into Freedmen," *Yale Review*, XVII (February, 1909), 418, 425.
[5] *Ibid.*, p. 415.

purchased their freedom and thus stood between slavery and freedom.[6] But there were often many reasons for a coartado slave not to purchase his full freedom. A coartado could not be held responsible for a debt, his master still taking responsibility, nor was the produce from his truck gardens subject to church tithes. If the coartado was a male, his slave status kept him out of the militia and free from other governmental burdens imposed upon the free colored community. And in times of sickness or other emergencies, the coartado could fall back on the master for sources of support.

The coartado pattern seems to have worked superbly well in the city, and it fit into the whole institution of urban slavery. For a coartado slave could not be sold beyond the amount of his purchase price, no matter what skills he had acquired. Thus for urban families or merchants who wanted skilled labor at the cheapest possible price, a coartado was a fine purchase. One-half to one-third of the price of even a raw black, the coartado was a proved money-earner and a skilled artisan or domestic as well. With the high prices existing for slave labor, a purchase price of $100 to $300 for the use of these skills for a five-year period was well worth the investment.

This is clearly revealed in newspaper advertisements in Havana in the nineteenth century. The *Diario de la Habana* of April 28, 1839, had listed for sale "A young Negro woman, very good laundress and ironer, very humble, agile and accommodating, at 300 pesos coartada." And in the same edition, another young Negro woman similarly described as a cook and general laundress, but not as a coartado, sold for 540 pesos. In another advertisement was listed "a negro woman of around 40 years, married, cook, laundress, and ironer, good house servant, coartado at 350 pesos," while another listed "a Criolla Negro woman, around 25 years old, recently delivered

---

[6] After the 1820's there also existed a class of semi-slaves known as *emancipados*, who were slaves taken from illegal slave-trade ships and were temporarily held as slaves for a fixed term, usually seven years, before gaining their freedom. It is estimated that there were some 25,660 of these captured illegal slaves brought to Cuba between 1824 and 1866. Ortiz, *Los negros esclavos*, pp. 322 ff.

three months ago, regular laundress and seamstress, coartado at 300 pesos and her child at 50." This last offering was an especially advantageous one since a woman with a newborn child often served as a wet nurse, which usually raised the price of such a woman to an extraordinarily high figure. In the same daily issue there also appeared a slave-wanted ad with the following remarks: "Desire to purchase a young Negro man, *calesero* [light chase] driver and cook, healthy and without marks, coartado at 400 pesos."[7]

The institution of coartación underwent many changes in its some three centuries of existence, from periods of a liberal attitude to those of government semi-hostility to the whole process.[8] But despite these constant shiftings, the process was never seriously challenged and it steadily fed energetic and able Negro slaves into the free colored population. One estimate of this input placed the annual rate of full coartación in the middle of the nineteenth century at 6.2% of the slave population, or around 20,000 slaves per annum.[9]

Coartación was obviously only for the more energetic and intelligent of the colored population and principally for the skilled and urban slaves. It was also primarily for the criollo slave, or native born, as opposed to the bozal, and in fact the bozales were not allowed to have their price set until they had been on the island for at least seven years. Nevertheless, although it was not for the masses, coartación served the vital function of abating slave discontent and constantly enriching the colored community with workers of the highest skill and

---

[7] This and other Havana newspapers for the 1830's will be found in Archivo General de Indias, Sevilla, Audiencia de Santo Domingo, leg. 1340. [Hereafter cited as AGI.]

[8] For conflicting royal attitudes toward coartación, see AGI, Santo Domingo, leg. 1142, no. 10, December 5, 1788; and leg. 1138, no. 3, February 17, 1778. In one case the crown fully supported the coartado by not charging him the alcabala tax when he purchased his freedom and by declaring that his original purchase price was all the coartado had to pay, no matter how much training he had received or how high slave prices had subsequently risen. At other times the crown declared itself opposed to wholesale coartación on a grand scale and held that children did not follow their mothers in coartación, but had to be purchased separately. Also see Aimes, "Coartación," pp. 415–16, 418–20.

[9] *Ibid.*, pp. 427–28.

ability. With energetic leaders thus drawn out of the slave class and with a large number of discontented and rebellious slaves easily becoming runaways or cimarrones, Cuba proved to be remarkably free of violent slave insurrections. A few bloody revolts are recorded in the mines in the early sixteenth century, and large numbers of cimarrones raids are reported in later centuries, but there seemed to have been very few rural-based slave insurrections and almost none in the urban environment. It was not until the general upheavals of Cuban society in the early decades of the nineteenth century that the island experienced anything like full-scale slave revolts, and these insurrections usually coincided with and were eventually absorbed into white revolutionary activities.[10]

Although manumission and coartación were primarily individual acts, the state also carried out emancipation on its own initiative. This occurred because of the crown's ownership of large numbers of slaves and because of its need to control the slave population in times of war and crisis. In the numerous invasions by corsairs and foreign troops, the local masters were often forced to arm their slaves to protect their own lives and property. To do this they often had to promise freedom for slaves who fought with distinction and, to guarantee support in any new crisis, the local governments often honored these promises after the conflict was over. The most dramatic of these instances occurred during the English invasion of Cuba in the 1760's, when the terrified local governor, fearful of slaves deserting to the English, armed hundreds of slaves and promised them their freedom if they fought for the crown.

[10] For the mild nature of slave revolts prior to this general upheaval see e.g. AGI, Santo Domingo, leg. 1329, letters dated November 10, and November 21, 1796; and AGI, Papeles del Estado, leg. 5, no. 15, 1795. In these two revolts, Negroes left their plantations in a body, marching first on the master's house and burning it, though killing no one, and then heading toward the nearest town, or simply melting into the countryside. In the second instance the Negro slaves marched toward the town believing that freedom had already been proclaimed for them and that the master was hiding the news. In both these revolts, no whites were killed, even though the slaves captured arms, and both movements were easily suppressed. See also Vidal Morales y Morales, *Iniciadores y primeros mártires de la revolución cubana* (Havana: Imprenta Avisador Commercial, 1901), pp. 131 ff.; and Ortiz, *Los negros esclavos*, pp. 425 ff.

The royal government, after retaking Havana, carried out this promise and several hundred slaves were freed by this action.[11] In another case, the crown liberated over 1,000 of its own slaves in the copper mines of Santiago del Cobre (or Pardo) in the late 1790's.[12]

By these several actions, a large body of freedmen was built up in Cuba and was continuously replenished throughout the history of slavery on the island.[13] Even after the tremendous growth of illegal slave importation in the nineteenth century, especially from 1820 to 1840, the free colored population continued to grow on the island and even recovered its percentage importance by 1861, as Table 2 clearly indicates.[14]

[11] José Antonio Saco, *Historia de la esclavitud de la raza africana en el Nuevo Mundo y en especial en los paises Américo-Hispanos* (Barcelona: Jaime Jepús, 1879), p. 317.

[12] For the government decision to free the slaves, which seems to have been written by Gaspar de Jovellanos, see AGI, Santo Domingo, leg. 1146, no. 29, October 31, 1799.

[13] As Alexander von Humboldt concluded in his famous visit to the island in the early years of the nineteenth century: "In no part of the world, where slavery exists, is manumission so frequent as in the island of Cuba; for Spanish legislation, directly the reverse of French and English, favors in an extraordinary degree the attainment of freedom, placing no obstacles in its way, nor making it in any measure onerous. The right which every slave has of seeking a new master or purchasing his liberty; . . . the religious sentiment that induces many persons in good circumstances to concede by will freedom to a certain number of negroes; the custom of retaining a number of both sexes for domestic service, and the affections that necessarily arise from this familiar intercourse with the whites; and the facilities allowed to slave-workmen to labor for their own account, by paying a certain stipulated sum to their masters, are the principal causes why so many blacks acquire their freedom in the towns.

"The position of the free negroes in Cuba is much better than it is elsewhere, even among those nations which have for ages flattered themselves as being most advanced in civilization. We find there no such barbarous laws as have been invoked, even in our own days, by which free negroes . . . can be deprived of their liberty, and sold for the benefit of the State, should they be convicted of affording an asylum to escaped slaves." Humboldt, *The Island of Cuba*, pp. 211–13.

[14] The population statistics for 1774–1827 are taken from Ramón de la Sagra, *Historia económico-política y estadística de la isla de Cuba* (Havana: Imprenta de las viudas de Arazoza y Soler, 1831), p. 7, except for the estimates of 1804 which were made by Humboldt, *The Island of Cuba*, p. 195. The census for 1841 and 1861 came from Julio Le Riverend Brusone, in Ramiro Guerra y Sánchez, *et al.*, *Historia de la nación cubana* (10 vols.; Havana: Editorial Historia de la Nación Cubana, 1952), VII, 187. These two years are somewhat undercalculated, since they omit persons over 60. The 1855 census is taken from José García de Arboleya, *Manual de la isla*

Freedmen could be found in every occupation and on every part of the island, but they were primarily concentrated in the cities. According to Humboldt in his estimates for 1811, 63%, or 72,000, freedmen were located in the major towns

TABLE 2

POPULATION OF CUBA BY COLOR AND STATUS, 1774–1861

Year	Free Colored	Slaves	Total Colored	Whites
1774	30,847	44,333	75,180	96,440
1792	54,152	84,590	138,742	133,550
1804	90,000	180,000	270,000	234,000
1817	114,058	199,145	313,203	239,830
1827	106,494	286,942	393,436	311,051
1841	147,787	421,649	569,436	408,966
1855	179,012	366,421	545,433	498,752
1861	213,167	399,872	613,039	748,534

and cities, although it should be noted that some of these urban freedmen were produce farmers in the environs of the various cities. On the eastern half of the island, the social and economic organization was distinctly flavored by a large rural free colored population. Divided equally between town and country, the rural freedmen represented 52%, or 36,000, of the total rural colored population of this area.[15]

The famous Cuban scholar Jacobo Pezuela listed in his extraordinary geographical dictionary a complete population and occupational census by wards for the major cities of the colony, which gives a truly fascinating picture of the economic position of the freedman Cuban society. For Havana in 1861, Pezuela had listed six of the city's districts and enumerated the occupations of the adult white and free colored popula-

de Cuba. *Compendio de su historia, geografía, estadística y administración* (2d ed.; Havana: Imprenta del Tiempo, 1859), p. 114.

There also exist censuses for 1846, 1849, and 1859 (see Jacobo Pezuela, *Diccionario geográfico, estadístico, histórico de la isla de Cuba* [4 vols.; Madrid: Imprenta Mellado, 1863–66], IV, 245), but these are shown by Thrasher to be grossly inaccurate as far as the slave populations are concerned (Humboldt, *The Island of Cuba*, pp. 206 ff). The 1855 slave figures should also be considered tentative, although accurate in other respects. Finally the 1827 estimate for free colored is obviously underestimated, with Humboldt's calculation of *ca.* 130,000 in 1825 being much closer to reality.

[15] *Ibid.*, p. 224 n.

tions in each. Table 3 is a compilation of these figures and lists the total number and percent of distribution of whites and free colored in each of the major occupational categories.[16] Aside from the major occupations listed in Table 3, there were innumerable small vendors and craftsmen, such as sail-

TABLE 3

DISTRIBUTION OF MAJOR OCCUPATIONS BY COLOR IN SIX SELECTED
DISTRICTS OF HAVANA IN 1861

| | OCCUPATION | DISTRIBUTION | | | |
| | | Free Colored | | White | |
		No.	%	No.	%
Males	Cigar-makers	1,611	27	4,318	73
	Day laborers	1,516	46	1,777	54
	Masons	760	58	555	42
	Carpenters	721	38	1,185	62
	Tailors	612	53	547	47
	Shoemakers	533	42	736	58
	Calash (2-wheel chaise) drivers	497	99	2	*
	Cooks	400	63	235	37
	House servants	278	24	893	76
	Landlords	274	6	4,322	94
	Musicians	210	65	111	35
	Wagon drivers	201	51	194	49
	Stonecutters	149	57	113	43
	Harness makers	146	46	168	54
	House-painters	121	42	166	58
	Small truck farmers	99	11	776	89
	Coachmen	91	28	238	72
	Bakers	79	36	140	64
	Coopers	66	43	89	57
	Blacksmiths	55	18	246	82
	Silversmiths	52	18	244	82
	Tinsmiths	44	23	147	77
	Butchers	40	25	117	75
	Barbers	32	15	177	85
Females	Seamstresses	3,685	51	3,533	49
	Washerwomen	3,525	78	977	22
	Non-working housewives	3,411	12	25,381	88
	Cooks	408	85	72	15
	House servants	93	90	10	10
	Dressmakers	14	8	160	92
	Midwives	6	50	6	50

* Less than one per cent.

[16] These figures are provided in Pezuela, *Diccionario*, III, 350–72.

makers and ropemakers, along with two schoolteachers and three dentists. One of the most surprising facts revealed by these figures is that the free colored male population did not have a monopoly on unskilled and domestic service labor. Although in the districts enumerated by Pezuela only 27% of the population were free colored, they were over-represented in the overwhelming majority of fields requiring skilled labor; but they made up only 24% of the domestic servants and only 46% of the day laborers, or unskilled workers. The free colored seemed actually to have dominated such trades as masonry and tailoring, and had a higher representation than their urban percentage (i.e., more than 27%) in 18 out of the 24 professions listed for men in Table 3.

Women, however, seemed to have had far less opportunity than men, although even here they worked alongside white women laundresses, cooks, and seamstresses. The fact that only 12% of the free colored women could afford to be full time housewives, as contrasted to 88% of the white women, indicates that the free colored tended to be clustered at the lower end of the economic scale.

The occupational pattern for the whole of Havana appears to have been unique on the island because of its heavy concentration of what were then called industrial workers, the 1861 occupational census listing 22,753 free colored industrial workers and but 2,180 small farmers. On the other hand, Santiago de Cuba, the second largest city on the island in 1861, listed 22,936 colored farmers and only 13,069 industrial workers. The two cities together had 104 colored teachers, 239 colored urban property owners or landlords, and 7,353 day laborers. They also listed a combined colored industrial work force of 35,822, and a total of 25,116 small-farm workers. The two cities listed the total of literate colored at 9,851 persons.[17]

Although the enumerated free colored population figures did not indicate any lawyers or doctors, late eighteenth and early nineteenth century records show that there were numerous instances of mulattoes who had university degrees and

[17] *Ibid.*, II, 166; III, 8.

were practicing law and medicine. But the individuals who reached such heights were almost always listed as whites, no matter what the color of their skins. And while it is obvious that only a few hundred or so, at most, did achieve such high status, nevertheless it was possible for the very skilled and very fortunate to gain such success, despite all the laws and the institutional opposition.

Initially the Spanish crown firmly believed in a highly structured society based on racial lines and did indeed attempt consciously to set up a caste-structured social system. From the very initiation of the free colored class, it began issuing prohibitions regulating dress and occupation to guarantee that the whites could be distinguished from the colored class. A royal code of 1571 declared that:

No Negresses, whether free, or slave, nor Mulattas, may wear gold, pearls, or silk; however if a Negress or Mulatta is married to a Spaniard, she may wear gold earrings with pearls, and a small necklace, and on her skirt a fringe of velvet. None may wear *mantos* or *burato* or any other garment, except short cloaks, which may reach a little below the waist, under penalty of having them as well as any gold or silk clothing, taken from them.[18]

The universities, jealous guardians of their own rights and privileges, were officially totally closed to all Negro, mulatto, or other mixed-blood candidates. While all classes were freely admitted by the church to its schools, the church only controlled primary and secondary education, for the universities were civilian, non-religious institutions controlled by their own faculties. In the days of mass illiteracy, a colegio, or secondary school degree, gained one entrance to almost anything, for the secondary education was of the highest caliber. It taught the most advanced science and humanities courses and enabled one easily to enter an intellectual career, government service, or just about any other occupation. It should also be

[18] *Recopilación de leyes de las Indias* (3 vols.; Madrid: D. Joaquin Ibarra, 1791), II, 369–70, Libro VII, Título V, Ley XXVIII. For other sumptuary laws see Richard Konetzke, *Colección de documentos para la historia de la formación social de hispanoamérica, 1493–1810* (3 vols. to date; Madrid: Consejo Superior de Investigaciones Científicas, 1953–1962), Vol. III, Book 1, pp. 124–34, 187.

remembered that the creole and peninsular white upper classes and the nobility at this time probably had no more than a colegio education. But for two key professions of status a university degree was still a prime requisite, and those were law and medicine. Both required university courses of many years duration, and both professions were controlled by the university examiners and professors, and the royal courts and officials. A potential lawyer or doctor had to be admitted to the university, get his degree, and carry out a period of practical work in an apprenticeship; then the lawyers had to be admitted to practice by the highest court of the land, the audiencia, and the doctors had to be examined by a *protomédico*, or royal medical examiner, before they could practice.[19] At all levels, the student had to prove *limpieza de sangre* or purity of blood. This meant that he could not be of colored or Indian ancestry, nor of Moslem or Jewish heritage (i.e., New Christian).

Nevertheless, despite these numerous and seemingly insurmountable obstacles to upper-class careers, time and again colored persons passed every one of these tests without being challenged, despite their dark skins. This occurred especially when illegitimate colored children received support, both in terms of recognition and inheritance, from their upper-class white fathers, a relatively common occurrence in Cuba but almost totally unknown in Virginia. There are examples too, of able and well-trained colored freedmen who, even when opposed, sometimes successfully overrode every one of these obstacles on their way up the social scale and successfully broke the color line for those who followed.

Probably the most outstanding instance of a Cuban mulatto achieving high economic and an even higher social position, even well beyond normal white upper-class expectations, was that of Don Julian Francisco Campo. A graduate of the University of Havana with a doctorate in civil law, Campo was licensed as a lawyer by the royal audiencia and not only practiced his profession but worked in many royal positions,

---

[19] For the regulations for lawyers and doctors, see *ibid.*, Vol. III, Book 1, pp. 192, 304–5.

probably amassing a fortune both through inheritance and his work. His father, who was white, was a high royal official on the island and must have left him well provided for. Because of his own and his father's service he petitioned the crown for a patent of nobility in honor of their outstanding service to the crown. It was only when the petition was presented that the crown discovered that he was a descendent of Negroes on his maternal side.[20]

Negroes and mulattoes seem to have gone farthest in medicine, for the number of petitions in this area far exceeds those for the law or other professions. A most important instance concerning a colored doctor was that of the mulatto Juan de la Cruz y Mena, who was a professor of medicine and surgery in Bayamo. For several years he battled with the University of Havana to have his two sons admitted to the university to take courses and degrees in medicine, although it seems he had little success.[21] More successful was the mulatto freedman Miguel Joseph de Aviles, also of Bayamo, who had obtained his medical degree from the Faculty of Surgery at the University of Havana, and then interned for a year at a Havana hospital. When the local royal medical examiner refused to let him take his final licensing exam on the grounds of his color, the crown interfered and forced the official to grant the examination.[22] An almost identical case was that of the mulatto Joseph Francisco Baez, who was the illegitimate son of a royal official, and who had graduated from the university and had been a practicing surgeon for some thirteen years before the local officials suddenly raised objections about his color. The crown strongly supported Baez' position, based on his recognized skill and service to the community, and ordered the royal medical examiner in Havana to permit Baez to practice his profession with all the rights it entailed.[23]

Along with medicine, the allied field of pharmacy seems to have been a profession practiced by many educated colored freedmen. Mathias Perez, a mulatto who had just appeared

[20] AGI, Santo Domingo, leg. 2236, October 1, 1791.
[21] AGI, Santo Domingo, leg. 1357, June 6, 1764.
[22] AGI, Santo Domingo, leg. 1607, July 29, 1763.
[23] AGI, Santo Domingo, leg. 1607, June 1, 1760.

before the royal medical examiner in Santo Domingo and had passed his apothecary examination, petitioned the crown in the 1740's to allow him to practice his profession in Havana without interference because of his color. He noted in his petition that his brother and another relative also practiced the apothecary trade in the city, and all had been licensed by the royal officials.[24]

There were also numerous freedmen who were *escribanos*, extremely important government officials whose duties combined those of a notary and a lawyer. Although the crown specifically prohibited mulattoes from being granted these positions,[25] time and again cases of mulatto escribanos arose. In the 1690's, Jeronimo Quesada, who had temporarily been admitted as an escribano into the Royal Treasury offices at the audiencia in Santo Domingo, was removed from the office because he was discovered to be a mulatto.[26] With the passing years, however, the opposition even in the royal bureaucracy seems to have diminished, and by the end of the eighteenth century the crown set up a series of dispensation fees whereby a colored person could, for a stated sum, have the color bar waived for the particular office or position in question. Thus in 1807, the royal governor of Cuba supported the petition of José de Salas for the position of royal notary escribano, with Salas stating his willingness to pay the 700-peso dispensation fee that this particular office required. In his supporting document, which the crown for its own reasons still rejected, the governor informed Spain that Salas was a young and intelligent mulatto who also knew French and English.[27]

But regardless of these rejections, free colored still man-

---

[24] AGI, Santo Domingo, leg. 426, no. 5, 1742.
[25] Konetzke, *Colección de documentos*, Vol. III, Book 1, p. 247, for Royal Decree of 1750.
[26] AGI, Santo Domingo, leg. 876, book 27, October 6, 1693.
[27] AGI, Santo Domingo, leg. 329, no. 38, 1807. Many Negroes and mulattoes were multilingual, but the most extraordinary case recorded of such linguistic ability was that of the bozal Negro Josef Gregorio de la Guerra. A native of Guinea, Gregorio de la Guerra was employed in the late eighteenth century by the Intendent of the Army in Cuba as an interpreter, primarily for Negro slaves used in military construction work. According

aged, like the unusual Don Julian Francisco Campo, to get a good general education and to enter civil government service as well. Don Joseph Maria Cowley, a mulatto from Havana, had served in the Poor Relief Office in the Quartermaster Section of the navy and in the Royal Tobacco Department in high offices never before held by a colored man. He asked the crown to grant him, for the usual monetary dispensation, the right to seek new and better offices, never before held by colored men, and to have his sons granted this dispensation. The Madrid official who answered this petition seemed to have felt that this was going too far, and he rejected the whole idea. He charged that the special dispensation fee now instituted by the crown for Negroes and mulattoes was for specific jobs and specific contemporary issues, not for future positions. He felt that there were already too many capable mixed-bloods in the Indies, and they severely threatened offices heretofore held only by whites. To grant future rights, he declared, would erode the white position altogether.[28]

Even the church, despite the multitude of laws and total opposition of the clergy, had its problems with mulattoes who attempted to pass into its ranks. In 1732 the crown bitterly complained to the archbishop of Santo Domingo, under whose jurisdiction came the island of Cuba, that at least seven if

---

to a royal official, he spoke, aside from Spanish, French, and Italian, both Latin and Arabic. AGI, Santo Domingo, leg. 1227, no. 131, November 22, 1777.

[28] AGI, Santo Domingo, leg. 328, January 30, 1797. Although upper class and wealthy persons tried to get around the restrictions on color by legal means, all classes seem to have done everything possible to change their legally declared status. The archbishop of Cuba reported to the crown in 1815, after numerous complaints about falsification of color on parochial birth records had led the crown to demand an investigation by his office, that even poor women seem to have resorted to stratagems to be listed as white. He noted, for example, that pregnant women, even though legitimately married, sometimes changed parishes before giving birth to confuse the new parish about the color and legitimacy of their children. "The determination of those of humble condition to see themselves listed in the highest classes of the parish book is undeniable," declared the archbishop, and this often led to the extreme of "bribing and corrupting the local parish priests and officials with money." *Informe del arzobispo de Cuba sobre la clase de libros,* April 8, 1815, reprinted in Richard Konetzke, "Documentos para la historia y crítica de los registros parroquiales en las indias," *Revista de Indias,* VII, No. 25 (Julio-Septiembre, 1946), 583–84.

not more of his newly consecrated priests, or those admitted to candidacy, were of Negro and mulatto descent. It informed him in no uncertain terms that all priests were to come from pure white and old Christian stock only.[29] Of all the branches of the royal government, this was the most jealously guarded, for the crown and the higher clergy feared the introduction of any nonwhite member within its ranks, though even here many colored men and women probably succeeded in passing.

Finally, of course, there was the whole field of popular culture and art. Negro influence in creating an Afro-Cuban language, folk music, dance, and even popular epic and drama is obvious. To every Cuban, of whatever color, this heritage is a Cuban heritage and its African aspects and contributions are fully accepted and praised.[30] But a few exceptional Negroes were also leaders in the first flowerings of a distinct creole literature in the early nineteenth century. In the first half of the nineteenth century, as white Cuban poets began to express a distinct Cuban idiom, there also appeared some eight free and slave Negro poets, working in themes identical to those of their white counterparts and participating with them in the same intellectual circles. Of these eight early colored poets, the two most important were José Francisco Manzano and Gabriel de la Concepción Valdes, known as Placido, both of whom have achieved an outstanding place in Cuban national literature. Contemporary critics hold Placido as the better poet, whereas Manzano achieved great fame for his extraordinary autobiography, which described the harsh 32 years of his slave existence. In fact, Manzano published his first book of poems in Havana in 1821 while he was still a slave, and it was primarily through the aid of his literary friends that this prolific writer was eventually freed. Several other early Cuban colored poets were also able to purchase freedom after achieving literary fame.[31]

[29] Konetzke, *Colección de documentos*, Vol. III, Book 1, pp. 185–86.

[30] On the concept of Afro Cubanism and its impact on Cuban culture see G. R. Couthard, *Race and Color in Caribbean Literature* (London: Oxford University Press, 1962), chap. 2.

[31] José A. Fernandez Castro, "El aporte negro en las letras de Cuba en el siglo xix," *Revista Bimestre Cubana*, XXXVIII (1936), 51–55. Fernandez

Thus despite all the sumptuary laws and regulations against university admission, the colored freedmen and their descendents succeeded time and again in breaking down the barriers. So successful were they, in fact, that by the end of the eighteenth century the crown had abandoned its sumptuary laws as utterly impracticable and had gone so far as to set up a system of cash dispensation payments, whereby persons of undoubted ability could be admitted to all offices and positions that had been previously open to pure whites only. The price was usually extremely high in every case, but this nevertheless indicated that the crown had finally recognized the impossibility of maintaining a caste system and had quietly dropped its barriers for those who could pay the price.

Innate intelligence or fortunate birth enabled the exceptional few to rise into the upper ranks of society, but there also existed another important area of mobility, the military. One of the most vital roles played by the free colored community of Cuba—and one of its most extraordinary—was that of voluntary military service, which opened up avenues for social mobility and for prestige for large numbers of artisans and lower-class colored persons.

Whereas the freedman of Virginia was disarmed and carefully isolated, the Cuban free colored citizen was a vital part of the Cuban military establishment. Long before the organization of the first volunteer militia companies, in fact, military service seems to have been a recognized part of the daily life of the Cuban freedman. Thus as early as the 1570's, in the famous ordinances of Cáceres, the military role of the free colored was singled out for comment. Whereas in ordinance 52 Cáceres had ordered that no Negro slave could carry arms, except for those working on the cattle estates, in the very next ordinance he decreed "that there are many free Negroes in this city [of Havana] who are *vecinos* [citizens] and officials,

Castro's view of the worth of the two leading colored poets is in sharp contrast to the more mature judgment of Max Henríquez Ureña, *Panorama histórico de la literatura cubana* (2 vols.; Puerto Rico: Ediciones Mirador, 1963), I, 166–69, 183–85. See also the famous edition by Francisco Calcagno, *Poetas de color* (Havana: Imprenta Soler, 1878).

and because this city is a port, if guard duty falls to them it is good that they have arms that they can bring" and declared that only a specific ruling by a judge could prohibit these freedmen from bearing arms.

As the crown quickly made it clear that it could not provide out of its own resources for the defense of its Indies, it had to rely on private individuals to guarantee the territorial integrity and internal peace of her New World empire. First came the privately financed conquistador armies and later the organization of volunteer troops from among the settled colonists of the region. Royal officers and cadres were sent out to train and control the locally organized militia companies that began to appear in the sixteenth century, and the bulk of the fighting forces until well toward the end of the eighteenth century were these civilian volunteers.

The civilian militia forces were to play a vital role in imperial defense, most decisively of course in the Caribbean, where Spanish authority was challenged almost from the first days of her settlement. In Cuba especially, imperial defense was an extraordinarily taxing problem because of the unusually exposed position of the island on the rim of Spain's empire and because of its domination of the European-American trade routes. From the middle of the sixteenth century onward, all of Spain's major colonial rivals at one time or another attempted to gain control over this gateway to the Caribbean. With long unguarded shorelines and a sparse population, Cuba invited constant attacks not only by veteran troops of established nations, but by a constant succession of independent privateers, pirates, and freebooters of all kinds, who infested its shore almost from the first days of Spanish colonization.

To provide the needed forces for defense, the crown, from the very beginning of its volunteer civilian companies, turned to its free white colonists and to its growing Negro and mulatto free male population for support. Recognizing its dependence on the free colored population in Cuba, the royal government went out of its way to guarantee to these freedmen the right to bear arms and it encouraged their volunteering by maintaining their coequal rights with the white militia companies, including, after their organization into separate colored military units, the right to select their own officers. Not only did the crown grant these militiamen the right to the *fuero militar*, which protected them from criminal prosecutions by civil courts,[32] but it also did everything possible to guarantee general community respect for these freedmen volunteers. This is well illustrated in an unusual document written by the king in 1714, in which he ordered royal officials to prevent these colored troops from being insulted. After the king pointed out their vital military role, the recognition of their necessity and efficiency by the captains-general of the island, and the self-sacrifice and zeal with which these "ancient and especially meritorious" colored militia companies served the crown, he went on to declare:

I have resolved that these colored militiamen be granted the good treatment which their actions deserve, considering them as my vassals, of whom I have full satisfaction for what they have always performed in my Royal Service; For this reason . . . I order and command the Governor and Captain General of the island of Cuba and the city of San Christobal de Habana, the Sergeant Major, Captains, and other persons of war; and the *alcaldes ordinarios, regidores* and other judges and justices of said city, that they give special care that the free mulattoes of these militia companies be attended with the good treatment that they deserve, not allowing any person to call them indecorous names in hatred, nor blemish their nation . . . because my royal desire and will is that they be treated with love and good friendship, not allowing them to experience the slightest abuse or contempt.[33]

With this attitude, the crown never had to fear the arming of its free men of color, and in fact the Spanish government used colored militia troops to excellent advantage, not only in Cuba where they were probably the most numerous in the New World, but wherever freedmen resided in Spanish America.

---

[32] See the Real Cédula of September 16, 1708, for the militia rights to the fuero and *preeminencias* in Konetzke, *Colección de documentos*, Vol. III, Book 1, p. 110.
[33] AGI, Santo Domingo, leg. 337, May 20, 1714.

The first organization of formal militia companies in Cuba was carried out in 1586 under the threat of an attack of English corsairs. The local governor at Havana created a force of some 1,000 armed civilian volunteers, in which some 400 men were organized into several permanent militia companies, "among whom were many men of color."[34] By 1600, with the constant expansion of the free colored population throughout the rest of the century, the governor at Havana was finally able to establish a completely independent 100-man colored militia company, which became known as the *Compañía de Pardos Libres,* pardos being the Cuban term for mulattoes.[35]

With the increased tempo of foreign invasions and corsair alarms in the late seventeenth century, the local officials created ever larger numbers of permanent militia companies, both white and colored, not only in Havana but in all the major provincial capitals as well.[36] By 1700, the one Havana pardo militia company had been expanded into four full companies, for a total of 400 men.[37] By this time as well, there were established pardo companies in Santiago de Cuba and other provincial centers, along with an almost equal number of *moreno,* or Negro, companies in the same cities.

Far from being ceremonial groups with bright uniforms who performed at parades and other social gatherings, these colonial militia companies were almost exclusively used as active military units. Observing strict military discipline when in service, these companies from the beginning were called upon, usually with no pay except when on full campaign, to engage in constant guard duty and military construction and to assist in local police work. They were used in military actions not only against invading buccaneers, privateers, and other irregular forces, but many times they also had to face veteran European troops in battle. Nor were their actions confined to the island, for on several occasions they

[34] Pezuela, *Diccionario,* II, 248.
[35] AGI, Santo Domingo, leg. 418, no. 7, 1714.
[36] Pezuela, *Diccionario,* II, 249.
[37] AGI, Santo Domingo, leg. 419, no. 8, 1715.

were engaged in major military expeditions beyond the confines of Cuba.

In fact, such was the experience of the pardo Antonio Flores, whose service was typical of the life of a colored militiaman. Volunteering as a common soldier in 1708, he served in the ranks for nine years before being promoted to sergeant, and after three decades he finally reached the rank of company captain. During this period he had served on guard duty over long periods at the outlying forts of Marianabo, Caleto, and San Lazaro. He had fought against the British ship "St. George," had been involved in the capture of two French ships, had fought in an engagement against pirates, and finally had gone on an expedition to East Florida, where he was taken prisoner and sent to France, not returning to Cuba for eighteen months. Next he fought in an expedition sent against the British islands, in which he served with distinction.[38]

Almost identical was the experience of the pardo, Joseph Sánchez, who had joined the militia a good half-century before Flores, that is, sometime in the latter half of the seventeenth century. He, too, had spent much time in guard duties at the fortress of Marianabo, which guarded the approaches to Havana. He served in the defense of Matanzas against European troops and had even been an auxiliary soldier of the Santa Hermandad, or rural constabulary, in its campaigns against the cimarrones. A major part of his service, he complained, was absorbed in time-consuming and non-remunerative guard duty at the various lookout posts around Havana. Like Flores, Sánchez had also been on an expedition to Florida, this time in defense of St. Augustine, and finally after an almost equal length of service to this country, he had risen to the rank of militia captain.[39]

As Florida and later Louisiana came under the jurisdiction of Cuba in the seventeenth and eighteenth centuries, more and more white and colored cuban militiamen were called upon to engage in overseas defensive operations for

---

[38] AGI, Santo Domingo, leg. 1455, no. 5, 1760.
[39] AGI, Santo Domingo, leg. 418, no. 7, 1714.

these territories. Thus when Alexander O'Reilly in 1769 gathered together a military force to take possession of Louisiana from the French, he took along 1,847 royal troops, and 240 volunteer militia, of whom 160 were Negro and mulatto militiamen from Havana.[40] Also late in the seventeenth century and early in the eighteenth, the crown sent Cuban Negro and mulatto troops on temporary service to Mexico and Yucatan.[41]

With the outbreak of the great series of colonial empire wars in the eighteenth century, the Spanish Empire in the New World came under increasing international pressure, and from the 1760's on, Spain was engaged, almost without pause, in one war after another with either England or France, in which the Caribbean was always a major theatre of military operations. The pressure of these incessant expeditions and international conflicts forced the island's government to expand its militia forces. This meant an increase in the number of armed free colored males and the creation of auxiliary labor batallions for the Cuban forces from among the Negro slaves themselves. Slaves were the obvious choice for military construction work, and in 1765 the local royal officials even established a *Compañía de Morenos Esclavos* of 100 Negro slaves to work in artillery.[42] Thereafter slaves were used for multiple purposes within the artillery corps, especially in the ammunition and storage sections.[43]

Probably the most momentous changes in the militia forces occurred as a result of the disasterous capture of Havana by the English in 1762. When the city was returned to Spain the next year, the local royal officials set about to completely reorganize and expand the island's militia. Under the enactments of Inspector General O'Reilly, issued from 1763–65, the scattered white and colored companies were organized into large batallion units with more permanent staffs and officer-training cadres. For the pardo and moreno militias

[40] AGI, Santo Domingo, leg. 1222, July 7, 1769; Pezuela, *Diccionario*, II, 251.
[41] AGI, Papeles del Estado, leg. 35, nos. 13, 73.
[42] AGI, Santo Domingo, leg. 1220, August 19, 1765.
[43] Pezuela, *Diccionario*, II, 260.

this meant the establishment of three full batallions of 800 men each, along with an expanded number of local provincial companies.[44]

By the time of the military review and census of 1770, there were over 3,400 colored militiamen out of a total insular army of 11,667. The entire army was divided into three roughly equal parts: the white militia who numbered 4,645, the Negro and mulatto militia who accounted for 3,413 men, and 3,609 paid royal veteran troops. Thus despite the increasing importance of soldiers from the peninsula, the militia was still the dominant military force on the island. The geographic and numerical breakdown of this army is shown in Table 4.[45]

From the single original company of pardo militia in 1600, the volunteer colored army had grown by 1770 to 3 full batallions and 16 separate companies. And although mulattoes outnumbered Negroes in the free community by almost two to one, the racial breakdown of this force was almost equal. There were 2 pardo batallions and 5 pardo companies equalling some 1,995 mulattoes, and 1 moreno batallion and 10 moreno companies totalling some 1,418 Negroes. As the total free male colored population of the island at this time was only about 15,000, this meant that roughly one out of every 4.4 free colored males was a member of the militia, which was an extraordinarily high figure, especially when compared to the white ratio which was only 1 out of every 10.3 free white males.[46]

By 1770, these military groupings not only constituted a major occupational area for the majority of the free colored adult population of Cuba, but they had also built up a powerful tradition of their own. Service was usually a lifetime affair for most of these militiamen, and the fact that they were almost all drawn from the same local community gave them

[44] *Ibid.*, II, 251.
[45] AGI, Santo Domingo, leg. 1222, June 1, 1770. The above figures do not include 545 royal troops who were listed as "detached." Cuba on the above list refers to Santiago de Cuba.
[46] For the population of the island in the 1770's see AGI, Indiferente General, leg. 1527, December 31, 1778; see also Sagra, *Historia económico-política*, p. 3.

an added measure of companionship, identity, and a true sense of defending their own homes.[47] With strong community identification and some 150 years or so of continuous existence, these companies and batallions developed a powerful esprit de corps and performed remarkably well, despite the constant lack of adequate supplies and full-time training. Finally, because these military organizations were officered by fellow colored freedmen who had worked their way up

TABLE 4

CUBAN MILITARY CENSUS OF 1770

Location	Name and Type of Unit	Number of Men
Havana	1 regiment of infantry of Seville	1,131
	1 regiment of infantry of Havana	697
	1 squadron of American dragoons	135
	3 companies of riflemen	242
	2 companies of artillery	166
	1 regiment of infantry militia, white	1,597
	1 regiment of cavalry militia, white	650
	1 batallion of pardos	799
	1 batallion of morenos	800
	1 company of noble cadets	18
Matanzas	1 regiment of dragoons	450
	10 infantry companies	484
	1 batallion of whites	798
Quatro Villas	3 cavalry companies	150
	4 companies of pardos	297
	4 companies of morenos	177
Puerto Principe	1 batallion of whites	800
	1 cavalry company	50
	1 company of pardos	99
	1 company of morenos	79
Cuba and Bayamo	1 batallion of whites	800
	1 batallion of pardos	800
	2 cavalry companies	86
	5 companies of morenos	362
	Total force present:	11,667

[47] Of the 800 men of the moreno batallion of Havana, for example, 566 came from the city itself and the rest from nearby communities. Change of residence seems to have been the prime cause for terminating service, for in the year 1772, the batallion listed 35 men as being discharged for this reason. AGI, Santo Domingo, leg. 1223, no. 360.

through the ranks, they represented an unusually open and democratic military pattern.

From the establishment of their formal battalions in the 1760's until well into the nineteenth century, the colored militia continued to play a major role. For during the last phase of colonial wars in 1779, Cuba became the scene of intense military activity. So desperate did things become that in 1808 and again in 1812, local officials went so far as to arm all male citizens and organize them into informal popular militia companies, whose chief work was to support the regular militia forces.[48]

With the development of the revolutionary wars of independence within the Spanish Empire itself, however, this dangerous expedient in popular undisciplined armies was quickly abandoned. In fact, after 1820 Cuba became a major staging area for royal troops engaged in putting down the numerous movements for independence on the American mainland. By the late 1820's the normal 3,000- to 4,000-man veteran component of the Cuban armed forces had grown to over 15,000 veteran Spanish troops.[49]

Nevertheless, as late as 1830, the colored militia still played an important part in the military establishment of the island. Of the 30,000-man army in that year, the paid royal troops made up 16 battalions, 11 companies, and 2 squadrons of cavalry. The various militia groups made up a force totalling only 11 battalions, but over 66 assorted companies and 8 cavalry squadrons. Of the militia total, pardo and moreno soldiers now made up 3 battalions and 26 companies (an increase of 10 since the 1760's), and along with the traditional infantry companies, the colored militia now also included 3 full companies of artillery, 2 being pardo and 1 moreno.[50]

But the tremendous buildup of royal veteran troops was not diminished after the end of the Spanish American wars for independence and from the 1830's on, the island was heavily garrisoned by peninsular troops. No longer burdened with a large empire and fearful of losing what remained,

[48] Pezuela, *Diccionario*, II, 252–53.
[49] *Ibid.*, II, 254–55.
[50] Sagra, *Historia económico-política*, pp. 323–25.

the royal government maintained a 15,000- to 20,000-man standing professional army throughout the next three decades until the outbreak of Cuba's own first major war for independence in the late 1860's. Because of these forces and because of the growing distrust of royal officials of the loyalty of the native Cubans, the role of the traditional militia was tremendously reduced.

For the colored militia, this growing conservative reaction by the government to local conditions had particularly disastrous results. Government officials were not only concerned over the local movements for independence and/or annexation to the United States, but they were also fearful of growing attacks against the institution of Negro slavery. In the 1830's and 1840's, the English example of emancipation and their increasing pressure against the illegal slave trade created fears of unrest among the slave population. This fear was greatly strengthened by a rash of local plantation uprisings in Cuba itself in 1842–43, and although these were essentially minor and discontinuous occurrences, they were probably the most violent slave revolts to date in Cuban history. Given these pressures, it was inevitable that the increasingly repressive and insecure Spanish government would turn its hostility toward the free colored population.

Late in 1843, a new captain-general, General Leopoldo O'Donnell, arrived on the island and in January of the new year was informed by a colored sergeant, one José Erice of the moreno militia company of Matanzas, that a revolutionary plot to free the slaves was being planned. Erice's statements, however, could not be collaborated and no evidence of unrest or sedition could be discovered. But once suspect, the free colored population especially became an ever greater concern to the harsh governor. When in March, 1844 a female slave also denounced the existence of such a plot led by the free colored population, the government took direct action. It raided several homes and rounded up a large group of free colored persons among whom the leading figure was the mulatto poet Gabriel de la Concepción Valdes, known as Placido. Another prominent figure accused of being a leader was a mulatto by the name of Andres Dodge who, it was charged, would be the overseas ambassador for the rebels, since he spoke Spanish, English, and French. Finally the government accused of being the key instigator the famous ex-British consul to Cuba, David Turnbull, who had been expelled from the island in 1842 for his ardent abolitionist statements. They claimed that he was behind this so-called race war that had as its aim to exterminate Cuba and to destroy its economy, which the Cuban government charged was the avowed policy of the British government.

Charging them with plotting a war of racial extermination, the royal officials had all the leaders executed in late June of 1844. Some eleven persons were sentenced to death, and dozens of others—slave and free, Negro and mulatto—were imprisoned, exiled, or whipped for their supposed complicity. But this was only the beginning, for under a corrupt military tribunal set up to deal with the "plot," a reign of terror soon set in and several hundred prominent freedmen were either killed, or exiled and forced to relinquish their property. The panicky government struck a heavy blow especially at the upper levels of the free colored community, which it almost succeeded in totally destroying.[51] It was inevitable that with its attack on the economic, intellectual, and social leaders of the free colored community, the government would also strike at the colored military establishment. Charging the militia with complicity, the government took the next logical step in its fear, and in this same month of June, 1844, it formally disbanded and abolished the pardo and moreno militia companies and battalions.[52]

Before very long, however, the peninsular authorities recog-

---

[51] For the government's position on the Placido affair see Justo Zaragoza, *Las insurrecciones en Cuba* (2 vols.; Madrid: Miguel G. Hernandez, 1872–73), I, 536 ff. A more balanced view is presented by Morales y Morales, *Iniciadores y primeros mártires*, pp. 147 ff. Morales y Morales estimated the total number of victims when all was finished at 78 executions, some 400 expulsions, over 1,000 imprisonments, and some 300 deaths due to prolonged punishments or other harsh treatments. The impact of the terror on the free colored population was extremely disproportionate and of the 1,800 persons variously punished, over 1,200 were freedmen, only 590 were slaves and but 14 were whites. *Ibid.*, pp. 155 n, 173.

[52] Zaragoza, *Las insurrecciones en Cuba*, I, 573. The very existence of the whole plot has been challenged not only by Morales y Morales, but by several more recent scholars; see Guerra y Sánchez, *La nación cubana*, IV, 71.

nized the utter stupidity and groundless fear behind this action, and even came to question the existence of the so-called Placido conspiracy, based as it was largely on perjured testimony and nonexistent documentary evidence. After tempers had cooled, the crown reestablished these famous militia companies in 1854 and even permitted the arming of the free colored fire brigades.[53] But the days of powerful professional militia companies were coming to an end, and in recognition of this and of the continued distrust of these potential revolutionary troops, the re-created colored militia companies were made subordinate to regular commands and placed under the jurisdiction of royal battalions.[54]

But even despite their reestablishment, the days of the militia were, for all intents and purposes, at an end, whether composed of whites or the colored freedmen. Not only was the island innundated from 1830 on with heavy concentrations of regular troops, but the royal officials even created a paid insular police force in 1851 modeled on the lines of Spain's Guardia Civil, which consisted of some 800 armed infantry and cavalry troopers. So reduced was the importance of the militia that the white and colored forces in the early 1860's had declined to some 4,170 troops, as opposed to some 19,561 royal soldiers, and this was not including the new constabulary force.[55] Thus by the outbreak of Cuba's first major war of independence in 1868, which began the famous Ten Years' War, the militia no longer played a significant role in the armies of the Cuban royal government. In fact, after 1868, the white, Negro, and mulatto militiamen would come to form the bulk of the troops in the Cuban revolutionary armies, and many a colored officer trained by the Spanish would rise to a position of prominence in the rebel armies.

After some two-and-a-half centuries of continuous existence, the famous colored militia organizations came to an end. Of tremendous military importance in the sixteenth, seven-

---

[53] Pezuela, Diccionario, II, 266.
[54] Zaragoza, Las insurrecciones en Cuba, I, 657–58.
[55] Pezuela, Diccionario, II, 276.

teenth, and eighteenth centuries, these colored soldiers had contributed vitally to the defense of the island against constant foreign attempts at conquest. Not only did they guard Cuba's shores, but they were constantly called upon to face better-equipped and veteran European-trained French and English forces in major battle. Yet these colored battalions performed their arduous tasks willingly and at great personal sacrifice. They also contributed to imperial defense far out of proportion to their numbers, well over twice as much in proportion to the free white settlers of the island. Since the militiamen were paid only on full campaign and received only moderate recompense for long years of service, their work represented a tremendous expenditure of unpaid time in the service of the state. Although militia officers received part compensation and many soldiers often received some type of pension or privilege, it would not be an understatement to say that the free colored community of Cuba heavily and positively paid on its own for a large part of the resources and manpower used by Spain to maintain Cuba within the Spanish Empire.

Although the free colored community never received the monetary rewards that its service demanded and that the other classes often received, it did gain substantial social benefits from its armed militia companies. For these companies provided one of the major avenues of social mobility for able Negro and mulatto freedmen through the existence of a large colored officer class. That this opportunity was widely available is attested to by the size of this group. In the 1770 census, for example, one pardo battalion had 34 colored officers, 25 sergeants, and even 1 colored military surgeon[56] for a force of 800 men.[57] This meant that for the 3 battalions and 16

[56] For the war experiences of a colored surgeon, see AGI, Santo Domingo, leg. 1455, no. 10, 1760.

[57] For the detailed organizational table and names of the officers of the pardo batallion of Havana, which included one company of mixed infantry and cavalry known as the Grenadier Company along with a ten-man white professional advisory and training staff, see AGI, Santo Domingo, leg. 1223, no. 359. Such organizational tables for the Havana pardo and moreno batallions for 1776 can be found in AGI, Santo Domingo, leg. 1225.

companies that existed in Cuba in that year, there were something like 130 colored officers, a not inconsiderable number when it is remembered that there were only 15,000 free colored males in the total population.[58]

Given this large officer population, the exceptionally gifted Negro and mulatto, through devoted service and the exhibition of skill and intelligence, had every expectation of reaching this position. Once they achieved this status, they gained enormous prestige and power. Not only were militia officers granted pensions and other honors by the state, but they were also accorded general respect for their rank in the community at large, and this enabled them to break through the social and economic barriers for themselves or, more usually, for their children.

The career patterns of some of the officers clearly show this to be the case. Antonio Flores, who began as a common soldier volunteer, after three decades of service finally achieved the primary position as battalion commander, and in so doing added an aristocratic "de" before his final name. An artisan by profession, he nevertheless gained enough stature through his position to be able to send his son to primary and secondary school. And in fact, he had his eldest son train not to be an artisan, like himself, but for the liberal professions. At the local Jesuit colegio of Havana, his son majored in theology and grammar and did well at these subjects. Not only did Flores demand the right for his son to enter the university if he wished, but he demanded from the crown that all his sons be exempt from any color bars to any professions they might wish to engage in or train for in the future. And in demanding this right from the crown, based on his long years of service and his prominent position, Antonio de Flores pointed out that the rise of militia officers' sons to high socioeconomic status was a common experience in Cuba.[59]

The existence of an armed colored militia not only pro-

---

[58] This was even large in proportion to the whole officer cadre of the Cuban army. Of the 448 field officers on active assignment in Cuba, which means sublieutenants to captains, 114 were colored.

[59] AGI, Santo Domingo, leg. 1455, no. 5, 1760.

vided an avenue of social mobility for the few but, most crucially, it granted a basic right of citizenship and humanity to the many. For, as the United States Constitution so aptly puts it, one of the fundamental rights of the free citizens of a state is "the right of the people to keep and bear arms. . . ." Not only did the creation of the colored militia of Cuba provide the free colored with the basic right as citizens to defend their state, but it also guaranteed to them one of the most fundamental of human rights, the right to human security.

With the Negro occupying this crucial position in the military establishment of the island, any attempt at wholesale deprivation of rights or even citizenship was doomed to failure. Nor did any agency wish to carry out such a deprivation. The free Negro above all else was a useful and very necessary member of the community. Although the white upper classes might bitterly resent the few exceptionally able freedmen who rose to challenge their own positions, this bitterness was incapable of finding concrete expression in the form of exclusion and apartheid policy. Negroes and more especially mulattoes could be found in almost every rank, class, and occupation on the island.

This is not to say that the Negroes and mulattoes as a class did not suffer severely in relationship to the other classes, nor that they were not disproportionately represented in the lower economic and social positions. But this was rather an inheritance of their slave condition and their lack of either education or capital rather than a preordained policy of oppression. They successfully competed with white labor, and in fact seemed to have blended in with the white lower classes on that level. They were neither shunted exclusively into unskilled labor roles nor did they lose out in the constant immigration of free whites. Artisans handed down their skills to their sons, and even upper class professionals, as in the numerous examples above, were very conscious of attempting to better their sons' positions, as well as maintaining the social conquests they themselves had made.

That the higher the Negroes went up the ladder the greater was the opposition is obvious. That derogatory caste terms were used and marriage exclusion policies at these levels were attempted is also obvious. Nevertheless it was still possible, even during the very height of the slave regime, for a colored person to break through almost all the barriers that existed. As slavery itself disappeared and creole society tended to level out more than under imperial rule, even these obstacles became less stringent and were less successful in maintaining a caste barrier against the colored. For the dynamics of an economic classification system had been firmly implanted in colonial Cuban society, despite the initial attempts to maintain a caste system defined by race. The unwillingness to deprive Negroes and mulattoes normal access to skills and capital worked toward redefining the structure of society to allow an open mobility class system.

One need not paint a racial utopia, which certainly never did exist, to recognize how different this system was from that of North America.[60] Racial antagonisms remained, invidious comparisons continued, and purity of blood still had great weight at the upper reaches of society. But the fundamental criteria for ranking an individual were not his racial attributes but his cultural and economic background.

This predominance of a normal class system was developed early in the slave period. At first through fortunate birth to an upper class white, then through trades and the military, avenues of mobility for the freedmen were constantly expanding. Although they might not scale the heights without undue stress, even the darkest colored found that some doors were never barred. Medicine, the arts, the learned professions were all open to men of ability, whatever their color. Although educational opportunity under slavery was distinctly unequal for whites and colored, there were enough schools to guarantee a minimum of opportunity for an important minority. Nor were successful artisanal and middle-class parents, regard-

---

[60] An excellent recent study on attitudes of Cuban workers has clearly indicated as an independent variable, a racial awareness among working class Negroes that modified their class consciousness, at least prior to the Cuban Revolution. See Maurice Zeitlin, "Economic Insecurity and Political Attitudes of Cuban Workers," *American Sociological Review*, 31, No. 1 (February, 1966), 35–51.

less of their color, slow in pushing their children to higher position.

Well before the end of the slave period, then, the free classes of Cuba, both colored and white, had evolved toward an open class system. The crown itself, in the late eighteenth century, finally accepted this reality of colored mobility and gave up its attempts to maintain a rigid caste structure. In short, the Cuban free colored had already created the beginnings of a class system that presaged the full development of such a social structure for all colored persons when slavery was finally abolished in the 1880's.

10. A World Apart: The Free Colored of Virginia.

Whereas slavery and emancipation were long familiar to the Cubans even before the arrival of the first Negroes, Virginia, like most of the English colonies in the seventeenth century, was in the unique position of having to define its attitude toward slavery and the Negro. While the colonists were aware that Negroes were being brought to the new world by Genoese and Latin traders for the purpose of slave labor, and while they even attempted to enslave the Indians, they were still heavily committed to the system of indentured white labor and seemed to have hesitated initially about the newly imported Negroes. Because planters were involved with head-right options to land and were accustomed to contracting for short-term indenture periods, it seems that a number of the first Negroes in Virginia were allowed, like their white servant co-workers, to pass into independence and citizenship.

Another major factor in creating this ambiguous situation in the first half of the seventeenth century was the rather small supply of Negroes arriving in the colony and the continued dependence of the planters on servant labor for the tobacco plantations. Whatever may have been the desire of Virginians for Negro laborers, the source of supply for a good part of the century was under the control of the rival Portuguese and

Dutch who held almost all the factories along the West African coast and excluded the English altogether.

The almost chance landing of a few Christian Negroes in 1619 at a time in Virginia history when a system of indenture labor had just been satisfactorily worked out, and the fact that England had not experienced slavery nor had any ready-made slave code available led the Virginians to treat these first Negroes as indentured servants.[1] Most of these very early Negro immigrants to Virginia seem to have been treated in the matter of labor and rights much as their fellow white servants, some receiving an education and most receiving their freedom dues. They appear also to have been accepted into the free community and to have possessed personal chattel, with a few even becoming over a period of years property owners and masters in their own right.

These few successful Negro planters, situated mostly along the Pungoteague River in Northhampton County, acquired their lands primarily through the head-right system as did most other Virginians. The first such grant was given to Anthony Johnson, a Negro who had come to Virginia prior to 1622, when in July, 1651, he received 250 acres for the importation of five persons.[2] In 1654 Richard Johnson, whose lands lay contiguous to the estates of both Anthony Johnson and another Negro freedman named John Johnson, was granted 100 acres for the importation of two white indentured servants.[3] John Johnson seems to have been the most successful of these three, for it is recorded that he acquired some 550 acres through the importation of eleven persons. Aside from these grants, in 1656 Benjamin Dole had received 300 acres in Surry County for six persons, and in 1667 Emanuel Cambew got 50 acres for one importation in James City County. Negroes also purchased as well as leased lands from whites. John Harris bought 50 acres in 1668 from the tailor

[1] John H. Russell, The Free Negro in Virginia, 1619–1865 (Baltimore: Johns Hopkins Press, 1913), p. 23.

[2] James H. Brewer, "Negro Property Owners in Seventeenth Century Virginia," William and Mary Quarterly, 3d Series, XII (October, 1955) 576–77.

[3] Philip Alexander Bruce, Economic History of Virginia in the Seventeenth Century (2 vols.; New York: Macmillan Co., 1896), II, 126.

Robert Jones in New Kent, and Philip Morgan, prior to 1676, leased some 200 acres in York County from John Parker for a period of ninety-nine years.[4]

Nor is there any question that these servant Negroes voted along with their white colleagues. When the suffrage was restricted by property qualifications, Negroes who possessed real estate were still free to exercise the vote.[5]

Even as late as 1673 appeared the case of Andrew Moore, a "Servant Negro" who was to be granted his freedom dues for five years of service.[6] By this time, however, the majority of references to the Negro bore the word slave with it, and as it became increasingly difficult for the Negro servant to prove his right to freedom, this class quickly disappeared.[7]

But even though there existed a period when slavery was not fully developed and when Negroes were sometimes given the status of servants and achieved freedom, Negroes themselves were never really treated as coequal to whites, for racial prejudice preceded the formal introduction of slave legislation. The Virginia codes reveal numerous instances of extreme reactions to racial miscegenation, of the doubling of penalties for Negro servants in crimes, and of the general tone of disrespect that indicate that the Negro from the very beginning was considered a unique and definitely inferior creature, one to be reviled and feared rather than understood.

As early as the 1630's and 1640's had come the famous cases of Hugh Davis and Robert Sweet who were whipped for having intercourse with Negro women, and this anti-miscegenation current was so strong that eventually all interracial contact of a sexual nature was brutally suppressed by a harsh series of laws. Not only were Negro men and women considered to be of a seriously different race from ordinary white persons, but Negro women were also held to an entirely different pattern of labor. Unlike white women servants, who never did field labor, Negro women were customarily used

---

[4] Russell, *Free Negro in Virginia*, pp. 37–38; Bruce, *Economic History*, II, 126–127.

[5] *Ibid.*, II, 127.

[6] H. R. McIlwaine (ed.), *Executive Journals of the Council of Colonial Virginia* (3 vols.; Richmond: Virginia State Library, 1925), I, 354.

[7] Russell, *Free Negro in Virginia*, pp. 29, 31.

as raw field hands on all the tobacco estates. So sharp was this distinction that when the colonial assembly wanted to tax Negro women and exclude white women from this law, they simply declared in 1662 that "woman servants whose common imployment is working in the ground [were] to be accompted tythable."[8]

This creation of a racial barrier and even of a work barrier was the sign of a sharpening racial prejudice against the Negro in Virginia. Once slavery was formally worked out after the 1660's in a regular slave code, this prejudice, combined with the end of the application of the indenture system to Negroes, made the life of the free colored person an increasingly servile and degrading one. Since freedom after servitude was no longer even a tolerated possibility and Negroes were reviled as lower status individuals, it was inevitable that as the iron law of slavery descended on Negroes as Negroes, the free colored would also lose their rights.

Thus by 1705, when the first general revision and collation of all laws pertaining to slaves and slavery was carried out, the freedman found himself seriously stripped of some of the most essential rights of citizenship and was left with little save the right to his own labor and to a restricted physical mobility. This degredation began as far back as 1639, when it was declared that "*all* persons except negroes were to be provided with arms and ammunition."[9] Not only were free Negroes now held in a lower status than white servants, who were specifically required to carry arms, but this also meant that Virginia would have only an all-white militia. Unlike Cuba where the free colored would prove such an important element in the colonial military establishment, Virginia was careful to guarantee the [white quality] of its militia. Faced with neither foreign invasion nor piratical expeditions of any serious nature and being largely outside the area of imperial

[8] William W. Hening (ed.), *The Statutes at Large: being a collection of All the Laws of Virginia from the first session of the Legislature in the year 1619* (13 vols.; Richmond: Samuel Pleasents, 1819–23), II, 170; see also Winthrop D. Jordan, "Modern Tensions and the Origins of American Slavery," *Journal of Southern History*, XXVIII, No. 1 (February, 1962), 26–27.

[9] Hening, *Statutes at Large*, I, 226.

conflict in the eighteenth and nineteenth centuries, Virginia had no need to rely on its free colored community for defense. In fact, the prime need for its militia, at least in the non-frontier areas and after 1700 when the Indian menace was confined to the borders, was to check and control the Negro slaves. Not only were the militia maintained to prevent slave revolts, but militiamen were successfully used in the extensive patrol system to hinder effective escape for runaway slaves. These patrols were established in all the counties to check the passes of the Negroes, to search for firearms, and in short to police the slave population and insure the enforcement of all regulations of the Assembly, not only in all general areas of the county but also on the plantations themselves if necessary.[10]

Again blurring the distinction between free and slave, the Assembly in 1661 declared that indentured servants and "all negroes male and female being imported shall be accompted tythable."[11] And although this was removed when freedom was granted to white servants, after 1668 the tax was to remain on Negro women. For, stated the law, "negro women, though permitted to enjoy their ffreedome, yet ought not in all respects to be admitted to a full fruition of the exemptions and impunities of the English. . . ."[12]

In 1670 Negroes were barred from purchasing white Christian servants,[13] and in 1705 came a whole code of laws depriving the freed Negro of many of the rights of a legal personality. In this year, in a newly revised edition of the law of 1680 regarding the striking of a Christian, the Negro and mulatto, bond and free, were now included:

if any negro, mulatto . . . , bond or free, shall at any time, lift his or her hand, in opposition against any christian, not being negro, mulatto or Indian, he or she so offending, shall, . . . receive on his or her bare back, thirty lashes, well laid on. . . .[14]

No Negro or mulatto could "bear any office, ecclesiasticall,

[10] James Curtis Ballagh, *A History of Slavery in Virginia* (Baltimore: Johns Hopkins Press, 1902), pp. 89–91.
[11] Hening, *Statutes at Large*, I, 84.
[12] *Ibid.*, II, 267.
[13] *Ibid.*, II, 280–81.
[14] *Ibid.*, III, 459.

civill, or military, or be in any place of public trust or power."[15] All Negroes and mulattoes were prohibited from being witnesses in any case whatsoever—this was later modified to allow them to appear in cases involving Negroes charged with a capital offense—because, read the preamble to this act, "they are people of such base and corrupt natures, that the credit of their testimony cannot be certainly depended upon."[16] It seems that the Assembly was belatedly reminded of the last right of citizenship that the Negro freedman possessed (besides that of property), for it was not until 1723 that he was denied the right to vote.[17]

When questioned by the London government over the legality and necessity of this action of disenfranchisement, the Virginia authorities, through a letter of Lieutenant Governor William Gooch, declared the following:

... I am well informed, that just before the Meeting of that Assembly, there had been a Conspiracy discovered amongst the Negroes to Cutt off the English, wherein the Free-Negros and Mulattos were much Suspected to have been Concerned, (which will forever be the Case) and tho' there could be no legal Proof, so as to Convict them, yet such was the Insolence of the Free-Negroes at that time, that the next Assembly thought it necessary, not only to make the Meetings of Slaves very Penal, but to fix a perpetual Brand upon Free-Negros and Mulattos by excluding them from that great Priviledge of a Freeman, well knowing they always did, and ever will, adhere to and favour the Slaves. And 'tis likewise said to have been done with design, which I must think a good one, to make the free-Negros sensible that a distinction ought to be made between their offspring and the Descendants of an Englishman, with whom they never were to be Accounted Equal. This, I confess, may Seem to carry an Air of Severity to Such as are unacquainted with the Nature of Negros, and the Pride of a manumitted Slave, who looks on himself imediately on his Acquiring his freedom to be as good a Man as the best of his Neighbours, but especially if he is descended of a white Father or Mother, lett them be of what mean Condition soever;

[15] Ibid., III, 251.
[16] Ibid., IV, 134, for reenactment of 1723 and this preamble. For the original law of 1705, see ibid., III, 298.
[17] Ibid., IV, 133–34.

and as most of them are the Bastards of some of the worst of our imported Servants and Convicts, it seems no way Impolitick, as well for discouraging that kind of Copulation, as to preserve a decent Distinction between them and their Betters, to leave this mark on them, until time and Education has changed the Indication of their spurious Extraction, and made some Alteration in their Morals.

After all the number of Free Negroes and Mulattos entitled to the Priviledge of voting at Elections is so inconsiderable, that 'tis scarce worth while to take any Notice of them in this Particular, since by other Acts of Assembly now Subsisting they are disabled from being either jurymen or Witnesses in any Case whatsoever, and so are as much excluded from being good and lawful Men, as Villains were of Old by the Laws of England.[18]

The Virginia Assembly also severely curtailed the availability and use of arms by free colored persons. In a 1748 enactment it declared "that no negroe, mulattoe, or Indian whatsoever [i.e., slave or free] shall keep, or carry any gun, powder, shot, club, or other weapon, whatsoever, offensive or defensive" and applied severe penalties for every infringement of this act.[19] The only exception to this were for free colored homeowners, who were permitted one gun under license of the local justice, or for colored persons living on the frontier.[20] But in 1806, all free Negroes or mulattoes, be they homeowners or living on the frontier, were prohibited from keeping or carrying any military weapon or any powder or lead whatsoever. By the 1830's, this restriction was backed up by the repeal of all gun permits ever granted to Negroes by local justices before that date and by the absolute denial of local justices to grant such licenses subsequently.[21]

A few slaves seem to have been caught inadvertently in the Revolutionary War, and one or two free Negroes served in the militia; but all records indicate that the free colored were not only denied admittance into the militia, but that they played little or no part in the military campaigns of the fron-

---

[18] *The Virginia Magazine of History and Biography,* 71 (1963), 414–15.
[19] Hening, *Statutes at Large,* VI, 108–9.
[20] *Ibid.,* IV, 109.
[21] Russell, *Free Negro in Virginia,* pp. 96–97.

tier, in such internal civil wars as Bacon's Rebellion or even in the great Revolutionary War itself.[22] The only exception to this policy was Lord Dunmore's famous desperate arming of several hundred slaves in 1775–76.

Dunmore's armed Negro force, however, integrated with loyal white troops was quickly defeated and dispersed within a matter of months by the patriot armies, and Dunmore's emancipation appeal for slaves to desert their disloyal masters was successfully suppressed.[23]

More crucial than the formal "rights of Englishmen" that were denied the freedmen were the laws and actions that attempted to isolate and degrade their humanity. The most famous of these, of course, were the anti-miscegenation laws. Beginning in the late seventeenth century, there had come several laws adding excessive penalites for white women having bastard Negro children, and finally in 1705 came a harsh law that totally prohibited legal marriages between the races. After listing the extreme penalties that free and bond white women suffered for having colored bastard children, the Vir-

[22] It seems that most of the Negroes who did participate were slaves who worked as wagoneers or as boatmen on board the ships of their masters. See e.g., W. P. Palmer (ed.), *Calendar of Virginia State Papers and Other Manuscripts. Preserved in the Capitol at Richmond* (11 vols.; Richmond: R. F. Walker, 1875–93), III (1782), 231; and *ibid.*, I (1652–1781), 588, for Negroes serving as crewmen in the Virginia State Fleet at Turkey Island. Typical of their use in the Revolutionary War is the following example given by a local officer to the governor in 1781. "As probably our Army will move in such a Part of the Country where a great deal of Pioneer worck will be wanted and the few regular Soldiers will have much Duty, and the Militia not very fond of such a kind of Worck, it will become necessary that Fifty or Sixty Negroes should be provided as Pioneers for the Army during such a time. . . .

"And as in a few days these negroes will be wanted, the most expeditious Way, in my humble Opinion, would be to send an Order to the Commanding Officers of the Militia from the nearest Counties, which are at present in Camp, to join, to propose to their men, that those who furnish a Negro, is to have fourlogh from Camp as many Days as the Negroe is employ'd as Pioneer. And as allways a covering Party will be with the Negroes when at Worck, there will be no danger of their running away." *Ibid.*, II (1781), 259–60.

[23] For Dunmore's "emancipation" proclamation against the rebel slave owners see *Tyler's Quarterly Historical and Genealogical Magazine*, II (1920), 323–24. For the history of the temporary arming and resistance of these some 300 Negro slaves, see *Virginia Magazine of History and Biography*, XIV (1906–7), 386–87; 135–36; and *ibid.*, XV (1907–8), 414; *William and Mary Quarterly*, 1st Series, XX (1911–12), 183–85.

ginia legislature was carried in its abhorrence of "that abominable and spurious issue" to prohibit interracial marriages and to provide extremely severe penalties for any ministers attempting such a ceremony.[24]

Even the very existence of the free colored class was being severely questioned by the end of the seventeenth century. In 1691 the Virginia General Assembly virtually ended the very process of emancipation when it declared that "great inconveniences may happen to this countrey by setting of negroes and mulattoes free" and provided, under pain of heavy penalty, that owners who emancipated their slaves had to pay for their transportation out of the country within six months.[25] Not satisfied with this restriction on the growth of the free Negro class, the legislature next made it impossible for a master to free his slaves even on his own initiative. By the law of 1721 all emancipation was prohibited whatsoever "except for some meritorious services, to be adjudged and allowed by the governor and council."[26]

By these extreme measures, the free Negro population, which probably numbered around 350 in 1691, was kept for the next century to its natural increase alone, and by 1782 there existed only some 2,800 freedmen in the state.[27] In this year, however, under the impact of the revolution and the growth of clerical opposition, a new law was passed that permitted open emancipation at the discretion of the owner.[28] By the first federal census of 1790, the number of freedmen had increased to 12,866. But even with this increase, the free colored population represented only 4% of the total colored population. Nor did the half-century between the first federal census and the Civil War indicate any major change. Although the percentage slowly rose from decade to decade, it only reached 11% in 1860. This percentage of freedmen to total colored compared to an extraordinary 35% in Cuba, or over

[24] Hening, *Statutes at Large*, III, 453–54.
[25] *Ibid.*, III, 87–88.
[26] *Ibid.*, IV, 132.
[27] Russell, *Free Negro in Virginia*, pp. 10–11.
[28] Hening, *Statutes at Large*, XI, 39–40.

three times as many freedmen (the absolute figures being 58,042 and 213,167, respectively). As for the percentage of freedmen in the total population, the Cuban figures were even higher, being 16% compared to only 4% for Virginia.[29]

TABLE 5

POPULATION OF VIRGINIA BY COLOR AND STATUS, 1790–1860

Year	Free Colored	Slave	Total Colored	White
1790	12,866	292,627	305,493	442,117
1800	20,124	345,796	365,920	514,280
1810	30,570	392,516	423,086	551,514
1820	36,883	425,148	462,031	603,335
1830	47,348	469,757	517,105	694,300
1840	49,842	448,987	498,829	740,968
1850	54,333	472,528	526,861	894,800
1860	58,042	490,865	548,907	1,047,299

As can be seen from Table 5,[30] a free colored class did not even begin to achieve any real importance or size until almost two centuries after the introduction of the Negro into Virginia. When the law of 1782 finally permitted him to expand, the free Negro found most of the economic opportunities already preempted. Land was no longer abundant, except on the harsh and very distant frontier, and all the major trades and skilled occupations were already occupied by newly arrived white immigrants. The latter continued to pour into the state, despite the growth of slavery, and the balance of population heavily shifted toward the whites, who represented 66% of the total population in 1860 as compared

[29] It should be noted that Virginia had the largest number and percentage of freedmen to colored population in 1860 of any slave state in the Union, except for Maryland, which was a unique border state.

[30] Source for above figures is: U. S. Bureau of the Census, *Negro Population 1790–1915* (Washington: Government Printing Office, 1918), Table 6, p. 57; and Table 13, pp. 44–45. The leading expert on the free Negro in Virginia estimated the declining incidence of emancipation in the nineteenth century in the following manner: "the chances of manumission of a slave living in Virginia through the generation preceding 1800 were about ten in a hundred; of one living through the period from 1800 to 1832, about four or five in a hundred; and of one living after 1832, about two in a hundred." Russell, *Free Negro in Virginia*, p. 82.

to only 59% in 1790.[31] The free Negro, with little possibility of acquiring land and largely devoid of highly trained skills, was thus condemned to unskilled labor in the slowly rising cities of the state, principally in Richmond and Norfolk, or more likely to being agricultural day laborers in the countryside.

Although the free colored had the highest urban percentage (22%) of any group in Virginia in 1860, in absolute figures freedmen were outnumbered by slaves in every town in the state; for 74% of the urban colored population (36,417) were slaves and only 26% (12,944) freedmen.[32] This meant that the vast majority of free colored persons were engaged in agriculture, working crops not grown on the commercial plantations. Or they lived and worked largely as unskilled laborers in the rural areas of the state in competition with slave laborers, and often in dangerous or unhealthy trades in which free colored overcame slave labor.

Nor did free Negroes, lacking skills or capital and being confined to the settled portions of the state, have much hope of actually owning the land upon which they labored.[33] In 1860 there were only some 1,194 free colored who owned their own farms and only about another 1,500 who were tenant farmers.[34] Even of the 1,194 free colored farmers, however, only 25% maintained a commercial type of agriculture, the other 75% being essentially subsistence farmers little above the level of sharecroppers. And the total number of farmers and tenant farmers among the freedmen class represented only 40% of all the free Negro heads of families in rural Virginia; the remaining 60% owned no property.[35]

[31] The white Cubans during this same period (1774–1861) actually declined from 56% to 55% of the total population.

[32] U. S. Bureau of the Census, *Population of the United States in 1860* (Washington: Government Printing Office, 1864), pp. 504–22.

[33] Of the 37 counties that listed 500 or more free colored in 1860, only one was not located in the Tidewater-Piedmont area. The entire tramontane region contained only 2,764 free colored.

[34] Luther Porter Jackson, "Free Negro Labor and Property Holding in Virginia, 1830–1860" (Unpublished Ph.D. dissertation, University of Chicago, 1937), p. 145.

[35] *Ibid.*, pp. 177, 179.

Not only were the vast majority of rural free colored propertyless, they were also homeless. The family structure in rural Virginia was, if anything, even weaker than in the urban areas. In the rural areas males predominated over females, and a large number of children did not live with either parent. It was common for free colored children in the rural areas to be indentured out until they reached adulthood. And in some areas these indentured, who were almost exclusively given to farmers, often received only food, clothing, and shelter for payment. Also after 1805, state law prohibited all masters from teaching their free colored indentured youth to read and write.[36] Most of the adult males seem simply to have hired themselves out on a yearly basis to farmers or even to plantation owners.[37]

Despite this overwhelmingly rural concentration of free Negroes (some 78% of the free colored population), in no county in Virginia, save one, did they even form a majority of the colored population. Most heavily concentrated in the southeastern and northcentral parts of the state, they were outnumbered by slaves in every county where freedmen resided, except in the county of Alexandria on the border of the federal capital. Wherever free Negroes resided, they were surrounded and isolated by the white freedmen and colored slaves who formed the bulk of the population. This isolation and splintering of the free colored population in the rural areas, especially, seriously curtailed the development of anything like a self-conscious and self-sustaining colored community that could succor the freedmen in times of stress or help preserve his unique cultural or personal attributes. In fact, it was only in the urban centers that anything resembling separate colored churches and fraternal societies existed, and these were few in number and under the control of whites.

For the free colored of Virginia, whatever economic and social mobility could be found was primarily to be located in the cities. But getting to the urban centers was a problem,

---

[36] Samuel Shepherd, *The Statutes at Large of Virginia* (*1792–1806*) (3 vols.; Richmond: Samuel Shepherd, 1835), III, 124.
[37] Jackson, "Free Negro Labor and Property Holding," pp. 100 ff.

since strict residence laws confined the free colored to the place of his emancipation. In fact, it appears that the slow but steady growth of the free colored population of the cities of Virginia, especially after 1830, was not due to external migration but was almost exclusively a product of internal growth. For after 1830, the process of emancipation virtually ceased in most of the rural areas of the state, whereas it accelerated greatly in the urban centers. Here the vast majority of freedmen came from the skilled, hired-out slaves who, for largely economic reasons, were freed by their masters.[38]

Therefore, unless the emancipated slave had the fortune to be freed in the cities or to be endowed with rural property by his benevolent master, his fate was an extremely miserable one. But even for those who were born in the cities, there were fairly limited opportunities. For unlike Cuba, Virginia had few industries and fewer positions for skilled labor, white or black. Despite the fact that Virginia ranked as the leading manufacturing state of the South and was fifth in the nation in many manufacturing pursuits,[39] her industrial growth was quite limited. For in Virginia there were no major public works projects for cities of over 100,000 strong, nor huge shipbuilding industries, large scale agricultural finishing industries, or clothing and shoe factories. Virginia's largest city in 1860 had only some 37,000 persons, and her largest industry, tobacco manufacturing, employed only 11,382 workers.[40] In contrast, tobacco manufacturing in Cuba in 1850 employed in all its branches some 23,900 workers, and it was not even the largest industry of the island, for many other industries employed several thousand more manufacturing workers.[41] In fact, the number of colored industrial workers alone in the three Cuban cities of Bayamo, Havana, and Santiago de Cuba

---

[38] *Ibid.*, pp. 214–16.
[39] *Ibid.*, pp. 56–57
[40] U. S. Bureau of the Census, *Manufactures of the United States in 1860* (Washington: Government Printing Office, 1865), pp. 638–39.
[41] José García de Arboleya, *Manual de la isla de Cuba. Compendio de su historia, geografía, estadística y administración* (2d ed.; Havana: Imprenta del Tiempo, 1859), pp. 178–80. The boot and shoe industry for example employed 39,000 workers. *Ibid.*, p. 183.

(37,824) was greater than the total number of industrial workers of all colors in the entire state of Virginia (36,174).[42]

Not only were urban centers smaller in Virginia than in Cuba, and manufacturing and skilled artisanal trades less in total numbers and percentages, but there was also heavier competition from skilled free whites for the upper strata positions in the labor market. Because of this competition, as all contemporaries noted, the Negro dominated the menial, non-skilled, irregular, and poorly paid occupations. As Virginia's Governor Smith declared before the legislature in the 1840's, in these types of jobs the free Negroes "wholly supersede by [because of] the smallness and nature of their compensation the employment of white men." As Governor Smith cogently noted, the free Negroes

perform a thousand little menial services to the exclusion of the white man, preferred by their employers because of the authority and control which they can exercise and frequently because of the ease and facility [i.e., cheapness] with which they can remunerate such services.[43]

Striking a key point, Governor Smith's declaration fully reveals the second class subservient role allowed by the whites to the free Negroes, which made them susceptible to far easier control than white laborers. In most cases liable to the same physical punishments as slaves for insulting or challenging a white person, a free Negro had little recourse against the exactions of a white employer. Also given the fact that a large number were out of residence and employed illegally, they could scarcely protest difficult labor conditions or low wages.

In areas where skills were required, white mechanics did all in their power to prevent free Negroes from learning a trade or entering an apprenticeship. Thus although large numbers of free colored were barbers and sailors in coastal and intrastate trade—sailing being a distinctly lower class and

---

[42] The Cuban figures are gathered from various tables in the several volumes of Jacobo Pezuela, *Diccionario geográfico, estadístico, histórico de la isla de Cuba* (4 vols.; Madrid: Imprenta Mellado, 1863-66). For the Virginia figures see U. S. Bureau of the Census, *Manufactures, 1860*, pp. 638-39.
[43] Quoted in Russell, *Free Negro in Virginia*, pp. 147-48.

hazardous occupation—very few free colored were black-smiths, building or clothing artisans, or other skilled trades-men. Of the 268 occupations for free workers listed in the state census for 1860, free Negroes could be found in only 72 of these occupations, and of these, they formed a majority of the workers only as barbers, boatmen, and washerwomen.[44]

In fact, this last seems to have been one of the most impor-tant urban occupations for free colored heads of families. For, in contrast to rural Virginia where the number of free colored males was much greater than that of free females, in the urban centers of the state the sex ratio was heavily weighted toward women. This meant that an unusually large number of free colored families, at least in comparison with the free whites, were fatherless. A good deal of this was simply the heritage of slavery, i.e. women freed without their hus-bands, or the lack of true marriage bonds in slavery, which meant that women were separated from men and only associ-ated with their children. Thus in Virginia's nine leading towns, the percentage of free colored females ran from a low of 56% to a high of 65%, which occurred in Norfolk. In this seaport town, for example, the 1860 census listed 189 heads of free colored families, 100 of whom were women—and of these 84 were washerwomen.[45]

Not only were social conditions as difficult in the city as in the countryside, but even despite the economic advantages and a relatively greater variety of skills, property holding seems to have been far less in the cities than in the rural areas, and apparently fewer Negro families in the cities lived in their own homes. In 1860 there were in the state only 635 free colored persons who owned town lots.[46] This meant that for the two towns with the largest free colored populations, Richmond and Petersburg, only 25% of the free Negro fami-lies in the former and 33% in the latter owned any real estate.[47] This total together with the total of rural real prop-

[44] Jackson, "Free Negro Labor and Property Holding," p. 132.
[45] *Ibid.*, pp. 120–21.
[46] *Ibid.*, p. 181.
[47] *Ibid.*, p. 193.

erty owners brought the number of free colored who owned real estate in Virginia in 1860 to 1,829, which was only 3% of the total free colored population, a figure low even by some southern standards.[48]

Despite the existence of a few free colored with fortunes over $1,000, the level of these highest income freedmen was low. Compared to the Virginia free colored who emigrated to Ohio, for example, the average upper-level colored farmer who remained in the state achieved nowhere near the level of wealth and land owned by those who migrated westward.[49] And all of these wealthy colored were either farmers or, more likely, artisans or small shopowners.

In Virginia there were no poets, lawyers, doctors, or pharmacists of colored skin. There was in short, no upper-class leadership of colored men. A handful of exceptionally industrious and fortunate artisans might achieve some wealth, but this in no way allowed them to enter the planter category or the upper class. There were no militia officers, no colored judges, and no colored vestrymen. In short, in Virginia, even wealth, when it was attainable, could never lead to either education or to an upper-class status. Such a concept was totally foreign to the whole structure of Virginia society. For neither money nor birth to a patrician father could break the rigid caste barriers of Virginia society.

Whereas a large number of colored bastard children of aristocratic Spaniards in Cuba could often emulate closely the educations and careers of their fathers—going to the university and practicing law and medicine—such recognition of bastard progeny was almost totally unknown in Virginia. At most, a white upper-class planter or master would free and pension his children or remove them from the state, but even this was extremely rare. In the vast majority of cases, illegitimate colored children were unrecognized by their fathers and

---

[48] This percentage was even smaller than the free colored real property owners in North Carolina; see John Hope Franklin, *The Free Negro in North Carolina, 1790–1860* (Chapel Hill: University of North Carolina Press, 1943), p. 158. In 1860, North Carolina with about half the total number of freedmen, had 1,211 freedmen who owned real estate.

[49] Jackson, "Free Negro Labor and Property Holding," pp. 151–52.

remained in slavery with their mothers, since both law and community mores were totally against this recognition. So intense was opposition to this practice that in the few recorded cases of its occurrence, the fathers were forced to take themselves and their children out of the state. Unlike Cuba, Virginia had no ambient of illegal unions common to all classes nor an entire set of special relations dealing with the numerous bastard progeny that resulted. In Cuba it was the rare master who did not at least manumit his children, and community mores encouraged those who wished to recognize their children and give them competitive advantage.

With birth even to white upper-class fathers giving no access to mobility, and with most trades closed on grounds of color, the Virginia freedmen also lacked the area of mobility through military careers. There existed no colored militia and therefore no free colored officer class that could enable successful free colored to elevate their children in rank and profession; nor was there a benevolent church willing to educate all classes and castes and corrupt enough at the lower level to certify that dark skins were white, even for a price.

There are enough instances of free colored artisans in Virginia acquiring money, like the colored barber Reuben West of Richmond who reportedly built up a fortune of several thousand dollars,[50] but none whatsoever of their sons buying their ways into the upper classes. Not only were Negroes unable to attend centers of higher learning in the state, it is even estimated that no colored persons ever graduated from any such institution of higher learning anywhere in the United States prior to 1828.[51] Thus the Negroes and mulattoes as colored persons had no possibility of successfully overcoming the laws regulating occupation and status. Unlike the Spanish crown, the Virginia Assembly never found itself willing to waive any of these regulations for colored persons on any grounds, for the laws and more importantly the customs of the white upper strata were so successful that no Negroes suc-

---

[50] Russell, *Free Negro in Virginia*, p. 151.
[51] C. G. Woodson, *The Education of the Negro Prior to 1861* (New York: G. P. Putnam's Sons, 1915), p. 265.

ceeded in forcing the barrier even with money. In this sense, Cuba was truly a thoroughly materialistic society in which money, connections, and breeding counted for everything; but in Virginia, these factors could never overcome that of the color of the skin. Virginia at first appeared to adopt an open mobility system at the time of its early Negro imports. But by the nineteenth century status had come to be defined by color, and endogomy was decreed through the total prohibition of legal intermarriage. With color as the primary determinant of ranking and with free access to economic and educational opportunities denied, Virginia had successfully established a closed caste system, which would be reinforced generation after generation until emancipation.[52]

Not only were the caste barriers firmly set by law and custom for the free colored "citizens" of Virginia, but the white population constantly found itself questioning the very legitimacy of and need for the free colored class. Although they recognized the labor done by the free coloreds as being of some importance and took into account the desire of the masters to free their slaves, the white Virginians of the nineteenth century found themselves ever more fearful and hostile to the free colored class and ever willing to chip away at every one of their minor rights and freedoms.

Whereas the reform movement that had given rise to the reopening of emancipation in the 1780's also saw the sudden flourishing of schools and churches for Negroes, by the 1820's and especially after the 1831 Turner revolt, these movements

[52] There can be little question that even by the most limited presently accepted definitions, Virginia had created a total caste system for free colored prior to 1860. Affiliation by descent, endogamy, institutional support for differential treatment and consequent acceptance of their status by Negroes,—the primary characteristics which are said to constitute a caste system—were all firmly established. For a recent definition of the differences between class, caste, and minority-majority systems of social stratification, see J. Milton Yinger, *A Minority Group in American Society* (New York: McGraw-Hill Book Co., 1965), chapter 3. For a definition that takes exception to that supported by Yinger and defines even contemporary southern United States race relations as a caste system consistent with contemporary Indian definitions, see Gerald D. Berreman, "Caste in India and the United States," *American Journal of Sociology*, LXVI, No. 2 (September, 1960), 120–27.

were effectively destroyed by harsh legislation. In fact, 1831 was a major turning point in the career of the free colored community of Virginia. For from this date until 1860, a severe antifreedmen reaction set in, which was equal if not superior to that of the pre-1782 period. Time and again petitioners from the Tidewater and Piedmont counties demanded that the state legislature after 1830 restrict every movement and action of the free Negro and attempt if possible the total extinction of this class through exportation. Petitioners from Westmorland County in 1831, for example, labeled the free colored "degraded, profligate, vicious, turbulent, and discontent" and charged that "their locomotive habits fit them for a dangerous agency in schemes, wild and visionary."[53] Probably the most universal sentiment was expressed by the citizens of Northumberland county, who in 1838 declared that

we can cordially bear testimony to the oft-repeated fact that free persons of color among us are the most degraded as well as the most wretched class of our population; and we believe nothing short of colonizing them in Africa, could be done to ameliorate this condition.[54]

This reaction, which set in and deepened as Virginia Tidewater and Piedmont planters began to defend positively the right of slavery against northern abolitionist charges, led to a more stringent enforcing of old laws against the free colored and a host of new, more dramatically restricting legislation. Particularly signaled out for greater enforcement was the 1806 law, which required newly emancipated persons to leave the state within twelve months.[55] There were also strong pleas from citizens of the state for tighter licensing of freedmen to prevent their accepting stolen goods from slaves, and most importantly of all, for the denial of their right to education.

Whereas various informal schools for educating free Negroes sprang up in all parts of the state at the turn of the century and important numbers of free colored thus achieved

[53] Quoted in Jackson, "Free Negro Labor and Property Holding," p. 15.
[54] *Ibid.*, p. 18.
[55] *Ibid.*, pp. 19–20.

literacy, these attempts had early come under intense opposition from the more conservative elements of the community. As early as 1819, the Virginia General Assembly grew apprehensive over this development and over the association of some slaves with free colored in educational matters, and in that year it prohibited slaves and freedmen from meeting together in groups for educational purposes.[56] In 1831, at the beginning of the new era of reaction, the Assembly took the next logical step and declared that "All meetings of free Negroes or mulattoes, at any school house, church meeting house, or other place for teaching them reading or writing, either in the day or night, under whatever pretext, whall be deemed and considered an unlawful assembly."[57]

This harsh law was fully effective, and all the efforts of the Quakers and of the various free Negro benevolent societies were harshly brought to an end by this code. When the free colored petitioned to have this law removed, the petition was rejected, and to curtail further the ability of free colored persons to obtain an education, a law of 1838 declared that any free Negro who left the state for purposes of getting an education could not return to Virginia.[58]

Prior to 1831 there had also developed a large and important body of Negro preachers who were creating the framework for an all-colored church within the state. There were also several traveling and even resident colored preachers who were administering to the needs of all-white congregations, especially in the Baptist and Methodist churches.[59] This crucial movement was also destroyed by the General Assembly when shortly after the Turner rebellion, it clamped down completely on Negro preachers and absolutely prohibited Negro clergymen from preaching in the state or any Negro from serving in the administration of a church.[60]

In this period there also came the abolition of trial by jury

[56] Woodson, Education of the Negro, pp. 159–60.
[57] Jackson, "Free Negro Labor and Property Holding," p. 23.
[58] Ibid., pp. 23–24.
[59] Woodson, Education of the Negro, pp. 85–86.
[60] Ibid., pp. 163–64; Jackson, "Free Negro Labor and Property Holding," p. 25.

for free Negroes in all cases except murder, the absolute prohibition of firearms, and the total restriction to purchase
slaves.[61] Nor was the repression confined to legislative action
alone, for the aroused white citizenry often took matters in
their own hands and drove out undesirable freedmen at will
by mob action. This procedure was explained by General
Broadnax to the legislature of 1831–32.

Who does not know that when a free Negro, by crime or otherwise, has rendered himself obnoxious to a neighborhood, how easy
it is for a party to visit him one night, take him from his bed and
family, and apply to him the gentle admonition of a severe flagel-
lation, to induce him to go away. In a few nights the dose can be
repeated, perhaps increased, until, . . . the fellow becomes perfectly willing to go away.[62]

That all of the public and private actions were effective can
be seen in the steady exodus of free Negroes out of the state
beginning in the 1830's. The eastern shore, where anti-Negro
sentiment was most violent, experienced a severe decline in
the number of freedmen in the decade 1830–40, despite a
slight increase of free colored in the state as a whole during
that period. Most of these freedmen migrated to Ohio, and
in the next decade, large numbers from Petersburg went to
Michigan, and when Alexandria was returned to Virginia
control in 1846, the majority of free colored moved across the
border into the District of Columbia.[63] Although after the
1840's there was a lessening of mass exoduses, nevertheless the
stream of refugees was constant, and it deprived the Negro
community of its ablest elements.

Not only did whites not oppose such emigration, which
they forcefully supported by much legislation, but they even
proposed wholesale exportation of the entire free community
to Africa. No such suggestions were ever made for slaves, but
the whites of all stripes felt that a free colored possessed a
self-contradictory status, and not only did they refuse the
freedman coequality in the economic and social sphere and

[61] *Ibid.*, pp. 26–27.
[62] *Richmond Enquirer*, February 14, 1832, quoted *ibid.*, p. 28.
[63] *Ibid.*, pp. 29–31.

deliberately bar him from all mechanisms for advancement, but they wished to remove him altogether for fear he would incite invidious comparison in the minds of the "docile" slaves. This, of course, was the major impetus behind the whole African colonization movement that had early and popular backing in Virginia. In fact, it was Jefferson who was one of the first proponents of emigration of freedmen out of the United States and whose major reasoning behind the proposal was that the free colored were an inferior, threatening race who could not be assimilated into the body politic.[64] Although Virginia was one of the staunchest early supporters of a return-to-Africa movement, the state leaders did not really wholeheartedly support the movement until the Turner rebellion of 1831. In fact, free Negroes were so terrified of the consequences of the resulting hysteria—remembering the colored bloodshed after the bloodless Gabriel scare of 1800— they willingly lent themselves to emigration, and in early December of 1831 some 350 colored Virginia freedmen fled to Liberia. Nor were those who remained behind made welcome by the Virginians. In this same year a petition by 180 citizens of Southampton County branded free Negroes "a most prolific source of evil," and they agreed to discharge all free Negro workers and evict free Negro families from the homes and land that they rented. Finally, they demanded transportation to Liberia for the entire county's free colored population.[65] That the essential element behind the colonization schemes, at least in Virginia; was complete hostility toward the freedmen can be seen from a memorial of the Virginia Colonization Society presented in February, 1833, which declared of free Negroes that "they are (with some happy exceptions), a thriftless and vicious race, degraded in the eyes of the public and their own; and ready accordingly for acts of violence and crime, etc."[66]

[64] For early Virginian proposals see P. J. Staudenraus, The African Colonization Movement, 1816–1865 (New York: Columbia University Press, 1961), pp. 1–4, 31.
[65] Ibid., pp. 179–80.
[66] Quoted in Joseph B. Earnest, Jr., The Religious Development of the Negro in Virginia (Charlottesville: Michie Co., 1914), p. 71 n.

Nor did this white hostility relent, even after the 1830's. If anything, hostility toward the freedmen on the part of rural Tidewater and Piedmont whites grew stronger in the years preceding the Civil War. In the new state constitution of 1852, for example, it was declared that:

The General Assembly may impose such restrictions and conditions as they shall deem proper on the power of slave owners to emancipate their slaves; and may pass laws for the relief of the Commonwealth from the free negro population, by removal or otherwise.

The General Assembly shall not emancipate any slave, or the descendant of any slave, either before or after the birth of such descendant.[67]

The object of this latter provision, of course, was to prevent the legislature in regular session from ever carrying out emancipation or abolition of slavery by making it a constitutional prohibition that could only be overturned by a constitutional convention. The intent of these two provisions was clearly to force the termination of all emancipation, although the constitution writers left this up to the Assembly. In the legislative session of 1852–54, the lower house of the General Assembly did actually pass a bill that would have required the removal of all free colored persons from the state, but this bill failed to pass the Senate.[68]

Nevertheless, the process of curbing the opportunities of the freedmen still continued unabated. In the 1840's and 1850's came measures against free colored owning or operating taverns and, on a county option basis, a law requiring Negroes who sold any commodity to have a license and to be bonded by two whites who guaranteed that the items for sale were not goods stolen by slaves. In the early 1850's also came a temporary special tax on free Negroes to pay for a colonization society scheme for the return of free Negroes to Liberia, with the state also providing $30,000 per annum for five years from its own general funds.[69]

[67] James Muscoe Matthews, *Digest of the Laws of Virginia* (2 vols.; Richmond: C. H. Wynne, 1856–57), I, 54–55.
[68] Jackson, "Free Negro Labor and Property Holding," p. 36.
[69] *Ibid.*, pp. 35–37.

So openly contemptuous of the freedom of the Negro did the Virginia whites become that in 1855–56 the Virginia General Assembly passed a series of laws that made it possible for a freedman to will himself into slavery. Interestingly, the Negro freedman who freely sold himself into slavery received absolutely no money for doing so and in fact forfeited all his property to the master.[70] Although these acts may have indicated how fully the whites accepted the mythology of the happy Negro slave and how disconsolate and impossible life for a colored person living as a freedman was, other provisions of the criminal code were more concretely designed to force the free colored persons either out of the state or back into slavery.

There existed the many criminal actions, especially those having to do with disturbance of the peace, assembly of Negroes, promotion of runaways, sabotage of property and inciting to riot, specifically applying to the Negro freedman penalties equal to if not exceeding those for a slave. The Assembly also provided that "if any free negro commit an offence for which he is punishable by confinement in the penitentiary, he may at the discretion of the court before whom he is tried, be punished, in lieu of such confinement in the penitentiary, by sale into absolute slavery."[71] Any Negroes who were found to be out of their place of residence illegally were, under the stringent vagrancy laws, sold by the local county officials for a number of months or years, and it appears from the county records that large numbers of free Negroes experienced this degradation.[72] The state was also not above leveling a discriminatory head tax on free Negroes. Several times in the history of the state, free colored were singled out for special taxes to which the whites were exempt.[73]

Because he was registered, controlled, taxed, and restricted in mobility, it was extremely difficult for a free colored per-

[70] Virginia, The Code of Virginia, including Legislation to the Year 1860 (2d ed.; Richmond: Ritchie, Dunnavant & Co., 1860), pp. 509–10.

[71] Ibid., pp. 815–16.

[72] Russell, Free Negro in Virginia, p. 148.

[73] Tipton Ray Snavely, The Taxation of Negroes in Virginia (University of Virginia, Phelps-Stokes Fellowship Papers, 1916), pp. 12–15.

son legally to earn an income. So hostile to the freedmen's very survival were these legal restrictions that despite the severe penalties which existed, it is estimated that from a fourth to a third of the free colored by 1860 were forced to engage in economic occupations or residence patterns that were prohibited by state law.[74]

Finally, where the entire world viewed color as an automatic indication of slave status, the freedman was extraordinarily vulnerable to being impressed into slavery. Thus, despite the fact that he was registered and known in the local areas, and despite harsh penalties to the contrary, the stealing and enslavement of freedmen seems to have been a common occurrence. Especially since the state's power extended only to the state border, stealing slaves across the state line was the accepted procedure, as the many instances of Maryland freedmen taken as slaves to Virginia and Virginia freedmen shipped out of the state as slaves bear witness.[75]

In short, the free Negro population was not respected, not permitted to live like other freedmen, and toward the last decades of the slave regime, was not even tolerated. The more the slave regime settled into its mold, the more the freedmen became an anomoly and an irritating element in the well-ordered view of the races held by the pre-Civil War southern whites. For this mold required that every colored person be a dependent being who could not function without a white master, and that he be considered part of an inferior race predestined to slavery by a superior white who would lead him to civilization. In such a world view, the conception of an independent, self-sufficient, and seemingly coequal colored person was impossible. The masters could deny slaves access to non-slaves, to literacy, and to mobility, and they could mold the personality of the slave in the direction of docility and subservience, ruthlessly destroying those who would not bend, but they could not so control the freedmen.

---

[74] Russell, *Free Negro in Virginia*, p. 156.
[75] See e.g. Palmer, *Calender of State Papers*, VIII (1798), 493, 510; IX (1799), 57; VII (1794), 376; VI (1792), 185–86. Freedmen, in fact, had grave difficulty in simply terminating ordinary indentured arrangements, which often seem to have ended in slavery. See e.g. *ibid.*, III (1782), 154.

Under such a system therefore, the free Negro represented a dangerous element who by his very existence challenged the legitimacy and threatened the stability of race relations. Going where he wanted, having a family and a private home, he represented an independence that was universally considered by the whites as a threat to the enforced dependency they had created between blacks and whites. That every southern state prohibited reading and literacy, the development of a social community in any but a very limited sense, and stressed as an ideal the isolated life of plantation labor with no force or circumstance interfering in the daily and lifelong interaction of master and slave meant that the free colored person was at most to be barely tolerated if not openly expelled, if "peaceful" and harmonious social relations were to be maintained between the races. By 1860 the majority of white southerners could conceive of the Negro in only one status, that of slave laborer.

Probably more than in any other relationship, the southerner's attitude toward the free colored person demonstrates the unique closed world of North American chattel slavery and indicates its sharp contrast to the Cuban slave system. In Virginia there were no sumptuary, or anti-university laws, there were no constant complaints of white upper classmen of colored mobility, for the free colored represented no conceivable threat to the whites as they severely did in Cuba. The only threat—economic, political, social, or military—that they exercised was to the stability of the colored slave population in that they indicated an alternative life to slavery, and this alternative example the white planters justifiably feared. Like their hostility to the freer patterns of urban slavery, the plantters opposed the free Negro as an example to the slave Negro. To picture him as a challenge to their own status would have been literally inconceivable.

Here, then, the two societies were most clearly opposed. Filled with every conceivable aspect of life and type of occupation from day laborer to medical professors and poets, from beggars to military officers, from professional musicians to mass processionals and holiday folk orgies, from local cabildos to African voodoo cults, the free Cuban community represented a thriving and integrated part of Cuban society. It was a perfect picture of what post-emancipation Cuba would be and it created a rich Afro-Cuban culture that all colored slaves would inherit with their emancipation, along with a distinctive national or Cuban mentality.

The free colored community of Virginia, degraded, despised and dispersed, isolated from the main movement of society, and expelled from the body social whenever and wherever politic, left only a legacy of hatred, bitterness, and contempt. Denied education, self-expression except in narrow and prescribed forms, and even economic skills and education, the free Virginia colored were an isolated and suppressed caste whose existence offered no lessons that the colored masses could profit by in the harsh world of post-emancipation America.

Conclusion

In this study I have tried to show the combination of causes that defined the two slave systems of Cuba and of Virginia and resulted in two sharply different slave regimes. These two systems most certainly did not represent all the varieties of slavery that developed in the Americas. Those in the British and French West Indies and in Brazil, although sharing many of the features of one system or the other, are unique enough to be treated and analyzed separately before all the ramifications of the comparative model can be fully understood. Nevertheless, I hope that my close comparative analysis of these two primary slave societies will be seen as an extension and refinement of the originally proposed comparative model.

At this point, I would like to suggest some implications of the differences in the slave systems for post-emancipation developments. The impact of these two regimes was quite dissimilar in terms of the retention and integration of African culture, of the norms of personality accepted for the Negro freedmen and slaves, and finally of social integration. This differentiation, I believe, seriously affected post-slavery race relations in a multitude of ways.

Virginia, it seems to me, developed a complete caste system, which essentially reinforced the slave system at all levels.

Because of this seeming interdependence, the Virginia whites fought all attempts to destroy slavery, even when it was shown to be uneconomic, on the grounds that the system of slavery supported the now highly crucial pattern of race dominance. It was thus necessary for civil war and outside intervention to destroy slavery in the South. To the initial surprise of the southern whites themselves, however, the caste system had been so thoroughly implanted that it survived the destruction of slavery. Rapidly accommodating themselves to the new system of free labor, the Virginia whites were able to rework the labor base without seriously changing the position of the lower caste. For the augmented urban free-colored element, always a divisive factor in the caste arrangements even under slavery, the whites further developed their system of physical and economic segregation that had been initiated for the freedmen. This rapidly elaborated segregation system, which was highly developed even before the end of slavery, successfully obviated the potential threat of the urban free colored to stable race relations.[1]

It would, in fact, require the mass migration of the colored out of the South in the twentieth century to begin to modify this caste system. But even with this mass migration and the corresponding impact of urbanization, along with the integration of the Negro into the modern industrial labor force, the caste system has shown a surprising resiliency. Class differentiation finally began to appear on an important scale after 1900, but the "black bourgeoisie" has been prevented, until recently, from integrating into the system of social stratification that exists among the whites.[2] Nor has a middle ground of mulatto assimilation been allowed to develop by which integration could be effected through miscegenation. The rules of color elaborated under slavery still operate today, defining a mulatto as a Negro and refusing to accept his as any mean-

---

[1] The origin of segregation under slavery has been clearly demonstrated by Richard C. Wade, *Slavery in the Cities. The South 1820–1860* (New York: Oxford University Press, 1964).

[2] The classic study on this nonintegrated class is E. Franklin Frazier, *Black Bourgeoisie* (Glencoe, Ill.: The Free Press, 1960).

ingful alternative position.[3]

The Cuban slave system, on the other hand, did not support a caste arrangement, but in fact had been functioning in the last decades alongside a developing class system in which the free colored were actively participating. Cuba was progressively able to eliminate slavery when it was shown to Cuban planters that slave labor was no longer profitable. Already in the late 1830's planters had begun systematically to introduce both European and Yucatecan Indian contract laborers. And beginning in 1847 came the famous importation of Chinese coolies, of whom over 124,000 would be introduced into the island by 1874, a figure far in excess of the most extreme estimates for illegal slave importations in this same period.[4] Cuban planters were thus already heavily engaged in purchasing new forms of labor well before emancipation was formally adopted.

This whole voluntary reworking of the plantation labor force coincided with a major technical and structural reorganization of the sugar industry itself, which by the 1860's was the last major employer of slave labor.[5] Divesting themselves of expensive and now doubtfully remunerative slaves, progressive planters were freeing their capital by purchasing cheaper contract coolies or Yucatecans, or simply renting their slaves from others, and were heavily investing in a vast assortment of new machines, from steam engines to new boilers, which were being introduced on a large scale by the middle decades

---

[3] Although the colored population of the southern United States had initially established among themselves a rank order based on lightness of color, this stratification scheme has completely broken down in the face of total white indifference and has been replaced in recent times, especially in the North, by a rank order based on occupation, income, and education. See E. Franklin Frazier, The Negro in the United States (rev. ed.; New York: Macmillan Co., 1957), chap. 12.

[4] Ramiro Guerra y Sánchez et al., Historia de la nación cubana (10 vols.; Havana: Editorial Historia de la Nación Cubana, 1952), IV, 189–95; also see Roland T. Ely, Cuando reinaba su majestad el azúcar (Buenos Aires: Editorial Sudamericana, 1963), pp. 607–17.

[5] By this time the coffee industry was in total collapse, leaving the sugar industry as the only major plantation system functioning in Cuba. At the same time, with new slave imports ended, the process of coartación was causing a decline in urban slavery. Thus, between the censuses of 1841 and 1861 the number of slaves fell not only in absolute terms, but its percentage decline was even greater, going from 43% of the total population in the peak year of 1841 to but 29% of the population in 1861.

of the nineteenth century. The large planters were also cutting down their actual plantings and concentrating on the construction of major refineries, or *centrales*, which in turn needed far more cane than a single planter could economically produce on his own. By 1880, this whole restructuring process was leading both to the constant consolidation of sugar mills into giant full-time centrales and to the introduction on a large scale of smaller, independent, nonrefining growers on surrounding estates and even of sharecroppers on the larger plantations themselves.[6]

Thus slavery was a dying institution even before the Ten Years' War (1868–78) erupted on the island and destroyed the very basis of the system. Primarily affecting the more traditional central and eastern portions of the island where slave labor was more entrenched, this first war for independence freed large numbers of slaves, who fought on both sides, and destroyed hundreds of sugar estates. At this same time, the progressive western section was going through the tremendous changes in structure and in labor noted, so that by the end of the war Cuba's sugar fields were being worked by a complex assortment of labor—from owned and rented slaves to coolie and Yucatecan contract laborers to white European and free-colored day workers and independent sharecroppers.[7] The law of 1870 that began emancipation by retroactively freeing all slaves born after September, 1868, all persons who were over 60 or who would reach that age, and all slaves who had supported the royalist forces in the war was greeted with little opposition.[8] It merely accelerated already established trends, and the slave population continued its rapid decline, dropping to 200,000 in 1877 and to but 150,000 by 1880.[9] By this latter date the Spanish government finally decreed total

[6] Ely, *Cuando reinaba*, pp. 504 ff; and Guerra y Sánchez, *La nación cubana*, IV, 198–208; VII, 164–69.

[7] *Ibid.*, VII, 152–56, 179 ff.

[8] For the complete text of the law, see Fernando Ortiz, *Hampa afrocubana: los negros esclavos* (Havana: Revista Bimestre Cubana, 1916), pp. 495–98. Negro slaves who fought with the rebels were also guaranteed their freedom by the terms of the *Pacto del Zanjón* of 1878, Guerra y Sánchez, *La nación cubana*, VII, 259.

[9] *Ibid.*, VII, 180.

abolition for the remaining adults with a tutelage system arranged to replace slavery, which in its turn was abolished in 1886.[10]

When abolition finally came to Cuba, it thus affected an institution that had long ceased to play a vital part in any aspect of the economy. The sugar industry, its last significant stronghold, experienced little disruption with abolition, but continued its phenomenal expansion and modernization. Neither was there any major shortage of labor nor mass exodus to the cities, since a wage system was fully functioning on almost all the estates well before the end of slavery, and the new freedmen were easily absorbed into the vast pool of whites, older freedmen, and Chinese wage laborers, or into the independent sharecropper system.[11]

All this clearly indicates that slavery for the Cuban whites was primarily a labor system that, when shown to be uneconomic, could be successfully abandoned by the planters. In Cuba there was no fear of emancipation changing racial relations, for the Cubans had long since accepted both racial miscegenation and an open-class system of social stratification. Even before slavery ended, economic and cultural attainments were becoming important elements in defining an individual's position in society, with color becoming more and more a secondary ranking tool.

Although after emancipation most full Negroes were initially found in the lower classes and the identification of color and class seemed quite strong, this was only a superficial relationship. Position in the class system of Cuba was never permanent, and social mobility was possible for even the darkest-skinned colored person. Within a few generations of

[10] Ortiz, *Los negros esclavos*, pp. 387, 389; the 1880 code is reprinted on pp. 510–14. For the history of the struggle in Cuba and Spain over enactment of the emancipation laws, see the forthcoming book by Arthur F. Corwin, *Spain and the Problem of Abolishing Slavery in Cuba, 1817–1873.*

[11] Guerra y Sánchez, *La nación cubana*, VII, 179–80. A similar process of the abandonment of slave labor prior to abolition also occurred in the coffee plantations of Rio and São Paulo. This was, however, a much later process and was neither on the scale nor intensity of the Cuban experience. For an analysis of these developments in Brazil, see Emília Viotti da Costa, *Da senzala à colônia* (São Paulo: Difusão Européia do Livro, 1966).

emancipation increasing numbers of full colored were to be found in the middle classes, and as even before abolition, mulattoes were located at every level of society.

Equally important, Cuban society organized itself around a tripartite color system that permitted mulattoes to think of themselves and be accepted by both whites and Negroes as a distinct group, not participating in many of the "traits" and disabilities of the latter group. To be a mulatto usually meant more economic and social mobility. Also, given money and education, the mulatto even if *obscuro*, or very dark, would be ranked in the white category, and the corresponding Negro would be classified as mulatto, for in Cuba as in the rest of Latin America, "money whitened." This categorizing of the mulattoes as a distinct group also meant that for the Negro, interracial marriage could mean simply marrying up into the mulatto class, with the resulting lightening of his children being a major social and sometimes even economic asset in prerevolutionary Cuban society. With a multitude of subcategories being recognized within each of the three major areas, and with heavy miscegenation blurring color and features at either end of the mulatto scale, there was no crisis caused by "passing." Most often a person's "color" was more easily determined by his education and income than by any physical features he possessed.

This open quality of color definition has led to heavy miscegenation and to a massive movement between color categories on the part of the Cuban population. Each generation has seen the progressive decline of Negroes, despite a constant Negro immigration from Haiti and the other Caribbean islands, and the progressive increase of mulattoes to the point that the majority of the Cuban colored now classify themselves by this term.[12] While Negroes were passing into

[12] By the 1907 census mulattoes already accounted for 54%, with their numbers rising to 61% by 1943. The census takers of 1943, in fact, were forced to the obvious conclusion that this rapid rate of growth of the mulattoes at the expense of the Negroes, "undoubtedly expressed the progressive mixture of the races, which produce over time an increase in the proportion of the mestizos [mulattoes]." República de Cuba, *Informe general del censo de 1943* (Havana: P. Fernandez y Cía, 1945), p. 743. At the same time, data for the United States, when available, shows a more or less stable

the mulatto category, mulattoes were continuously passing into the white group. Thus the percentage of total colored population has been steadily decreasing since the last decades of slavery, falling from 45.0% in 1861, to 26.8% in the census of 1953.[13] This decline can only be explained in terms of a constant passing, since the growth rate of the colored population was internally as great as the white population and its own additions from immigration counterbalanced white immigration. As early as 1899, the Cuban colored had a slightly higher birth rate than Cuban whites and were far more urbanized, thus enjoying the same, if not better, health standards.[14] Nor did any major immigration of whites occur, except from 1919 to 1931, and this was even offset by a heavy colored migration into the island accounting for one-quarter of the total immigrants. In fact, in 1943, foreigners made up 4% of both the white and the colored populations.[15]

Thus the Cuban Negroes have been steadily moving into the majority mulatto grouping, and the mulattoes, in turn, have been defining themselves in ever larger numbers as whites. This process seems to be aiming toward a multicolored "white" population for the island, and in fact such an amalgamation process has already occurred with far smaller nuclei of colored populations in the La Plata and Andean regions, where known colored populations of the colonial period have simply disappeared into a homogeneous and multishaded white population.

From all the available evidence, the possibility of this color assimiliation occurring in North American society seems unlikely. In all probability, miscegenation is on the decline, and whatever small percentage of complete passing into all-white society that has been occurring is more than offset by a tremendous birth rate that has seen the steady expansion of

mulatto population, which even seems to be on the decline, going from 21% in 1910 (its highest figure) to only 16% in 1920. Frazier, *The Negro in the United States*, p. 186, Table VIII.

[13] República de Cuba, *Anuario estadística de Cuba 1956* (Havana: P. Fernandez y Cía, 1957), p. 71.

[14] U. S. War Department, Office Director Census of Cuba, *Report on the Census of Cuba, 1899* (Washington: Government Printing Office, 1900), pp. 140–41.

[15] Cuba, *Censo de 1943*, pp. 753, 755.

the colored population. While the caste system has been breaking down everywhere and an intermediate pattern of relationships has been emerging between caste and class systems that some have tried to label majority-minority relations,[16] color per se is not disappearing, nor has color ceased to be a primary ranking device in American society. Since 1930, the percentage of the colored population out of the total population of the United States has ceased its slow decline and has been on the increase.[17] And its internal rate of expansion has been higher than that of native-born whites in every census since 1910, reaching almost double the native-white birth rate from 1930 to 1950.[18] Although this dramatic difference in birth rates will probably decrease as the colored population gains in economic position and status, demographers, in their most recent estimations, still project a percentage increase in colored out of total population, from 10.6% in 1960 to over 12% by 1968.[19] Even if the percentage expansion of the Negroes in the United States is slowed or stabilized, one cannot predict on the basis of present knowledge that there will be anything like the major absorption of colored into the white classes that has been steadily and inexorably occurring in Cuba. In sharp contrast to Latin America, intermarriage is extraordinarily low,[20] and no intermediate ground is recognized in the movement toward eventual total assimilation. Color in the United States is still a black or white proposition.

As with color, so with social mobility. It is true that occupational stratification, especially since the 1940's, has been steadily taking place within the Negro community, and a more

[16] See J. Milton Yinger, *A Minority Group in American Society* (New York: McGraw Hill Book Co., 1965), chap. 3.

[17] Frazier, *The Negro in the United States*, p. 175, Table VII.

[18] These percentages refer to the expansion of persons in the productive age group 25–44 years; see Conrad Taeuber and Irene B. Taeuber, *The Changing Population of the United States* (New York: John Wiley & Sons, 1958), p. 74.

[19] Karl E. Taeuber and Alma F. Taeuber, "The Negro Population in the United States," in *The American Negro Reference Book*, ed. John P. Davis, (Englewood Cliffs, N. J.: Prentice-Hall, 1966), p. 158.

[20] Totally outlawed in a large number of states, racial intermarriage, even in the largest northern cities, has not gone beyond 3% and is more often much less than that figure. See Frazier, *The Negro in the United States*, p. 698.

normal system differentiating classes on the basis of occupation, income, and education has been developing. Nevertheless,
the full integration of the upper strata of the colored community into the white community has not taken place, and
the "black bourgeoisie" still largely depends on a colored
clientele.[21] And while occupational differentiation is rapidly
occurring in the unskilled and skilled blue-collar occupations,
there has been stability and even decline in the colored professional classes.[22] Although the drift is seemingly toward an
open mobility system and socioeconomic integration on a class
basis, there are still major obstacles to be overcome before this
system can begin to function normally.

But in Cuba, the rudiments of a class system had already
been established under slavery, and a more normal class breakdown very rapidly developed in post-emancipation society.
Here, the distortions of a separate "black bourgeoisie" dependent upon a segregated clientele did not occur, and despite the
differing rates of industrialization and urbanization in the two
nations, occupational mobility came earlier and more successfully for the island's colored than it did for North America's.
Although a complete demonstration of these differences in
mobility is impossible to present here, an approximate idea may
be obtained from the comparisons made in Table 6.[23]

The Cuban colored-male work force had attained a per-

[21] For an excellent survey of upper-class northern colored attitudes toward
real socioeconomic integration, which are identical no matter what the
profession, the origin, or schooling experience, see David H. Howard, "An
Exploratory Study of Attitudes of Negro Professionals toward Competition
with Whites," *Social Forces*, 49, No. 1 (September, 1966), 20–26.

[22] See Eli Ginzberg and Dale L. Hiestand, "Employment Patterns of Negro
Men and Women," *American Negro Reference Book*, pp. 219, 233, Table XV.

[23] The 1943 Cuban census used the 1940 U. S. census classifications but had
fewer categories (e.g. its *obreros no calificados* included domestic service
workers and non-farm laborers). The U. S. 1960 census in turn modified
the 1940 definitions (e.g. separating sales and clerical and putting protective
service workers under the general service workers category). I have therefore used the 1960 terminology, but have combined several major categories
as they appear in the 1943 Cuban scheme. The sources for these statistics are
Cuba, *Censo de 1943*, pp. 1113–14; U. S. Bureau of the Census, Sixteenth
Census of the United States: 1940, *Population*, Vol. III, *The Labor Force*,
Part I: *United States Summary*, pp. 89–90, Table 62; U. S. Bureau of the
Census, Census of Population 1960, Vol. I, *Characteristics of the Population*,
Part 1: *United States Summary, Detailed Characteristics*, pp. 1–544 ff.,
Table 205.

TABLE 6

PERCENTAGE OF ALL EMPLOYED COLORED MALES BY MAJOR
OCCUPATIONS FOR CUBA AND THE UNITED STATES, 1940-60

Major Occupations	Cuba, 1943	U.S., 1940	U.S., 1960
Professional, technical, and kindred workers	1.8	1.8	3.1
Farmers and farm managers	36.9	21.1	4.2
Managers, officers, and proprietors except farm	5.4	1.3	1.7
Clerical and sales workers	8.0	2.0	6.2
Craftsmen, foremen, and kindred workers	21.3	4.4	9.8
Operatives, private household workers, and laborers except farm and mine	20.0	36.6	45.5
Service workers except private household workers	3.4	12.3	13.9
Farm laborers and foremen	3.2	19.8	7.0
Occupation not reported	...	.5	8.4
Total employed Negroes	100.0	100.0	100.0[a]

[a] Totals do not add up to 100 because of rounding.

centage in high status, non-rural occupations (i.e., as skilled laborers, craftsmen, and in the professions) four times as great as the colored males of the United States in 1940 (36.5% to 9.5%), and almost twice as great as United States colored males had achieved by 1960 (20.8%). When colored men and women are taken together, as in Table 7, the percentages

TABLE 7

PERCENTAGES OF ALL EMPLOYED COLORED WORKERS, MALE AND FEMALE
COMBINED, FOR CUBA AND THE UNITED STATES, 1940-60.

Major Occupations	Cuba, 1943	U.S., 1940	U.S., 1960
Professional, etc.	2.6	2.7	4.7
Managers, officers, etc.	5.0	1.1	1.4
Clerical and sales	8.4	1.8	7.3
Craftsmen, foremen, etc.	20.3	2.9	6.1
Totals	36.3	8.5	19.5

are even greater. If one takes into account that Cuba, since 1943, has experienced a total social revolution that resulted in rapid upward mobility of the lowest classes and the deliberate breakdown of the last vestiges of color impediments, it must be recognized that the differences in the two societies are even greater today than two decades ago.[24]

But regardless of how much the recent Cuban revolution may have accelerated the process of social integration and color amalgamation, these trends had already been clearly initiated even before the end of slavery. On the other hand, the heritage of North American slavery established patterns that were opposed to such a process of integration, and although these patterns have been seriously modified they continue to have an important impact on contemporary race relations.

[24] The successful appeal of the Cuban Revolution to colored working class Cubans is clearly revealed in the study by Maurice Zeitlin, "Economic Insecurity and the Political Attitudes of Cuban Workers," *American Sociological Review*, 31, No. 1 (February, 1966), 45–48.

Index